In the Shadow of Tobacco Row Mountain

Elon, Monroe, and Other Villages

Florence Marion Foster Nixon

BLACKWELL
PRESS

©2010 by Florence F. Nixon
All rights reserved. No part of this book may be reproduced in any form or by any electronic or mechanical means without permission in writing from the author.
Published 2010

First edition

ISBN: 978-0-9830482-0-6
Library of Congress Control Number: 2010939073
Printed in the United States of America
Published by Blackwell Press, Lynchburg, Virginia

BLACKWELL PRESS

Contact Blackwell Press at:
311 Rivermont Avenue
Lynchburg, Virginia 24504
434-528-4665
www.BlackwellPress.net

Email: hfnixon@verizon.net

Contents

v	Acknowledgments
vii	Dedication
viii	About the Author
1	Amherst County's 250th Anniversary
3	History of Amherst County
5	History of Elon
11	Lyle and Massie Foster Family Move to Elon
13	Elon Churches
21	Elon Presbyterian Church Bible School
23	Elon Elementary School
33	Elon Houses
49	Elon Organizations
59	Elon Stores, Service Stations and Other Businesses
69	Small Stores and Filling Stations in Elon Area
73	Elon Water Sources
77	A Village Divided
79	The Home Front During World War II
87	Elon Honors War Veterans
89	The Unwelcome Guests
93	Entertainment and Fund Raisers
99	Recreation/Games
109	Happenings and Accidents in and Near Elon
113	Some Elon People
119	The Dameron House
121	David Hugh Dillard
127	The Miracle On Cedar Gate Road
129	Queena Stovall and Triple Oaks Schools
133	Views of Elon and Areas on Route 130 in 1930s and 1940s

137	Agricola/Mt. Tabor
139	Allwood Area
145	Bethel/Salt Creek
149	Riverview/Monacan Park
151	Burford and Burford's Mill
153	Cedar Gate Farm/Laurel Cliff
157	Chestnut Grove Baptist Church and Area
159	High Peak Road Area
163	Long's/Taylor's Mill
165	Madison Heights High School
171	McIvor Station and Area
173	Monroe, Virginia
181	Monroe Churches and Schools
185	Monroe Stores and Businesses
187	Some Monroe People
191	The Monacan Indians
193	Naola and Area
199	Orchards
207	Pearch Ferry and Pearch Station
211	Pearch School and Area
213	Pedlar Lake and Dam
219	Pedlar Mills
225	Churches, Schools and Other Buildings at Pedlar Mills
233	Pera
237	Pleasant View/New Prospect
247	River Road Area
253	Snowden and Area
257	Frank Padget Story
259	Tobacco in Amherst County
263	Waugh's Ferry and Area
267	Businesses in Area in 1880s
269	Do You Remember?
271	Some Sources of Information
272	Index

ACKNOWLEDGMENTS

About thirty years ago I got interested in genealogy and began to talk to people and started my research. After securing family genealogy for several generations, it seemed important to find out more about the way of life back in those days. My husband, Holcomb, and I went out and took pictures of existing mills, schools, churches, and other buildings, and gathered history, especially in the Elon area of the county.

We found a lot of pictures of people and places that no longer exist and when we assured the owners that we would have them copied locally and not send them out of town with the possibility of losing them, they were willing to share them with us.

Fortunately we had a photographer friend, Calvin Mason, who would take a picture of the original so it could be returned the owner. Some people who didn't know me would take their original by Calvin's house and he would take a picture and let them go on their way with their original. He would then make a negative and picture. This was much more expensive than the machines that are available these days, but I am thankful he was willing to go to this trouble for me.

In the early 1980s, many people in the community, who are no longer living, shared history of the area with me. Some of them were Broadus Foster, Ed Taylor, William Morris, Mrs. Lena Wills, Ruth Harris Foster and Mr. Roy McIvor, I am very grateful for this information. I am also grateful for the many pictures that have been shared with me for my collection over the last thirty years. Some of these are in the public domain. Some people shared so many pictures that were taken in the village of Elon and other places, that in some cases I am not sure who furnished which pictures to enable me to give individual credit for each picture. Some of the people who shared pictures are: my sister-in-law, Doris Foster; Mary Foster, Ruth Foster, Lois Foster, Ann and Spence Correll, Daisy Oblinger, Margaret Camden Weeks, John Dillard, Elizabeth Ogden, Jackie Mann, Marita Taylor, Ethel Pick, Ruby Stinnette, Catherine Moore, Robert Floyd, Helen Connelly, Carolyn and Abbitt Horsley Jr., Peggy and Gerald "Jerry" Thomas, Shelby Floyd, Celia Richeson, June Howard, Eleanor Campbell, Garland Huffman, Kathryn Spencer Pixley, and Nancy Marion. I am fortunate to have copies of Mildred Purvis' photographs which she took of the Monroe area in 1940. If anyone shared pictures with me that I did not give credit to either here or at the location of the picture, I do apologize.

I would also like to thank the many people who helped me identify some of the people in the pictures. Some of the ones who helped were: Charles Singleton, Malcolm Wills, Bob Morris, Tom Burford, and Marilyn Burch Harris. If I have not properly identified all the people in the index, I apologize.

My main interest in publishing this book is to preserve history and pictures for future generations. I have strived to be as accurate as possible with information that has been given to me, as well as with research. I hope that any inaccuracies will be outweighed by the history and pictures preserved.

I would like to thank Charles Stinson for sharing information as to how to go about having this book published.

I would like to give a special thanks to Kathryn Spencer Pixley, and Nancy Marion for proofreading my stories, and also to Nancy Marion for formatting my stories, scanning pictures, etc., and helping me get this book published.

—Florence Foster Nixon

DEDICATION

This book is dedicated to my husband, Holcomb Rogers Nixon. He has been very supportive and has an interest in genealogy and history. In recent years he has become a member of the National Society Sons of the American Revolution, having proved an ancestor on both his father's and mother's line. He has been my photographer for buildings, and other places of historic interest. Not only has he been patient when I have been having conversations to gather information, he has been willing to go through some rough terrain to locate old mill sites, cemeteries, etc. I would not have so much material and pictures for this book if it hadn't been for his interest and his assistance.

Holcomb Rogers Nixon and Florence Foster Nixon

ABOUT THE AUTHOR

Florence Marion Foster Nixon has spent all her life in Amherst County. She attended Elon Elementary School and graduated from Madison Heights High School in 1954. She then attended Phillips Business College and graduated from there. On October 26, 1957, she married Holcomb Rogers Nixon. They are the parents of sons, Alan, who has two daughters and two grandsons; and Scott, who has three sons.

Over the years Florence has been employed by Barker-Jennings Corporation; Lynchburg Foundry Company/Mead Corporation; the law firm of Edmunds, Williams, Robertson, Sackett, Baldwin and Graves; and retired from Central Virginia Training Center after 24 years of service as SSI Coordinator.

She is a member of Elon Baptist Church where she has served in a number of capacities over the years including: Training Union director; Sunday School teacher; and president of the W. M. U. (Women's Missionary Union) for over 25 years. She served as co-chairman on both of the book committees when the *Amherst County Virginia Heritage* Vol. I & II, were published. She is currently a member of the Amherst County Museum and Historical Society where she serves on the activities committee; the National Society Daughters of the American Revolution, where she served as regent of the Amherst Chapter; the National Society Colonial Dames XVII Century, where she served as registrar of the West of the Falls Chapter, and has proved a number of armorial ancestors; the National Magna Charta Society Dames; and the Plantagenet Society.

–Courtesy Ann Correll or Ruth Foster

–Courtesy Ties magazine

AMHERST COUNTY'S
250th ANNIVERSARY

A mherst County's 250th anniversary will be celebrated in 2011.
In observance of the 200th anniversary of the founding of Amherst County, The Chamber of Commerce engaged architect Charlie L. Vail Jr., of Madison Heights to design a seal since there was no record of one for the county. Mr. Vail along with the committee that included Harold Singleton, Rev. Bailey F. Davis, and Alfred Percy, author of

IN THE SHADOW OF TOBACCO ROW MOUNTAIN

The Amherst County Story, received suggestions from many people for the seal that was hung in the county courthouse. The interpretation was written by Charlie L. Vail Jr. as follows:

CHARLIE L. VAIL, JR., A.I.A.
ARCHITECT
R. F. D. No. 3, BOX 600
MADISON HEIGHTS, VIRGINIA

AMHERST COUNTY SEAL

THE CREST OF THIS COAT OF ARMS IS FORMED BY CROSSED SHEAVES OF WHEAT RESTING ON THE BLOOM OF A DOGWOOD AND TOPPED BY A TOBACCO PLANT. ON THE LEFT SIDE OF THE CREST IS THE SWEET BRIAR ROSE WITH OAK ACORN SITTING ON THE RIGHT SIDE.

THE SHIELD'S UPPER LEFT AND BOTTOM RIGHT QUARTERS WERE TAKEN FROM LORD JEFFREY AMHERST'S COAT OF ARMS, AS HE WAS THE FIRST GOVERNOR OF VIRGINIA; THE UPPER RIGHT QUARTER IS FROM THE FIRST EARL OF ALBEMARLE'S ARMS BECAUSE AMHERST COUNTY WAS CUT FROM THE COUNTY OF ALBEMARLE IN 1761; THE LOWER LEFT QUARTER IS FROM THE VIRGINIA COLONIAL COAT OF ARMS AS IS ALSO THE MOTTO.

THE CENTER SHIELD IS FROM GEORGE WASHINGTON'S COLORS TO REPRESENT THE UNITED STATES OF AMERICA, WITH THE SHIELD OF THE CONFEDERATE STATES OF AMERICA IN THE CENTER.

THE SUPPORTERS ARE THE BLACK BEAR ON THE RIGHT, THE WHITE TAILED DEER ON THE LEFT WITH THE RABBIT AND SQUIRREL SUPPORTING FROM THE BOTTOM. THE BASE IS FORMED BY THE BLUE RIDGE MOUNTAIN RANGE OFTEN KNOWN TO THE PEOPLE OF AMHERST AS THE "SLEEPING GIANT", AND IS CRADLED BY THE RIBBONED MOTTO MEANING "GOD AND MY RIGHT".

DESIGNED BY CHARLIE L. VAIL, JR.

HISTORY OF AMHERST COUNTY

Amherst County was formed from Albemarle County in 1761. It got its name from Lord Jeffery Amherst who was born in Kent, England, in 1717. He was appointed commander-in-chief of the British army in America in 1758. After many successful campaigns, he was made governor of Virginia by the king of England. He preferred his native land and when it was required that he reside in the colony, he resigned the post and was succeeded by Lord Botetourt.

The population growth in the southern portion of Albemarle County and the distance from local government justified forming a new county. Leaders, having great respect for Lord Jeffery Amherst, named the new county for him.

The first courthouse for Amherst County was located near Cabellsville (now Colleen)

Early courthouse with bars at entrance to keep cows and horses off the lawn – *Courtesy Jake Motley*

in Nelson County. Through the research and auspices of Rosemary Dunne, a marker was erected beside Route 29 at Colleen where it is thought the first courthouse stood.

In 1807, Nelson County was formed from a portion of Amherst County when it was divided in order to have a courthouse more centrally located. At that time the courthouse was moved to a place called "The Oaks;" some publications say "Five Oaks." Shortly after that the village began to grow and became known as Amherst. The town of Amherst has continued to grow and is not only the county seat, but has its own town government.

The present courthouse was built in 1870. There have been additions and renovations made to the building over the years. In 1935, additions were made to the rear. Further additions and improvements were made in 1961. The courtroom on the second floor was completely renovated in 1973. Beginning in the summer of 1996 and continuing into the summer of 1998, renovations were made and a large addition was completed to the back of the courthouse with this becoming the main entrance. A portion of the wall surrounding the courthouse was removed due to its deteriorated condition.

Courthouse taken in 1999 – *H. R. Nixon*

HISTORY OF ELON

This early history of Elon was written by Dorothy Moore in her senior year. She was one of four people who graduated from Elon High School. The others were: Margaret Morris, Elmo Page and Mary Lou Page. This was the only graduating class. After that the higher grades were sent to Madison Heights High School and they graduated from there. Below is an exact quote of the Elon history written by Dorothy Moore.

THE HISTORY OF ELON

April 14, 1924

INTRODUCTION

Long, long ago in the days before the invention of automobiles, phones, electricity and other modern conveniences began the history of a little village now called ELON. As we think of the history of any events there comes to our mind the greatest historian the work has ever known, "Hypocrates." As we, the Seniors of the Elon High School endeavor to trace the history of Elon, we do not expect to become great as Hypocrates, or to relate as interesting events as he, but those who have lived in this little village and learned to love it feel as much interest in its beginning and growth as in the development of our country.

CONDITIONS OF COUNTRY AND LOCATION

The location of this place is about two miles back from the James River in Amherst County, Virginia. When the first thought of settlement entered the minds of the people, the land was a forest with small streams running through. Then there was no thought of this forest ever becoming the progressive village that now stands about ten miles from Lynchburg and two miles from the foot of the Tobacco Row Mountains. About this time, the conditions of the country were different from the conditions that now exist. The people were busy with their mode of existence and gave not a thought to ever living in the times of many modern conveniences that are now in use. The farmers labored hard in their way, not realizing that soon into their lives would come a great change to make their labor easier.

SETTLEMENT AND GRANTS

At this time the rule in England was carried on by kings who had sent colonies over to America. In this band of settlers came Lord Fairfax who had been granted a large tract of land, now Amherst County. He granted a part of this territory (from the top of the mountains to Lynchburg on the right hand side of the road) to the four Shelton brothers. The left hand side he granted to Mr. Harding. A few cabins were built at this time. The one which is now owned by Mr. Camden opposite the store was the first to be built.

NAME AND WHY

In 1856, Mr. Harding, the man who owned the left hand side of the large territory awakened to the need of a place of worship in this little community, and for this purpose gave a tract of land.

The question of what to call the church arose. It was decided to call it after one of the Judges in the Bible who was named Elon. This reference may be found in the 13th Chapter of Judges, verses 11-12.

In a short while the surrounding place took the name from the Church, and since then has been known as Elon. For fifty-one years, this church of Elon served as a Union Church. It then became a Presbyterian Church and has remained so until the present time. In 1858, Mr. Keaton repaired the church and built the benches that are now used. The first person buried in the cemetery of this church was the child of Mr. Harding. The grave was surrounded with a brick wall and marble slab on top that still stands as a sacred Memorial to the child. In 1860, a stage coach road was established from Lexington to Lynchburg, but was later abandoned.

FIRST BUILDINGS

Gradually, the ideas of settling this place entered the minds of many people. In 1857, the forest begun to be cleared, houses begun to be built and new life seemed to dawn on the few owners of property around. Several cabins were built and a store was built on the corner of the road leading to Salt Creek and Elon road. Later in this same house, Doctor Sutphin lived and has his office.

TRANSFERS OF PROPERTY

In the advancement of civilization in this community the land began to be transferred from one to another. The Shelton brothers sold part of their property to the Camms where the Baptist Church now stands. He sold to Mr. Grubbs who built a house where the Wiley's house now stands. A tract of Mr. Harding's land was sold to Mr. Ned Fletcher who sold to Mr. Dameron. Soon Mr. Grubbs sold part of his land to Mr. Ed Hudson, the remainder to Mr. Tinsley. The Pascos bought a portion of the land on the right hand side of Elon from the Sheltons. They soon sold it to Mr. Curd, but retained the tract where the Baptist Church now stands. Mr. O. P. Morris, in later years, bought this property from Mr. Curd, and on the left hand side bought from Mr. Hudson. Thus the land came down from one to another until now Elon is practically owned by Messrs. Morris and Camden.

EDUCATION DEVELOPMENT

As we look back into history of any place, we see a lack of educational development at the beginning of its growth. Thus it was with Elon. The educational advantages at first were poor. The first school was conducted in an old Academy which stood between the Presbyterian Church and the old school building that now stands. The name of the first teacher was Mr. Arnold. At this time, the girls attended school in the Academy and the boys in a little cabin that stood on the macadam road, a place now owned by the Wiley's. This old Academy was moved on a wagon up on the macadam road for a barn. A two-story school was built which served as a teacher's dwelling as well as a school. Later this was moved down to the school known as "Flint Hill."

In 1916, a new school was built; with the building of this school came an improvement in education. The schools have continued to be better until it has now reached the standard of a four-year high school. The first generation of people in Elon believed in getting along with just as little education as possible, but now the educational standards have grown and the younger generations are striving for a more complete education.

MAIL AS A MEANS OF COMMUNICATION AND ESTABLISHMENT OF JAMES RIVER POST OFFICE

When the village first begun its growth the Post Office was kept in the store and was known as Elon Post Office. Later the James River Post Office was established.

ESTABLISHMENT OF RURAL ROUTES

1904 found the establishment of a rural route on the James River through Elon. The Post Office was in Madison Heights and soon the route was changed from James River route to Madison Heights.

BUILDING OF BAPTIST CHURCH

In 1907, a group of religious people decided it best to worship to themselves rather than continue with the Union Church. They then built a church and the following year dedicated it as the Elon Baptist Church. Mr. Cowherd was the first pastor.

INDUSTRIAL DEVELOPMENT

The industries of any village are responsible in a greater or lesser degree for the development of that section. We cannot say there were fewer industries in earlier Elon than are carried on now, because there were many, but of a different kind from those of today. The first store was built in 1876 which formed the central place of the neighborhood. This store is now used for a dwelling house and owned by Mr. Camden. In this house was kept a barroom by Mr. Musselman. A few yards from the store was a shoemaker's shop in the house where Mr. J. E. Ramsey now lives. Though these were considered profitable industries, agriculture was the chief industry. Soon another store was built by Mr. Hudson. Also, Mr. Vest built a store on the corner of the Salt Creek and Elon Road. Industry was then fast developing. In 1876 the first "Home Comfort" stove was introduced into Elon by Mr. Williams.

The Montrose Fruit Farm, a very profitable industry, was established in 1898. At the present time, a blacksmith's shop, a garage, a store, and a saw mill form the chief industries. Agriculture is still considered a profitable industry and is preferable to the new industries in many instances. The Elon farmers are now grasping the new ideas of farming and are using newer methods. Thus they are breaking away from the old way and keeping up with the times.

SOCIAL ACTIVITIES

In the earlier days of Elon there was a great deal of the Cavalier spirit. The people were carefree; They loved to visit. There was not so much formality as now exists. Friends went to spend the day rather than an "afternoon call." The people knew nothing of such things as car riding, but soon into their lives came a surprise. The first automobile was brought through the little village, and oh! What a sensation it caused. In a short time they became more common, and now nearly every citizen of Elon owns one.

Horses and buggies are fast going out of use. About nine years ago, a very helpful contribution was made to Elon. It was a fund appropriated by Mr. Colgate, and the people were to decide what to do with it. They finally decided to get a nurse to come into the neighborhood who would also be a community worker, thus helping mentally and religiously as well as physically. This fund brought a most useful and intelligent lady from New York, "Miss Davis." While here she did a great deal for the social development. When she left another nurse was secured, "Miss Hawkins," who remained only a short time, but during that time started a most useful organization, "The Girl Scouts."

LATER RELIGIOUS GROWTH

Of the earlier days of religion we know little, but we do know they only had preaching service, no other means of religious worship. Into their midst in a time of religious depression and gloom came a wide awake Presbyterian preacher, "Mr. Thomas," who started new life in the Church. He not only started the men to work with vim and vigor, but the ladies also got busy. They organized a Ladies Aid Society and entered the work. After several years of hard work here, Mr. Thomas saw his duty elsewhere, and then came the dearly loved friend and pastor of the church now, "Mr. Clyde Walsh," who has done a great deal for this community. An organization was formed by him for the young people, known as the "Get-together Club." Also, the Boy Scouts were organized which is one of the many organizations Elon is so very proud. The Sunday school has also seen a great change. More members are joining, more interest shown, and good work is being done.

THE BUILDING OF THE LIBRARY

The two public buildings of which Elon boasts are the library and high school. For years the Elon-nites had dreamed of these buildings, planned and worked for them until finally their aim was accomplished. In a later paragraph, I shall discuss the building of the high school, but now let us look back to the beginning of the library. This building is the result of the efforts of a most intelligent and public spirited lady, "Mrs. Lea," who when sick in the hospital planned some way of establishing a public library in Elon. When she came home she presented her plans for this project to the people and with their cooperation and the help of The Colgate Fund, a way was found by which they might begin this work. A house was rented (where Elmer Ramsey now lives) and books were contributed by people from all over the county. Frances Elder was the first librarian. This house served as a library for about two years. Then it was discovered that a building could be put up for this purpose with a contribution from the people and the Colgate Fund.

Work was contributed on the building, as well as money. The foreman was Mr. Davis. In 1917 the building was completed and is still used. It has aided greatly in developing the minds of the people, and formed entertainment for the children. The library contains many excellent books.

THE BUILDING OF THE HIGH SCHOOL

The building of the high school was begun in 1921. The contractor was Mr. Patterson. For many years the parents longed for a high school where their children might complete their education without having to go from home. At first, it seemed they would never reach this height, but by hard work and energetic spirit they finally convinced the Board of the need of a high school. The Board promised to appropriate a certain sum of money if the people would make up an amount necessary.

A loan was made for this purpose, and soon the work of building was commenced under the supervision of Mr. Patterson as contractor. In 1922, the school was opened with about 160 pupils on roll.

From that time until the present the people have had to work hard to pay off the school debt. In the summer of 1923 a community worker was secured. Many plays, minstrels, and other entertainments were held under this community worker, "Miss Hubbard," for the purpose of paying off the debt. The Elon High School is to be congratulated more this year, than ever, since its first graduate class is to pass from its doors.

CONCLUSION

From the sketch I have given you of Elon, you can see that it started from a very simple beginning, like the beginning of our country. The land was granted, then the forest cleared, and buildings gradually erected. As we look back over the history of this village, let us appreciate the fact that it has developed so much, and let us each endeavor to aid in the further development, rather than stop and say, "We've accomplished our aim, we have finished our work," but let us each do our part in bringing about the future possibilities which are in store for our dearly loved and honored village, "Elon." As Lowell tells us "New occasions teach new duties; time makes ancient good uncouth; They must upward still and onward, who would keep abreast of truth." So may the citizens of Elon keep abreast of truth by striving upward and onward.

In about fifteen years hence there will be a great many events to take place, and much to be added to this history. Things of which we now have no conception of what are in store for Elon, but we know she has a great future.

Written by: Dorothy Moore
April 14, 1924

LYLE AND MASSIE FOSTER FAMILY MOVED TO ELON

My family had lived near Pleasant View when I was born. When I was three years old our family moved to Pedlar Mills and were there for a year. During that time, my brother James graduated from Pleasant View High School. At that time students only had to go to school for a hour on so on their last day. I was almost four years old by then and James took me to school with him. I have been told that Mildred White, Helen Coffey, Ruth Harris and some of the girls entertained me.

We moved to Elon in the fall of 1941. My sister, Eleanor, was in the ninth grade at Pleasant View School and transferred to Elon School since grades 1-9 were taught there at that time. She then attended Madison Heights High School and graduated in the spring of 1944. My brother Gordon was in the fourth grade at Pedlar Mills School and transferred to Elon School where he went through seventh grade and then on to Madison Heights High School and graduated. Shortly thereafter Elon Elementary had only grades 1–6, and so I attended Madison Heights High School for grades 7–11 and graduated in 1954.

As time went on, we married and had families of our own.

In September, 1972, Lyle and Massie Foster celebrated their 50th wedding anniversary, with their children, grandchildren and their spouses attending.

Holcomb Rogers Nixon and I were married on October 26, 1957, and have spent all our married life at Elon, except for the first year and a half. We celebrated our 50th wedding anniversary at Winton Country Club on October 27, 2007, with family and friends.

l.–r. back; Massie Foster, Lyle Foster, and children; middle: Eleanor, James, front: Florence, Gordon

IN THE SHADOW OF TOBACCO ROW MOUNTAIN

50th wedding anniversary of Lyle and Massie Foster l.–r.: Holcomb Nixon, Florence Nixon, Eddie Foster, Ray Foster, Bill Foster, Alan Nixon, Connie Foster, Lyle Foster, Gordon Foster, Massie Foster, Doris Foster, Debbie Foster, James Foster, Gerry Morris, Eleanor Morris, Bobby Morris, Dale Foster, Bennett Foster; front: Scott Nixon, Judy Foster

50th wedding anniversary of Florence and Holcomb Nixon

Sons, l.–r.: Scott Rogers Nixon, Florence, Maurice Alan Nixon, Holcomb

Scott with family, l.–r.: Scott; his wife, Jacqueline (Hopchak) Nixon; and sons: Dylan, Dakota, and Drake Nixon

Alan's daughter, Kelly (Nixon) Wall, with her husband, David Wall and children, l.–r.: David, Bryce, Turner, and Kelly Wall

Alan's daughter, Jennifer Nixon, with her fiancé, Mark Woodard

ELON CHURCHES

A plat of division of the estate of Edward Fletcher dated Sept. 1883, made by M. H. Garland, shows that a large percent of property surrounding Elon was owned by Mr. Fletcher.

There was some acreage east of Bethel Road (now Monacan Park Road), continuing west of Bethel Road, beside the Turnpike to Lynchburg (Elon Road), almost to Rucker Road (now Ambrose Rucker Road). On the north side of Turnpike to Lynchburg his property adjoined Rucker Road it then extended north to branch of Graham Creek. From Rucker Road it extended back east to the far edge of Homewood Farms at what is now Manse Road.

The plat shows a number of houses and businesses in the community. Also shown on Road to Court House (now Cedar Gate Road) are the church (brick church, location of present Elon Presbyterian Church), and the Academy (the early school).

By the early 1900s, Mr. O. P. Morris owned much of the land in the village of Elon.

RED BRICK CHURCH

Sometime after the original settlers had come to this section of Amherst County, they began to feel the need of a house for the worship of God. To supply this need, in 1856 they erected the Red Brick Church. This church was deeded and built to be a union church with all denominations having the privilege of using it. It was erected on the site where Elon Presbyterian Church now stands.

Apparently, the first regular minister was the Rev. Mr. Teese, a Presbyterian. He owned "Cloverdale," farmed, and ministered to the spiritual needs of the people for a number of years. After Mr. Teese, Mr. Massie, a Baptist minister, preached for the union church for some time. Also, there were Episcopal ministers on stated Sundays. At one time, three denominations were observing their regular appointments each month.

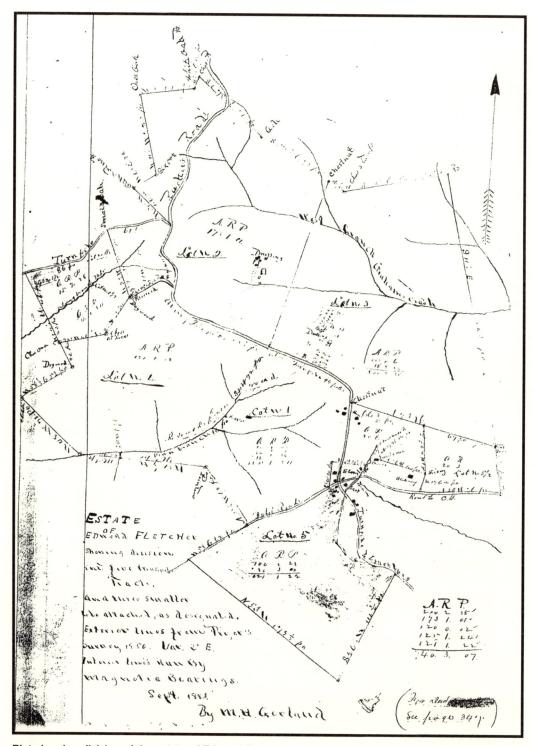

Plat showing division of the estate of Edward Fletcher – *Amherst Co. Circuit Court Clerk's Office*

Elon Baptist Church – *Courtesy of Nancy Marion*

ELON BAPTIST CHURCH

After worshiping at the Red Brick Church (Union Church) for almost 20 years, the Baptist congregation organized Elon Baptist Church on November 2, 1877, and continued to worship in the little Red Brick Church for a period of thirty-one more years.

In 1896, Elon Baptist Church united with three other Baptist churches: Cornerstone, New Prospect, and Midway (this was called a field of churches), for the purpose of calling a pastor with each church having services, once or twice a month. In 1897, a parsonage was built in Pleasant View for the pastor's home in our field. The same year we were admitted into the Albemarle Association (which later became Piedmont Association), and in July 1964, our church joined the newly organized Lynchburg Baptist Association.

We were finally able to build our own church, and in 1908 our white frame church building was dedicated. Since we were in a field of churches, we had worship services only one Sunday morning and one Sunday night a month. On the Sunday mornings we didn't have a preacher, we would have Sunday School at our church and then most of our congregation would go down to the Presbyterian church. Rev. George Bird Talbot was the preacher.

At that time, the preachers did not receive a very large salary. It was customary for different families to invite the preacher and his family home for Sunday lunch. We did this for Mr. Talbot, as well as our own preacher. Sometimes Patty Bird, who was just a little girl, would tell us at church that she was going home from church with us.

Elon Baptist Bible School – 1954 Back row: l.–r. Rhonda Davis, Earl Collins Wiley, Bessie Moss, Florence Foster, Ethel Pick, Helen Foster, Carol Langley, Mrs. Nannie Layne, Ronnie Foster, Freda Davis held by Gloria Throneburg, Edith Foster, Mrs. Shumaker, Cecil Foster, Barbara Stinnette, Mary Foster, Middle row: In front of Edith Foster, ?, ?, ?, Sylvia Kaye Wiley in front of Cecil Foster, Front row: Rebecca DeLancey, Sharon Bailess, Shelby Bailess, Delores Green, Bernard Gowen, Tommy Joe Foster, Douglas Inge, ?, Sissy Inge, Talmadge Foster Jr., David Delancey, Carl Ray Davis, Robert Moss, Linda Bailess, Walter Pick, Linda Foster, ? – *Mary Foster*

IN THE SHADOW OF TOBACCO ROW MOUNTAIN

W. M. U. Ladies – April, 1958 l.–r. first row: Jane Davis, Connie Foster, Doris Tyree, Middle row: Mary Foster, Dossie Elliott, Bessie Moss, Barbara Stinnette, Mary Moss; Standing: Martha Moss, Cecil Foster, Edith Foster, Ethel Pick, Clara Tiller, Opal Eubank, Gloria Throneburg, Doris Foster, Virginia Ware, Barbara Massie. – Courtesy of Mary Moss Turman

1950s church with walkway to Sunday school building in background l.–r. Front row: ?, Cynthia Humphries, Carolyn Foster, ?, Patty Ware, Debbie Foster, Rosa Whitehead, Stephanie Throneburg, ?, Betty Moss, Back row: Ellen Gowen, ?, Billy Johnson Jr., ?, ?, Ryland Peters, Sam Davis, III

Sunday School class l.–r. Front row: ?, Beth Connelly, Rene Coleman, Scott Nixon, Kelly Eubank, Christy Throneburg, Back row: Lisa Eubank, Laura Davis, Judy Foster, Becky Sigmon, Valarie Martin, Margaret Jean Tiller.

Old church and new educational building

Up until in about the 1960s, whenever you had a series of revival services, different church members would board the preacher, and then different ones would invite the preacher and his family and the visiting preacher into their homes for supper.

In 1949, feeling we could make it on our own financially, we decided to withdraw from the field of churches in order to have more services at our church. We gave our part ownership in the parsonage at Pleasant View to the churches remaining in the field. That same year, Randall P. Layne, a layman from Lynchburg, came as our preacher, and we had worship services on Sunday morning and Sunday night, as well as prayer meeting on Wednesday. Training Union, W. M. U., Mission Friends and G. A.'s were organized. Women's Missionary Union and Training were first organized in around 1933. We have had vacation Bible school at our church since 1952. Prior to that, we attended Bible school at Elon Presbyterian Church.

Our educational building was constructed in 1951, and our parsonage was built in 1959, after which a call was extended to Rev. Eugene C. Campbell to come as our first full time pastor.

Picture of old church and new sanctuary in 1964 – *Lois Foster*

Present Elon Baptist Church – *H. R. Nixon*

Our present sanctuary, with additional Sunday school rooms was completed in February 1964, and the old building, erected in 1908, was torn down. In 1995 the educational building was replaced by our present one.

The pastors we had after joining the field of churches, up to present are: Rev. E. R. Root, Rev. K. Cowherd, Rev. R. P. Ellington, and Rev. E. E. Lamb. For a few years we only had supply pastors and laymen, including Rev. Talmadge Magann, Tyler Fulcher, and Rev. Kirkwood.

After them our pastors up to present have been: Rev. T. E. Goad, Rev. R. A. Oliver, Randall P. Layne (layman), Rev. E. C. Campbell, Rev. S. W. Elliott as interim pastor, Rev. Joe Knowles, Rev. Walter Mayes as interim pastor and then as pastor, Rev. Edward O. Temple as interim pastor, Rev. Carroll B. Welch, Dr. Marvin C. Gold as interim pastor, Rev. Charles Jolley, Rev. John Bowles as interim pastor, and Rev. Steve Tyree, our present pastor.

Something that has stuck with me most of my life is a statement that Rev. Oliver made over and over. He said "Keep on keeping on." Also, Mr. Randall Layne impressed upon us as young people, "Don't be afraid to be different." If you feel that it is something you shouldn't do, and that it would not be pleasing to God, don't mind being different. This concerns me so much in today's world. Society accepts so many things that were frowned upon when I was growing up. It is the Bible (God's word) and the Holy Spirit, that should control our decisions.

ELON PRESBYTERIAN CHURCH

In 1838, land was sold to W. O. Harding making specific exception of 1¼ acres of land on which the Pedlar Ford Church was already standing.

Apparently, the Red Brick Church built in 1856 was the second building on the site. The Rev. David Teese moved to Elon in 1870 and preached there from time to time until his death in 1894. He

Old Elon Presbyterian Church

Young people of the community l.-r. front: Jack Litchford, Beth Younger, Margie Litchford holding ?, Betty Harris, Eleanor Foster, Middle row: Doris Morris, Lois Brown, Margaret Dillard, Frances Morris, Back row: ?, Frances Belk, Raymond Wills, Ned Harris, Harry Horton – *Doris Foster*

was the first Presbyterian minister of whom they have any definite knowledge.

According to tradition, Elon Presbyterian Church was organized in 1873, but no records have been found to substantiate this. After an exhaustive search of records at the Presbyterian Historical Foundation, Montreat, N.C., it was found that on April 16, 1902, the clerk and Rev. George H. Ray were appointed to investigate the history of Elon to determine whether it had ever been formally organized as a church. In August, 1902, the Presbytery approved of Rev. Ray's action in organizing a church at Elon and ordered that the church be entered on their roll of churches.

The Presbyterian Manse was completed in 1924 and first lived in by Rev. Walsh and his wife. In 1964, the original property was sold and a new manse was built on Camden Drive.

They had different organizations, such as the Ladies Aid Society, and prayer circles. The Talbots were there during WWII and they had programs with the young people. One group met on Sunday nights at the church. I was just a little girl and I thought my sister was saying they were going to attend the "Christian and Devil" meeting. After I was a little older, I realized they were saying "Christian Endeavor."

Back in those days you didn't have air conditioning. In the hot summer you would usually open all the windows you could. This was also true with the churches. Most of the time there would be a supply of paper fans, compliments of one of the local funeral homes. One night during a revival a snake crawled through a window where the choir was sitting and caused quite a commotion.

I remember in the 1940s seeing the Torodes come to church in their horse-drawn buggy. They would leave it across the road in the shade, a little ways back from the church while they attended the service. Also Mr. Tom Burch and his daughter, Lena, would travel to church in their Model T Ford. June Wills said sometimes they would pick her up, along with her brother, R. H., and give them a ride to church.

The church was badly damaged by fire in July 1969, resulting from a severe thunderstorm. The basement under the left wing addition was gutted and the main floor, sanctuary, and other rooms were damaged by water, heat, and smoke.

Services were held for a short while in Elon Elementary School, and then in the American Legion Hall, while the church was being reconstructed. After much studying and planning, the old "Red Brick Church" was razed, to make room for a larger building with a fellowship hall, and kitchen in the basement. The left wing and other rooms were left standing and renovated.

In recent years, the right wing of the church has been razed and a fellowship hall with a folding partition (which can be opened if needed for additional seating), kitchen, and rest rooms have been built.

Bible school group – 1940s l.–r. front: Cathlene Horton, June Wills, Helen Jean Loving, R. H. Wills, Nancy Carol Morris, Fred Stinnette, Robley Loving, Calvin Burford, Fritz Belk; row 2: Malcolm Wills, Frank Wills Jr., Virginia Morris, Betty Jean Coffey, Snooks Stinnette, James Marshall Brown, ?, Shirley Loving, Ethel Pick, June Rucker; row 3: Billy Burford, Bobby Morris, Glen Coffey, cousin of Glen Coffey, Frances Morris, Ann Younger, Madeline Horton, Beth Younger, Frances Belk, Vernell Morris; back row: George Burford, ? looking over shoulder, Frances Hudson, Mac Smith looking over shoulder, Rufus Coffey, Martha Smith, Thelma Shrader, Bill Walker, ?, Dot Loving, Marshall Burford, ?, Arlene Horton, ?, Mrs. Hoge Smith, Miss Alpha Dameron, Doris Morris seated in doorway.

Ministers of the church have been: Rev. David Teese, Rev. George H. Ray, Rev. J. A. Thomas, Rev. Clyde Walsh, Rev. Jonathan Edwards, Rev. J. Hoge Smith, Rev. George Bird Talbot, Mr. Haywood L. Wooldridge (layman), Rev. R. R. Ramsey, Rev. Charles E. Sutton, Rev. J. Renwick Kennedy, Rev. Harold V. Kuhn, Rev. Wayne Meredith, and Rev. Barry Tucker, present minister.

Old Elon Presbyterian Church showing old manse in right background – *Jackie Miller Mann*

Current Elon Presbyterian Church – *Rev. Barry Tucker*

ELON PRESBYTERIAN CHURCH BIBLE SCHOOL

As I mentioned in the Elon Baptist Church history, during the early 1940s, we were in a field with three other churches, and, therefore, had preaching at our church one Sunday morning and one Sunday night each month. We would go to Elon Presbyterian Church after Sunday School on the days we didn't have preaching and worship with them.

The community children would attend Elon Presbyterian Church Bible School. For a number of years, a group from Rivermont Presbyterian Church would come to Elon to help

Bible School group circa 1945, l.–r.: Back row:?, Mrs. Carrie Burford, Virginia Morris, Mrs. Will Hicks, Ann Younger, Lois Burch, ?, ?, Ethel Dawson, June Rucker, Gloria Wiley, ?, Miss Alpha Dameron, ? ; Row 3: Mr. Talbot, Marilyn Burch, ?, Carolyn Horsley, Helen Jean Loving, June Wills, Warren Rucker, Neil Peters, Beth Younger; Row 2: Junior Wills, Robley Loving, Fred Stinnette, Snooks Stinnette, Calvin Burford, R. H. Wills, Sylvia Loving, N. J. Thomas, James Brown, ?, Betty Jean Coffey; Front: George Talbot, ?, Johnny Layne, Charles Wills, Wade Talbot, Florence Foster, Vera Loving, Nancy Wills, Barbara Wills, Earl Collins Wiley, Barbara Ann Wiley, Connie Stinnette, Nancy Morris, Lois Layne,? – *Ann Correll*

with conducting Bible School. Helen Nowlin was one of the group who came to help.

Frances Belk Morris would drive Mr. Belk's big car and pick up some of the local children. Others would bring children from below Elon. Mrs. Guy Lewis would bring the Wallace girls, Kate and Isabelle, when they were visiting their grandfather, Colonel Hyatt, at Red Hill at Pedlar Mills.

Miss Alpha Dameron, who grew up at the Dameron house near Elon, would come out from Lynchburg, and teach. She was born blind, so she would have her Bible in Braille to read the scripture and teach us. She could play the piano, and even gave piano lessons. Barbara Ann Wiley took lessons from her and at different times has served as pianist, and choir director at Elon Baptist Church.

l.–r. back: Mrs. Carrie Burford, Mrs. Lula Wills, Mrs. Will Hicks, Miss Alpha Dameron, Mrs. Talbot; front: Mrs. Mildred Thomas, Mrs. Talbot's sister, Rev. George Bird Talbot – *Ann Correll*

Miss Alpha would stay in Elon the full two weeks, and different people would give her dinner and supper and have her spend the night. My mother, Massie Foster, would usually keep her for a night. Fried chicken was one of her favorite dishes, so mother always had that on her dinner menu. Usually there would be some chicken left over for Miss Alpha to have some for supper. As children, we would get tickled, because, she would laugh and say, "If there is anything I like better than fried chicken, it's more fried chicken!" With her keen hearing, I am sure she could hear us snickering.

The bedrooms were upstairs, so she would count the steps as she went up. Before she got into bed she would remove her glass eyes and place them in a little box. The next morning when she got up, she would put them back in. When she got to the stairs, she would remember that there were thirteen steps and count them as she came down. Soon after breakfast, she would be picked up to go back to Bible School, and after teaching, she would go to a different home for the night.

Bible School would last for two weeks. There were teachers for all age groups, and the older children were expected to memorize a chapter of scripture. Also, we had to study the Catechism. We made crafts, learned new songs, and played games. Mr. Talbot was the preacher, and he usually directed the games. When we finished with the games, we usually would go across the road and go onto the foot log to get a drink of water from the community spring.

At the end of the two weeks, we would have a commencement program at night, so our parents could attend. This would involve reciting scriptures we had learned, and singing the new songs.

ELON ELEMENTARY SCHOOL

Old, old, Elon School

This two-room school was located on what is now Cedar Gate Road, a little beyond Elon Presbyterian Church. It was used until a new Elon School was built in 1921. The building has had several owners and some additions, and it is still standing and is the home of Toppie Sigmon.

ELON ELEMENTARY AND HIGH SCHOOL

Old Elon High School – completed in 1922 – *H. R. Nixon*

Students first attended the new school in 1922. The first and only graduating class from the High School was in 1924. They were Dorothy Moore, Margaret Morris, Elmo Page, and Mary Lou Page.

After that, students in the tenth and eleventh grades went to Madison Heights High School and graduated from there. In the school year 1943, Tyler Fulcher was teaching ninth grade at Elon and was moved to Madison Heights High School as principal. He took his ninth grade class with him and taught them until the end of the school year. The next year, Mrs. Catherine White, who taught chemistry and physics at Elon went to Madison Heights to teach.

I started to Elon Elementary School for the school year 1943–1944.

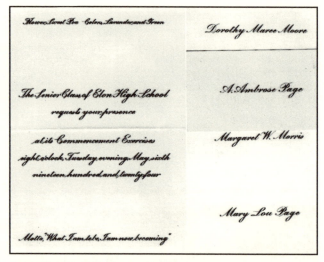

Graduation announcement and personal cards – *Courtesy Jackie Miller Mann*

Graduates and others at Elon Betterment League fund raiser in 1950s: l.–r. Gilbert McGlothlin, Harold Throneburg, Elmo Page, Dorothy (Moore) Page, Mrs. Etta Brandt (first principal), Margaret (Morris) Wiley, and Mary Lou (Page) Burch – *Marita Taylor*

ELON ELEMENTARY SCHOOL

Elon School 1943–44 students' pictures arranged to show 'ELON') Identified as follows: top of "E" – Calvin Burford, Betty Jean Coffey, ?, ?, down: Dorothy Ogden; middle of "E" – N. J. Thomas, June Wills, James Brown; down: Gene Peters; bottom of "E" Nina Harris, Snooks Stinnette, Audrey Riley, ? Whitehead; top of "L" – Gordon Foster, Dot Brown, Robert Sigmon, Earnest Mays, Helen Jean Loving, Theodore Mays, Marie Garrett, Caleb Stowe; "O" – clockwise: Janice Brown, R. H. Wills, Joan Eggleston, ?, Connie Stinnette, Robley Loving, Ollie Mae Stowe, Floyd Whitehead, Fred Stinnette, Joyce Brown, Lois Layne, ?, ? Higginbotham, ?, Carolyn Horsley, ? ; "N" – bottom left: Cecil Higginbotham, Betty Jean Garrett, Ray Watts, Nancy Wills, Wade Talbot, Florence Foster, Johnny Layne, Flora Campbell, Billy Ogden, ? Stinnette, ?, Harold Stinnette, ?, Withers Whitehead, Gene Sigmon, ? – *Courtesy Catherine Sigmon Moore*

At that time there were two grades to a room: first and second with Miss Ethel Tinsley as teacher (who also served as principal); third and fourth with Mrs. Mildred White as teacher; and fifth and sixth with Miss Eloise Wilsher as teacher. Miss Florence Lewis was the teacher for seventh grade, and the eighth graders were sent to Madison Heights High School.

As I already mentioned, my first year in school was the 1943–44 school year. We had to walk to school which was a little less than a mile. I missed some that year due to the fact that I had the German measles and the red measles. By the time I started second grade, Mr. Hannon Rucker drove his own bus over our road and picked us up in front of our house. I remember that Nancy Johnson and

L.–r.: Mrs. Mildred (McIvor) White, Miss Ethel Tinsley, Mrs. Catherine White, Miss Florence Lewis, teachers – *Courtesy Ann Correll*

Miss Eloise Wilsher– *Courtesy Helen Foster Connelly*

the Blanks children had to walk from a long distance on Winesap Road to the intersection of Cedar Gate Road to be picked up by the bus, for several years. Then the bus went all the way through and came out to the intersection of Winesap Road and Route 130/ Elon Road (now Winridge Road and Elon Road) and met the bus from Elon to exchange students going to Madison Heights High School. After the county bought school buses, Mr. Rucker continued to drive until his retirement in June, 1977.

Mr. Hannon Rucker with last school bus he drove – *May Rucker collection*

The school had quite a large auditorium and a nice stage with curtains. Many community functions and fund raisers were held there. You didn't have social halls in the churches then.

We had pot-belly stoves in the classrooms for heat. They had to be stoked with coal during the day. We had outdoor bathrooms/toilets. The one for the boys was down at the edge of a big field at Mr. Camden's orchard. The girls' was a little closer to the school. One year we had a lot of locusts. Boys being boys would try to put them on the girls. I remember one time that we had run to the girls' toilet and one of the boys yanked the door open and threw some locusts in. Unfortunately, one of the girls was using the toilet, but I don't think anything was exposed. (By the time my older son, Alan, started school, they had installed indoor plumbing in the school, so no more outhouses!)

5th & 6th grade students about 1948: l.–r. Front: ? Campbell, Ronnie Stowe, June Peters, ? Eagle, Billy Ogden, Carl Higginbotham, William Watts; Middle: Miss Eloise WIlsher, Barbara Ogden, Jackie Miller, Nancy Wills, Betty Garrett, Margaret Campbell, Charles Wills; Back: Johnny Layne, ?, Michael Taylor, ? – *Florence Foster Nixon*

One day one of my classmates didn't come to school, and one of her neighbors brought a note for the teacher. That morning, the principal called us out of the classroom to check our heads. Apparently at recess in playing hide and seek, cooties had traveled from one girl's head to another. After checking our heads, the principal checked the head of the brother of one of the students, and they were sent home to get rid of their cooties. My friend was back at school the next day.

Around 1948: L.–r. Front: Shirley Mays, June Peters, Helen Foster; 2nd Row: Cecil Watts, William Watts, Eleanor Wills, Barbara Ogden; 3rd Row: ?, ?, ?

L.–r. Florence Foster, Betty Jean Garrett, Nancy Wills

Mr. Talbot, the Presbyterian preacher, would come about once a month to have a program with some scripture and some songs. We would maybe sing a hymn or two, but then we would sing fun songs, such as "John Brown's Baby Had a Cold Upon His Chest," and use all the appropriate motions. We sang many others, including "My Bonnie Lies Over the Ocean."

Some of the principals at old Elon School were: Mrs. Etta Brandt, Nay Rucker, Tyler Fulcher, Miss Ethel Tinsley, June (Rucker) Bibb, Mrs. Loop, and Henry Emerson.

NEW ELON ELEMENTARY SCHOOL

New Elon Elementary School – *H. R. Nixon*

The first year in the new Elon School was 1968–1969. This school was built behind the old school which stood at the crest of the hill. This school was built with a cafetorium, office, and separate rooms for 1st through 7th grades.

FIRST GRADE 1968–69

l.–r. 1st row: Rita Sexton, Carolyn Turner, Glenda Campbell, Miss Addie Eley (teacher), Douglas King, Tommy Mason, Johnny Mays; 2nd row: Ricky Branham, Roy Johns, David Johns, Linda Watts, Gail Humphreys, Donna Hamilton; 3rd row: Eddie Turman, Mark Ogden, Marshall Branham, Lee Wood, Donald King, Sharon Staton, Sandra Watts – *Elon School Yearbook*

SECOND GRADE 1968–69

l.–r. 1st row: Brian Pick, Dwain Branham, Jeff Ferguson, Virgil Coleman, Tony Stinnett, Helen Rucker, Mike Wooldridge; 2nd row: Rose Freeman, Teresa Carson, Kim Davis, Mrs. W. R. Williams (teacher), Susan Harris, Linda Mays, Angela Campbell; 3rd row: Jimmy Davis, Lori Ogden, Alicia Hill, Wanda Watts, Jackie Huffman, Amy Waugh, Lisa Garrett, Lori Roberts (Absent – Robert King) – *Elon School Yearbook*

THIRD GRADE 1968–69

l.–r. 1st row: Scottie Throneburg, Rodney Taylor, Lynn McConnell, Becky Tabor, Nancy Foster, Mrs. R. T. Campbell (teacher), Kathy Mays, Cathy Sigmon, Herman Branham, Glenn Duff, Everett Donigan; 2nd row: Vicky Campbell, Dennis Branham, Wayne Harris, Barry Clarkson, Danny Hill, Gary Pick, Chancer Humphries, Judy Smith, Norma Jean Hamilton, Tracy Ferguson, Walter Wooldridge; 3rd row: Debbie Carson, Gary Watts, Darlene Branham, Kenneth Watts, Larry Stallings, Rosa Stallings, David Crews, Cheryl Connelly, Shelia Wills, Junior Watts, Dennis Turner – *Elon School Yearbook*

FOURTH GRADE 1968–69

l.–r. 1st row: Annie Waugh, Vicky Loving, Deborah Burch, Melissa Tabor, David Mays, Bob Stovall, Mark Moser, Sam Stinnette, David Freeman, Sharon Jones; 2nd row: Ted Miller, Freddie Sexton, Tommy Hill, Mrs. V. A. Coleman (teacher), Alan Nixon, Edward Donigan, Gerald Sexton; 3rd row: Randy Staton, Cheryl Hall, Angela Woodruff, Delia Branham, Betty Coles, Hugh Bolton, Edith Branham – *Elon School Yearbook*

FIFTH GRADE 1968–69

l.–r. 1st row: Danny Johns, Phil Ware, Mike Ogden, Jimmy Nuckles, Mayo Knight, Greg Connelly, Tommy Ranson, Shirley Sexton, Anne Staton, Debbie Hodnett, Patsy Womack; 2nd row: Greg Loving, Ray Foster, Kevin Bernard, Jimmy Mays, Mrs. D. D. Dillard (teacher), Billy Mason, David Fifer, Jimmy Sellick; 3rd row: Harry Clark Rucker, David Clark, Mike Wills, Beveley McFaden, Evelyn Donigan, Ray Branham, Kathy Harris, Lois Jean Duff, Carolyn Branham, Linda Branham – *Elon School Yearbook*

SIXTH GRADE 1968–69

l.–r. 1st row: Annmarie Vosburgh, Fay Jones, Leah Coleman, Debbie Sales, Kaye Sellick, Gail Branham, Faye Campbell; 2nd row: John Tucker, Charles Sales, Stanley Garrett, Mr. King (teacher), Mike Ware, Ronnie Davis, Eddie Foster; 3rd row: Sue Foster, Anne Rucker, Pam Cash, Darlene Humphries, Mike King, Kenneth Smith, Tommy Ayers, Luke Hudson (absent – Edna Stinnett) – *Elon School Yearbook*

SEVENTH GRADE 1968–69

l.–r. 1st row: Daryl Loving, Melanie Harris, Diane Ogden, Rhonda Hodnett, Sharon Mays, Darlene Eggleston, Rebecca Hall, Marilyn Branham, Bonnie Foster, Ruth Sigmon; 2nd row: Oneal Sandidge, Timothy Stinnette, Hugh Bailess, John Garrett, Mrs. E. C. Campbell (teacher), Larry Branham, Danny Connelly, Jimmy Burch; 3rd row: Jerry Johns, Richard King, David Coles, Gil Moser, David Massie, Gary Sexton, Debrell Foster, Yevonne Crews, Susan Miller, Rillie Johns, Kathy Sexton, Douglas Ayers (absent – Don Mays). – *Elon School Yearbook*

ELEMENARY BAND AT ELON

l.–r. 1st row: Ruth Sigmon, Rebecca Hall, Faye Campbell, Eddie Foster, Leah Coleman, Kaye Sellick, Debbie Hodnett; 2nd row: Harry Clark Rucker, Ann Rucker, Rhonda Hodnett, Debrell Foster, Hugh Bolton, Tim Stinnette, Miss Joyce Whitehead (instructor), Beverly McFadden, Pam Cash, Diane Ogden, Mayo Knight, Alan Nixon – *Elon School Yearbook*

They had started band programs in the elementary schools, and this was very beneficial to the high school band.

By 1972, the new school was over populated, and students from Elon were sent to Amherst Elementary School for the 7th grade. The next year they attended Amherst Junior High School for the 8th grade.

The Amherst County High School was overcrowded by the time they were in 9th grade. A portion of the old Amherst high school was renovated and 9th graders went there for a split day. Some students had classes at the Annex (the old high school) in the morning, and others at the high school. They would switch at the middle of the day. Additions have been made to the high school, and now all students go to Amherst County High School for grades 9–12.

Some years after the completion of Elon School in 1968, an addition was made with a library being built, as well as a number of classrooms. About twelve years ago, another addition which included a computer lab, teachers' lounge, a larger library and seven or eight classrooms was made, and it gave the building a "T" shape. In June 2004 renovations were made to the office, and a gymnasium was built and in use for the 2005–2006 school year. Now even with the additions, etc., kindergarten through grade 5 are taught at Elon, and then students go to Monelison Middle School for grades 6–8.

Principals for the new Elon Elementary School have been: Mrs. Pekar, Ardie Bumgarner, Bobby Flowers, Betty Douglas, Jane Andes, Ralph Steele (filled in for a while), Kathy Nance, Ashley Wallace, and Kimberly Anderson.

Over the years, both of my sons, Alan Nixon and Scott Nixon have attended school at Elon. Also, their children (my grandchildren) attended Elon School. They are: Kelly Nixon, Jennifer Nixon, Dylan Nixon, Dakota Nixon, and Drake Nixon.

Present Elon Elementary School – *H. R. Nixon*

ELON HOUSES

MISTOVER

House when auction was being held – *H. R. Nixon*

This house is located on what was Townley family property. Their property was next to the property where the Dillard Mansion "The Shelter" is now located, before Route 130/Elon Road was changed. According to Jean (Dillard) Neblett, the Townley house was a big white house which was on the curve just a little down, and in front of where Mr. Scott built his house in 1942. It is now named Mistover Mansion Road, which is a little west of Ambrose Rucker Road. There was an old school on the property, run by a

Mrs. Jones. Mr. Scott also, ran Mistover orchard. The old Townley Tan Yard was located on this property. In recent years the Freeman family built a house and used some of the rock from the old Townley chimney.

DEARING MANSION/SPEED-THE-PLOW

Speed-the-Plow – **H. R. Nixon**

According to Amherst County records, Col. Charles Ellis of Richmond bought the property in 1835. His daughter, Jane, married William Dearing of Rappahannock County. On November 16, 1850, Mr. Dearing bought the property (located on what is now Ambrose Rucker Road) from Mr. Ellis' widow. It is reported that the Shelton brothers helped build the mansion house shortly after 1850, using bricks made on the property. It is a Greek revival–style house, originally built as a three-story, six-room brick house.

The Dearings had three children: Clarence, William Alfred, and Jane. Clarence was an active member at Elon Baptist Church, and Alfred married Florence Scott who grew up in the home named "Riverview," which was where Monacan Park is now located. Jane married a Cox.

In 1925, Rowland Lea purchased the property, and he and his wife, Theadora Stevens Lea had an addition built to the north side of the house for a kitchen and dining room.

In 1938, Rowland Lea's nephew and his wife, Phillip and Mary (Mae) Girling came to Speed-the-Plow and managed the orchards until the 1990s. Now the Girling's son, Rowland Lea Girling, and his wife, Lorriane Shiels Girling, live there and are restoring the house and making changes to the grounds.

THE ROCK HOUSE AT SPEED-THE-PLOW

In 1932, George Stevens, brother of Theadora Lea, wanted a little refuge from Wall Street in New York City. He had a rock house built close to Speed-the-Plow, as well as some other buildings on the farm.

Mr. and Mrs. Sam Belk, along with their children, Fritz and Frances, moved to Amherst County for him to build the Rock House for Mr. Stevens.

Rock house at Speed-the-Plow

THE SHELTER

"The Shelter" – *Elizabeth Dillard Ogden*

This mansion house which is located at the corner of Ambrose Rucker Road and Route 130/Elon Road is a residence of native stone which was built in 1940–42 for David Hugh Dillard and his wife, Leonora Rosa van Gelder Dillard.

This house was built by Sam Belk, who had built the rock house for Mr. Stevens. Most of the rocks were obtained from Tobacco Row Mountain and area. The Dillards chose the location because of the scenic view, and there is a large cupola on the house with a pineapple on the top. From there they could look over Homewood Farms.

There is a cornerstone on the house which reads:
SHELTER
BUILT BY
DAVID HUGH DILLARD
1942
ARCHITECTS BUILDER
J. EVERETTE FAUBER Jr.
SAMUEL E. BELK
TRUEHEART POSTON

The house was built using large amounts of metal, concrete, stone, and very little wood. Upon entering the foyer, there are three large rooms with open arches. There is a black marble fireplace made by Italian cutters, in one of the rooms, and there are wide plank floors. The rooms have marble window sills. There were black-and-white-tile baths for all the bedrooms. A large garage is on the lower level, and a room with a drugstore-type soda fountain. Shortly after the Dillards moved into their new house, Mrs. Dillard invited the Elon ladies to tea, and showed them through the home.

The present owners named the house "Stonehurst."

1939 view of Homewood Farms from location where The Shelter was to be built – *Elizabeth Dillard Ogden*

ALEX MORRIS HOUSE

Alex Morris house in 1957 – *Ann and Spence Correll*

Mr. and Mrs. Morris' farm was located across the road from where "The Shelter" was built.

Mr. Morris had a farm and orchard, as most of the local people did at that time. If they didn't have a commercial orchard, they raised fruit for their own family use.

In August, 1951, there was a terrible thunder storm that caught Mr. Morris outside. When some time had passed and he didn't come to the house, they went looking for him. They found his body. Apparently lightning had struck a metal button of his overalls.

Shortly thereafter the family sold the farm to Mr. Dillard, and built a brick home in Elon.

MOUNTAIN HOME/JOHN DILLARD HOUSE

In a conversation I had with Jean (Dillard) Neblett in April 1992, she said she grew up on the property at Elon which was known as Mountain Home where her Grandma Dillard (Mrs. Ella Dillard) had purchased the farm. Mrs. Dillard was the mother of John Dillard, David Hugh Dillard, Queena Stovall, and others. Jean said this property adjoined Mr. and Mrs. Fletcher who lived on what we know as Homewood Farms. The Fletchers lived in the big house which, in later years, was lived in by Melvin Bailess and his family.

Mrs. Dillard named the place "Killey Kranky Farm" and her son, John Dillard, and his

ELON HOUSES

John Dillard family house – *John Dillard Jr.*

family lived in the house located between where the mansion house was later built and the Fletcher house. Some years later she sold the property to her son, David Hugh Dillard. He built a pool and pool house in the bottom down from the house where John and his family lived.

Margaret (Dillard) Camden Weeks told me that her father contracted tuberculosis and at the doctor's suggestion, moved to Elon where he could

John Dillard house in background and D. H. Dillard pool in foreground – *Lou Basten*

breathe clean country air. She also told the story about her parents driving from Elon into Lynchburg one rainy night to see a movie, not knowing that two old hens were on the bumper of their Ford car. Her father was known for his slow driving. As he poked along, cussing the flickering lights, the old hens were flapping their wings trying to stay on the bumper. Upon arriving on Main Street, he checked the front of the car and found the hens. He put them in the trunk of the car and he and Ruth went on to the movie.

FLETCHER HOUSE/DILLARD HOUSE

This house was once occupied by Frank Fletcher, son of Ned Fletcher and his wife, Betsy. She was the daughter of Mr. Musselman, the grocery man at Elon.

After Mrs. Ella Dillard bought the "Killey Kranky Farm," she lived in this house for some time. She later sold the property to her son, David Hugh Dillard, which he operated as

Fletcher house with Dillard family in front – *Margaret Dillard Camden Weeks*

Homewood Farms. She moved to Pedlar Farm and lived there for a number of years. Some years later David Hugh purchased the "Wigwam" and fixed it up and she moved there to be nearer family. Her daughter, Queena Stovall, and her family moved in with her. Ella lived there until her death in April, 1945, at age 89.

Notice the rock wall at the edge of the farm road. In some areas, the rock wall was on both sides of the road. For years, Melvin Bailess and his family lived in the house on Homewood Farms.

The house was located across from the Dairy House, and was torn down in 1992. The property is now owned by Gen. Albert and his family.

House taken in later years – *Lou Basten*

THE OLD MANSE

Old Presbyterian Manse – *H. R. Nixon*

This house is located at the corner of Route 130/Elon Road and Manse Road.

In 1919, Oscar Preston "O. P." Morris donated an acre of land, and the Elon Presbyterian Church trustees purchased an additional acre and one-half of adjoining land from him to build a Presbyterian manse. Rev. Clyde J. Walsh, who was the preacher at that time, oversaw the construction from 1920 until 1924. The church members did most of the building. The rocks for the living room fireplace and the

Rocks being hauled by horses and wagons from mountain for chimney and fireplace – *Mrs. Lena Wills*

chimney were hauled from the mountain by horse and wagon.

After the Manse was completed, Rev. and Mrs. Walsh moved in. He was instrumental in starting a Boy Scout troop for the Elon area. The manse over the years was a meeting place for the women and youth of the community.

There were several preachers after Mr. Walsh. Mr. Bird Talbot and his family came in the 1940s. Mr. Talbot had been a missionary to China, and left because of WWII.

Front porch of manse in 1920s: l.–r. back row: Lena Belle Crist, Lizzie Younger, Alpha Dameron, Ragland Ballowe, Ola Moore, Cassie Lee Smith, Mrs. Ruth (John) Dillard; middle row: Mrs. Alma Walsh, Mrs. Bratton, Mrs. George Ewers, Zelma Moore, Miss Virgie Ballowe, Mrs. George Jackson; Front: Margaret Morris, Dorothy Moore, Hazel Hicks, Frances Ballowe, Daisy Smith, Cornelia Smith – *Courtesy Daisy Oblinger*

Side yard of manse in 1940s l.–r. Standing: Mrs. Massie Foster, Mrs. Annie Morris, Mrs. Clara Morris, Mrs. Sadie Harris, Mrs. Eva Harris, Mrs. Annie Tomlin, Mrs. Annie Sigmon, Mrs. Essie Phillips, Mrs. Guy Lewis, Mrs. Vernie Wiley, ?, Mrs. Lillian Hicks; Kneeling: Maggie Brown, Mrs. Lizzie Younger, Mrs. Pearl Brown, Mrs. Eva Burch, Mrs. Talbot, Mrs. Mattie Belle Belk, Mrs. Addie Foster, Mrs. Lula Wills

He served the whole community during the war, and then left with his family, and went back to China as a missionary in 1947. They had another daughter after they moved from Elon.

In 1964 the church decided to build a new manse. The old manse was purchased by Maurice William Nixon and Amy Rodgers Nixon, who planned to move there after their retirement. They continued to rent the house to the current occupants, and did not move into the manse until 1967. They connected to the county water system (the house had been on the community spring), upgraded the electric system, added central heat and air conditioning, insulated the house, and made other improvements, including adding a second bathroom.

In 1979, Maurice Nixon sold the property to his grandson, Maurice Alan Nixon and his wife. They raised their two daughters, Kelly and Jennifer, there. Since then, Alan has made improvements to the house and grounds, including installing a pool.

MARTIN/THOMAS HOUSE

This house is located on Manse Road, just a little ways off Route 130/Elon Road.

The house was built in the 1920s. A back corner of the property adjoins Speed-the-Plow property. At one time it was owned by Bruce Younger and his brother, Lawson Younger. It was then purchased by Claude

Martin/Thomas house – *H. R. Nixon*

Martin and his wife, Willie, who owned it for many years. I have been told that Mr. Martin was the only person in Elon who raised tobacco. The Martins sold the property to a young couple, who kept it for a few years. Grover and Janet Thomas purchased the farm in the 1970s. Grover and Janet owned and operated Janet's Salads, and later sold the business to Mrs. Giles' Salads.

They continue to raise cattle on the farm, as well as hay fields.

EARL MORRIS HOUSE

Earl Morris family house with Annie Morris at right – *Mary Foster*

The Earl Morris family lived in a house that at one time had belonged to the Ramsey family. That house burned around 1930, and they lived in a tent on the property for about a year and a half while the new log house was being built. The logs were covered with shingles in the 1960s. Mr. Morris served in WWI and their son, Earl Grey Morris Jr., was a German prisoner of war for a while, during WWII. Their other son, Robert Preston Morris, served in the Korean Conflict. They had a small peach orchard, and Mr. Morris ran a little store, where he sold gas for a while. Later he worked at Camden & Younger Store and sometimes drove their school bus.

WILLIAM MORRIS/WILL HICKS HOUSE

This house stood at the corner of what is now Route 130/Elon Road and Cedar Gate Road. It was owned for many years by William Morris and his family. For a year or so, with the rationing of gas during WWII, the family moved into Lynchburg for him to be near his job with Appalachian Power Co. After the war was over, they moved back to Elon to their house.

Talbot family taken in front of Earl Morris House, l.–r.: Mr. Talbot in Militia uniform holding Patty Bird, Mrs. Talbot with Wade in front of her, George beside her

At that time, there were no houses on Elon Road between their house and the manse. There was a small orchard beside the house, and there was a large barn at the back of the house (with the end toward Cedar Gate Road) between their house and the Presbyterian Church.

At the front of the house which faced Elon Road, there were no houses between the Crist/Thomas house and the Earl Morris house. You could see as far as the Alex Morris house.

William Morris house – *Doris Foster*

Frances Morris holding cat in front of barn – *Doris Foster*

Doris Morris with wide open spaces and Alex Morris house in far right background – *Doris Foster*

The property where the house and barn were located was purchased by Elon Presbyterian Church. Some years later the house and barn were torn down. The church sign is near the corner, and they have extended the parking lot up the hill, almost to Elon Road.

CRIST/THOMAS HOUSE

Mrs. Lena Belle (Watts) Crist was a sister of Mrs. Lizzie (Watts) Younger. She was widowed while she lived there. Gerald J. and Mildred Thomas bought the property in 1940 and lived there with their two sons, Gerald and N. J. In 1948, Mr. Thomas built a store beside the house. They sold the house to A. B. and Winnie Dodd in 1959.

Crist/Thomas house – *H. R. Nixon*

SAM BELK HOUSE

Samuel "Sam" Erastus Belk and his wife, Mattie Belle, along with their children came to Amherst County for Sam to build the rock house on Speed-the-Plow for Mr. George C. Stevens. They decided to stay in Elon, and Mr. Belk built a rock home on Cedar Gate Road. In early 1940s he built The Shelter for Mr. and Mrs. David Hugh Dillard.

Belk house taken in 2010 – *H. R. Nixon*

The picture on the right shows the Dick Wills house in the far left background. You can see how rural Elon was in the 1940s. The background is where the Hunt Club Subdivision on Cedar Gate Road is now located.

CAMDEN HOUSE

This house is located at the corner of the Bethel/Salt Creek Road (now Monacan Park Road). This was the home of Bernard Camden. His mother, Virginia (Rhodes) Camden, lived with him. His sister, Sadie (Camden) Harris, moved from Allwood to Elon to live with him after the death of her husband.

l.–r.: Ann Younger, Fritz Belk, Beth Younger – *Doris Foster*

It is said that the portion of the house which had the rock chimney was built of logs, and was one of the oldest houses in the village of Elon. Some years ago there was a storm and the chimney fell down. The house has had some additions and improvements, over the years.

Camden house – *H. R. Nixon*

Front of Camden house, standing on porch: (Miss Margaret "Maggie" Rhodes, sister of Virginia (Rhodes) Camden; l.–r. back: Bernard Camden, Hiram "Plunk" Camden; Middle: Betty Cassidy, Mary (Camden) Waidelich, John Camden, Robert Camden; front: Dewey Camden, Virginia (Rhodes) Camden, Sadie (Camden) Harris. – *Ruth Foster*

Section of house with old rock chimney – *H. R. Nixon*

O. P. MORRIS/BRUCE YOUNGER/GUGGENHEIMER HOUSE

House which was a little below Camden and Younger Store –*Mary Foster*

By the early 1900s, Mr. O. P. Morris owned much of the property in the Village of Elon.

The O. P. Morris family lived in this house, until he sold most of his Elon property and moved to Lynchburg. Bernard Camden and H. P. Camden bought the store and house property from Mr. Morris. Bruce Younger bought H. P. Camden's share and the Younger family lived in this house until they built a new brick one on the loop of old Elon Road, which is now named Younger Drive. After Max Guggenheimer purchased Camden and Younger store property, which included the old house, the Guggenheimer family lived in this house until they sold the property.

KEITH/BURFORD/TABOR HOUSE

This house is located across Route 130/Elon Road from Camden and Younger's Store. It was built circa 1914 by Harry Keith. He was the father of Lewis Keith, whose mother died when he was only 19 months old. Mr. Keith bought the Keith home place near Agricola and moved there with his sons, Wilson and Lewis, where his unmarried sisters could help raise his children. He sold the Elon property to Willie Burford and Carrie (Keith) Burford. Most people called her "Aunt Carrie," whether they were actually related to her on not. For many years, Mr. Willie Burford was the janitor at Elon School. A number of families have owned this house since the Burfords. They include the Tinsleys, and Mr. and Mrs. Ed Foster. The Tabors have owned the house and lived there since in the late 1960s.

Keith/ Burford/Tabor house – *Courtesy Eleanor Tabor*

BROWN FAMILY HOUSES

From the time my family moved to Elon, there were two families of Browns on the loop of old Elon Road (now Younger Drive). One was Mrs. Ila Brown with some of her grown children. The other was Addie Brown and his wife, Pearl, along with their children, Helen and James. The Addie Brown house is across Younger Drive from Elon Baptist Church. It is now owned by a Rucker family.

Addie Brown house – *Courtesy Helen (Brown) Camden*

HUNT CLUB HOUSE/GREAT OAKS ESTATE

This house was probably built in the later 1800s. A plat prepared in 1895 shows a house and 133 acres. It also shows Elon Post Office. Some of the owners over the years have been: Mrs. Grubbs, the TInsleys, John Stuby, John Stuby and William and Lily Webb, Bruce Wiley, Bruce and Rosa Dobyns, E. V. Perry, Bernard Camden, David H. and Rosa L. Dillard, R. Cary and Judith S. Fairfax. The present owners are Alfred and Rebecca Coleman.

During 2009–10, they have made changes and additions, including columns on the front of the house. East of their house on Route 130/Elon Road is a section of Hunt Club Subdivision.

Hunt Club house, circa 1910; l.–r. William Webb, Lily Webb, John Stuby – *Courtesy Becky Coleman*

Great Oaks Estate – *Rebecca Coleman*

THOMAS JEFFERSON FOSTER HOUSE

The Tom Foster family moved to Elon in the late 1920s. The property adjoined the Wigwam property on the east. It adjoined Bernard Camden's orchard property on the south and west. On the north side it adjoined the Hunt Club property. When improvements were made to Elon Road in the 1940s with some of the curves taken out, some of their property became D. H. Dillard property. Across Elon Road from the property is a portion of the Hunt Club Subdivision.

Thomas "Tom" Foster house – *H. R. Nixon*

Mason house – *Lois Mason*

MASON HOUSE

This house was located on the left, headed east, a little ways down Route 130/Elon Road from the Tom Foster house. Mr. and Mrs. Joe Mason moved to the farm in 1939. Mrs. Mason's mother was a Shelton. The long building pictured below is where they raised turkeys. It is similar to the one used by Mr. W. M. Hicks for his chickens.

This property is where the Nottaway subdivision is now located. The farm house is still standing.

Mason turkey house – *Lois Mason*

THE WIGWAM

(See: QUEENA STOVALL AND TRIPLE OAKS SCHOOLS story).

CLOVERDALE

Cloverdale

It is thought that property was acquired in 1802 by the Rev. John Camm of Williamsburg. Rev. Camm's son, John Jr., married a local girl, Elizabeth Powell, and they raised their family there. John Jr., died in 1818, and his widow took over management of the farm and stayed to endure the hardships of the Civil War. There were a number of owners until 1918 when Dr. Arthur Deekens sold the house and 220 acre tract to W. T. Tabor of Welch, W. Va. He was the father of Lena Tabor who married W. P. "Buck" Wills.

The house is strong and well built with the joists and main beams on the foundation made of large oak timbers about 10 inches square. Originally it was fitted inside with hand-hewn laths covered with plaster containing horse hair. The kitchen and dining room were originally in the basement but the Willses changed them to the main level. The two three-story chimneys are the originals, built from brick fired on the plantation.

Since Civil War days the original front and back porches have been replaced with a masonry version, and the front and back double doors replaced with single ones.

Mr. Wills was very active in the American Legion, Post 100. For many years the American Legion Annual Lawn Party was held on the large lawn at Cloverdale.

At Mrs. Lena Wills' death in 1989, she left the property to her two sons.

RED LEVEL

Red Level – *H. R. Nixon*

This house is located on what was old Trent's Ferry Road, now Graham Creek Road (across Route 130/Elon Road from John's Creek Road), and was the home of Mr. and Mrs. T. W. Hicks. According to Mrs. Edna (Ballowe) Hicks, in the 1960s, the house stands on a portion of land granted by Lord Fairfax to four Shelton brothers.

Captain E. L. Shelton willed this house and a tract of land to Mrs. Fannie (Shelton) Ballowe, who was the mother of Mrs. T. W. (Edna Ballowe) Hicks. Mrs. (Fannie Shelton) Ballowe was the daughter of Major Jack Shelton and Sally Bell Shelton

The house has had additions and renovations. The house has stayed in the possession of Shelton descendants over the years. Teddy Hicks farmed, and at one time ran a saw mill.

Teddy and Edna were very active participants in the Elon community and were members of Elon Presbyterian Church. The house was sold, out of the family, following the deaths of the Hickses. Their daughter Aileen Hicks Miller was living with them when she had "The Unwelcome Guests" at her house.

ELON ORGANIZATIONS

ELON CIVIC BETTERMENT LEAGUE

On November 23, 1915, some Elon ladies met to form a club with the general object for the betterment of the Elon district. Originally named Civic Betterment League of Elon District (later named Elon Civic Betterment League), the dues were five cents per month. There were thirty-one charter members, men and women, as follows: Mrs. John Dillard, Mrs. A. W. McFarland, Mrs. John Long, Mrs. Willard Ballowe, Mrs. T. W. Hicks, Mrs. James Moore, Mrs. Dave Watts, Mrs. J. B. Stovall, Mrs. Oscar Morris, Mrs. George Ewers, Mrs. Tilden Keith, Mrs. Cox, Mrs. A. H. Deekens, Mrs. John Webb, Mrs. James Dillard, Mrs. Edgar Wood, Mrs. Abner Grant, Mrs. Aubrey Smith, Mrs. Charles Dameron, Mrs. Jim Ballowe, Miss Sallie Long, Miss Virginia Ballowe, Miss Caroline Harrison, Miss Atala Creasy, Mr. Tallifero Crist, Mr. E. G. Stevens, Mr. and Mrs. Rowland Lea, Mr. and Mrs. John Berry, and Mr. and Mrs. Ned Wortham.

They decided to start a free lending library. They rented a log building from C. W. Dameron which was located at the corner of Bethel Road, now Route 130/Elon Road and Monacan Park Road, for $2.00 a month for a library and meeting place.

They sponsored Christmas pageants, held at one of the community churches. Each child received a bag of candy.

They held fund raisers which included sponsoring Elon Horse Shows. These were held at Homewood Farms.

Other fund raisers were: talent shows, minstrels, womanless weddings, beauty contests, and male beauty contests.

In 1917, the League decided to affiliate with the Cooperative Education Association, and became an auxiliary of Amherst Red Cross and helped with WWI efforts. (During WWII they held classes teaching nursing, rolling bandages, etc.)

Members were urged to visit Riverdale, Elon, and Morris schools to report on conditions. Mrs. J. B. Stovall was asked to organize a Girls Club, and Mrs. Jim Ballowe, a Little Folks Club. A Pig Club was organized by the County Agent for the boys. In May, 1918, the County Agent, Mr. Crawford, and Mr. Bradshaw delivered pigs to the boys of the Pig Club at Elon as follows: James Ballowe, Ambrose Page, Hunter Day, Ned Ewers, Ross Burford,

Harry Rucker, Donald Davis, Harry Ewers, and Harry Duff. There was only one Club from Amherst County to receive pigs. Elon District was given preference as more interest and enthusiasm in community work was shown than any other sections of the county.

In 1918, Mr. Dameron donated one acre of land for a library. The Colgate Fund was

Some of the early League members in 1950s, l.–r.: Rowland Lea, Mrs. T. W. Hicks, Mrs. Willard Ballowe, Mrs. Queena Stovall, Mr. T. W. Hicks – *Marita Taylor*

used for the library, and a community nurse, Miss Davis. Most of Miss Davis' visits were made on horseback. From 1918 to 1923, through club efforts spearheaded by Mrs. Theodora (Rowland) Lea, the nurse assisted the doctor in births. Her charges were as follows: assisting the doctor in births $5.00; use of knife on boils, abscesses, etc. $0.25 to $1.00; dressings $0.10 to $0.25; and sick calls, including simple medicine $0.25.

The League was instrumental in the building of a new school, completed in 1921. Over the years, they have supported many of the school activities, including repairs, and equipment for the building and playground, hot lunch facilities and food, and painting the school.

The League continued to function until the PTA was organized in the early 1960s.

THE ELON VILLAGE LIBRARY

The Elon Library opened in a log cabin in the village of Elon in 1915. The Elon Civic Betterment League felt that a free circulating library and other projects would be of great benefit to the community. The library was stocked with books given by Elon residents. The shelves held a set of encyclopedia, a number of the classics, and some fifty volumes of fiction. In the winter of 1915–16 Mrs. Rowland Lea met with Dr. McIraine, State Librarian of Richmond, for advice as to cataloging, and any information he could give in running a small library. He was most helpful and encouraging, and gave her twenty volumes from his own shelves. He said so far as he knew, Elon had the first rural lending library in the state.

As mentioned, earlier, Mr. Charles Dameron deeded an acre of land to the Elon Civic Betterment League as a site for a permanent library. The records are not clear as to the exact date the building was completed, but it was no later than 1919.

Elon Village Library sign – *H. R. Nixon*

The library was kept well equipped and various civic groups and individuals donated books, and at one time there were more than 2,000 volumes. The furnishings in the library were most unique with a small round table and chairs, and, long benches that once were in the Triple Oaks School.

Elon Village Library – *H. R. Nixon*

The library was used by the community as a meeting house. It was used sometimes on Election Day.

The library was operated by volunteers, and served Elon School children and citizens of the community almost continuously for a number of years. N. J. Thomas, who lived in the Elon community told me about one summer in the 1940s reading a lot of books from the library. The library was temporarily closed in 1965. Miss Phyllis Lea, long associated with the library in capacities ranging from unpaid librarian to fund raiser, was unwilling to accept closing of the library, and began working with other library friends, on a fund raising drive. Necessary repairs and renovations were made, and again it was in operation. Volunteer librarians opened the building one day a week for a while.

Election Day; l.–r.: Hannon Rucker, Ambrose "Shep" Shepherd, Bruce Younger, Sadie Harris, Pearl Brown – *Ruth Foster*

More friends contributed to the library operation including PTA, Elon Ruritan Club, and American Legion Post 100, Elon Presbyterian Church and Elon Baptist Church, and the building was painted. The library closed in the 1970s.

It is a picturesque landmark in the Elon community. It is now owned and maintained by Elon Baptist Church. The building has been painted and the roof was replaced several years ago.

ELON EXTENSION HOMEMAKERS CLUB

The organizational meeting for the Elon Home Demonstration Club, later called the Elon Extension Homemakers Club, was held in the home of Mrs. T. W. Hicks at "Red Level" in late 1922 or early 1923

It is believed that the first members were: Mrs. T. W. Hicks, Mrs. Rowland Lea, Miss Virgie Hicks, Mrs. John W. Dillard, Mrs. J. B. Stovall, Mrs. George Ewers, Mrs. Ola Moore, Mrs. Willard Ballowe, Mrs. Charlie Dameron, Mrs. Cassie Smith, Mrs. John Ballowe, and Mrs. O. P. Morris.

Elon Home Demonstration Club display at Amherst Co. Fair in 1926

Some of the members, l.–r.: Mrs. Mason, Lois Camden, Mitzi Thomas, Daisy (Smith) Oblinger, Phyllis Lea, Cecil Foster – *Collection of Ruth Foster*

They held their meetings in the Elon Library. The county agent and some of the members would give demonstrations. They had day meetings and would bring uncooked food, canned fruit, and vegetables, and different ones would take care of doing the cooking and serving the meal.

They shared information about canning, etc., as well as ideas for making over old garments, updating the style or dying items. They explored different ways of being conservative.

They joined in with the Elon Civic Betterment League in fund raising projects for items for the school. Later they met in places other than the Library.

ELON ORGANIZATIONS

They continue to meet, but the name has been changed several times. It is now known as Elon-Sinai Family and Community Education Club.

1970s in the home of Mrs. Sam Belk; l.–r.: Gwen Campbell; Mrs. Addie Foster, Mary Foster, Mrs. Pearl Brown, Ethel Pick, Mrs. Bruce "Miss Lizzie" Younger

ELON AMERICAN LEGION POST 100

The "American Legion Stewart-Morris Post No. 100" was organized February 7, 1952. The Legion was named for two people from the Elon areas who served in wars and lost their lives. Mr. Stewart lost his life in WWI and Morris in WWII.

The charter members were: Samuel Fritz Belk, Samuel W. Burford, Charles Waidwich Camden, Talmadge R. Coffey, Claude Melvin Eubank, Broadus A. Foster, James A. Foster, Joshua Lyle Foster, William Massie Foster, Harry Wayne Horton, John R. Litchford Jr., Daniel V. Loving, Elmer H. Loving Jr., Walter P. Martin Jr., Lloyd M. Miller, Charles Houston Morris, Earl Grey Morris Jr., Earl Grey Morris Sr., Clayton Andrew Moss, Alfred Percy, William Henry Moss, Charles William Singleton, Edward Woodruff Taylor, Charles Raymond Wills, Walter P. Wills, and William Edward Wills.

They purchased a lot on Elon Road and then had a Buy-A-Block campaign at fifty cents per block to build the foundation for the American Legion Hall. They borrowed some money to complete the building. The building was dedicated on May 17, 1958, with William E. Sandidge serving as master of ceremonies.

American Legion building – *H. R. Nixon*

One of their main fund raising activities was the annual lawn party held on the lawn of Lena and W. P. "Buck" Wills home.

They built a community swimming pool in the 1950s which is still in operation and enjoyed by pool members. Bathing Beauty contests at the pool with water shows being presented under the direction of Joanne and Dick Ricketts were other fund raisers.

ELON RURITAN CLUB

The Elon Ruritan Club was organized in 1958 with their meetings first being held at Elon Elementary School and later in the Elon American Legion Hall. Over the years they were involved with many worthwhile projects with the school and community. The club disbanded in January, 1965.

In June, 1968, the second Elon Ruritan Club was organized. The club continues serving the community to make it a safer place to live. One of their projects is to support the local rescue squad and fire department. They were instrumental in helping secure property for the Elon branch of the Monelison Fire Department. Over the years they have helped the school with securing and maintaining playground equipment.

Elon branch Monelison Fire Department

An early fund raiser was making apple butter outside the Homewood Farms packing shed.

After the apple butter project had been going for a few years, the Home Demonstration Clubs were inspired to sell crafts. From that it grew into what is today the Fall Apple Harvest Festival. (See "ORCHARDS")

The club continues to meet in the American Legion Building Post 100. In 2003, the trustees of the American Legion transferred the property to the Elon Ruritan Club for them to assume the responsibility and maintenance of the building. The American Legion Post 100 retained the right to meet in the building.

The Elon Ruritan Club continues to grow. They have made improvements and renovations to the building, including bathrooms on the first floor, and new windows.

BOY SCOUTS

Rev. Clyde J. Walsh came to Elon Presbyterian Church as pastor in the 1920s. He and his wife were very active in the community. Rev. Walsh was instrumental in organizing a Boy Scout troop. Daisy (Smith) Oblinger shared some pictures. Some of the scouts were her brother Aubrey Smith, Sherman Caldwell, Triggy Tabor, Rice Scott, Dick Wills, Roy Wills, Ashby Wills, Ned Ewers, Donald Watts, Burgess Duff, Randolph Morris, Robert Tabor, Jack Smith, Bob Wiley, and Earl Wiley.

A group of boys along with their leader, drivers and chaperons went to Washington, D.C. for a Boy Scout Jamboree in 1923, and camped at Haines Point with the government furnishing the tents. According to Sherman "Sherry" Caldwell, Route 11 between Buena Vista and Lexington was being built and the road was so muddy they had to buy chains, and then go by a blacksmith shop to have them lengthened. At some places the boys had to get out and push the truck.

They spent the first night at Staunton. They then went on to see the Luray Caverns and spent the second night in Luray. The third night was spent at Little Washington, and the

H. P. "Plunk" Camden driving car and James Ballowe driving truck, going to Haines Point – *Courtesy Daisy Oblinger*

next day they went on into Washington, D.C., and set up camp. Traveling was not so easy in 1923!

In 1923, the Boy Scouts were ready to leave for an outing at Holcomb Rock. Rev. Walsh is in his scout uniform on the front row.

Taken in front of Crist house, later owned by Gerald Thomas – *Courtesy Daisy Oblinger*

Boy Scouts in James River at Holcomb Rock with power plant in background – Triggie Tabor at front of boat – *Courtesy Daisy Oblinger*

Elon adults at Haines Point, l.–r.: Rev. Walsh, H. P. "Plunk" Camden, Jessie Tabor, Frank Tabor – *Courtesy Daisy Oblinger*

Rev. Walsh with Boy Scouts on Eagle Rock at Holcomb Rock – *Courtesy Daisy Oblinger*

Over the years there have been active Boy Scout troops, Girl Scouts, as well as Cub Scouts in the community.

At present there is an active Boy Scout troop sponsored by Elon Presbyterian Church. One of the community services provided by this troop is placing American flags at the graves of veterans in our local cemeteries. There is a local Girl Scout troup and they recently cleared and fenced in a small cemetery near Elon.

l.-r.: Alan Nixon, Gary Pick, Tony Stinnett, Edward Hume, Dennis Turner, Brian Pick, Wayne Harris, Tommy Faust, Rodney Taylor and Dwayne Chaplin. Not pictured – Barry Clarkson – *News & Daily Advance*

CUB SCOUTS

Elon Presbyterian Church sponsored two Cub Scout dens organized in 1968. The den mothers were Rita Wills and Florence Nixon. Some of their helpers were: Barbara Massie, Connie Foster, and Ethel Pick. Some of the cubs were: Hugh Bolton, Dwayne Chaplin, Barry Clarkson, Greg Connelly, Beverly McFadden, Tommy Faust, Ray Foster, Wayne Harris, Edward Hume, Mayo Knight, Randy Massie, Chris Moser, Alan Nixon, Mike Ogden, Brian Pick, Gary Pick, Tony Stinnett, Sam Stinnette, Rodney Taylor, Dennis Turner, Phil Ware, and Mike Wills.

There were weekly meetings with a special theme for each month. A pack meeting was held once a month with the Cub Scouts from both dens attending, along with their parents.

Some of the Cub Scouts participated in a tour of the Lynchburg Municipal Airport. They took an airplane ride on Cardinal Airlines and flew over the Elon area. David B. Shelton was the scoutmaster of the troup at that time. Some of their other outings were a visit to the Lynchburg Fire Station on Fifth Street, a father and son cook-out at Boy Scout Camp Monacan in Nelson County (this is now a part of Wintergreen property), and went fishing with a cook-out at Ricketts' lake.

They also participated in the Pinewood Derby race. Each boy built his own car.

PARENT TEACHERS ASSOCIATION/ PARENT TEACHERS ORGANIZATION

In the early 1960s the PTA was organized at Elon School, so there was no longer a need for the Elon Civic Betterment League. The PTA functioned in the school for a number of years. They had fund raisers, and worked with the school in providing playground equipment, etc. National dues for the PTA became so expensive, and their guidelines so strict, that the teachers and parents decided to organize a Parent Teachers Organization (PTO) in order to make decisions at the local level.

The PTO encourages the parents of students to join the PTO and actively participate in school activities. At times they have contests to see which class can get the most parents to join. They continue to have fund raising projects, and make contributions to the school in different ways. Over the years, some of the things they have provided are: stage curtains, a sound system, play ground equipment, and instructional materials. They also give financial aid for children who otherwise would be unable to go on field trips.

They volunteer in many ways, and sponsor "Theater Four" which is an acting group that comes from Richmond to perform. They work with Field Day at the school in the spring, and pay for blow-ups (shaped large balloons) and other extra things.

Each year, they ask the teachers for a wish list for something they would like for the school to have, and then provide an item from the list. Also, they make a donation to each teacher at the beginning of the school year to help her with the purchase of her school supplies.

ELON GARDEN CLUB

For many years there was an active garden club. A lot of the ladies had flower gardens. Some of the ladies grew prize-winning roses.

ELON STORES, SERVICE STATIONS AND OTHER BUSINESSES

According to information in a history of Elon written by Dorothy Moore in 1924, the Elon Home Demonstration Scrap Book prepared in the 1960s, and *The News*, a store was built in Elon in about 1876. Also, Mr. Musselman operated a bar room in early days in a building near the corner of what is now Elon Road and Monacan Park Road.

Soon after 1876 Mr. Frank Hudson built a store on Route 130/Elon Road in the vicinity of where the large brick building in Elon is now located. After Mr. Hudson's death, the business passed on to his son, W. E. Hudson. In 1912, Mr. O. P. Morris purchased the store from W. E. Hudson.

CAMDEN AND YOUNGER STORE

Mr. Morris kept store in the same building as Mr. Hudson, and then in 1920 sold it to Bernard H. Camden and his brother H. P. "Plunk" Camden.

In 1924, H. P. "Plunk" Camden sold his interest to Bruce Younger, and from that time it became known as Camden and Younger.

In 1928, Bernard Camden and Bruce Younger erected a new Camden and Younger building with living quarters on the second floor.

It was quite a large store that sold most anything a person would need. They had fabric, sewing supplies, boots, groceries, feed for stock, coal oil, and all kinds of

Old Camden Store, l.–r.: Ambrose Page, Bernard Camden, Mary Camden (daughter of John Camden), H. P. "Plunk" Camden, Calvin Wiley, Bertha (Camden) Wiley – *Ruth Foster*

Old Camden & Younger Store: l.–r. Bruce Younger, H. P. "Plunk" Camden – notice horse on left and gas pump on right

supplies. They had high shelves with a rolling ladder to get to the top shelves. They had a grabber for reaching boxes of cereal, etc. from shelves that were not so high.

I especially remember the stalk of bananas that ripened as they were hanging. You could buy as many as you wanted. Like most all of your larger country stores, they had a wheel of cheese from which they would slice off whatever size chunk you wanted.

Sometimes the voting polls were in the store.

On September 1, 1948, the business was sold by B. H. Camden and M. B. Younger to S. E. Belk and Earl Grey Morris Jr., a grandson of an earlier owner, O. P. Morris. A little over a year later on October 1, 1949, the business was purchased by Max Guggenheimer of Lynchburg.

On November 14, 1949, a repairman was working on something in the store using a blowtorch and caused a fire which burned the store and several nearby buildings. They had a bucket brigade from the com-

New Camden and Younger store with gravity-type gas pumps

ELON STORES, SERVICE STATIONS AND OTHER BUSINESSES

New Camden and Younger store with old store building to the left. Building on far left was used by Bernard Camden to keep his equipment for his orchard, etc.

Inside store, l.–r.: Addie Brown, Bernard Camden, Charlie Camden, Bruce Younger

Election Day, l.–r.: front: Gerald Thomas, Gladys Dodd, Lizzie Younger, Bruce Younger, Walter Dawson, Rebecca (Keith) Rutledge, Tilden Keith, Will Dodd, Bernard Camden, George Ewers, Teddy Hicks, back: Tom Burch, Oscar Rutledge, Bob Camden, Sam Belk, Pearl Brown

munity spring, but with the ferocity of the fire and the lack of water the buildings could not be saved. The two apartments on the second floor of the store were occupied by two couples, Harry and Mary Horton, and Bobby and Eleanor Morris. They lost all their possessions.

MAX GUGGENHEIMER'S/ VIRGINIA STORE GENERAL MERCHANDISE

l.–r.: Max Guggenheimer, Earl Grey Morris Jr., B. H. Camden, M. B. Younger, O. P. Morris

After the Camden and Younger store burned Mr. Guggenheimer had a one-story brick store erected and the store was given a new name. He also had a cinder block storage building erected. He stocked some specialty items. One item was flour where the bag stated "Made Expressly for MAX GUGGENHEIMER'S VIRGINIA STORE ELON, VIRGINIA – AT BRIGHTWELL'S MILL."

Also, they were able to have an Elon Post Office once again. It was in the store where locals could pick up their mail.

Some years later Mr. Guggenheimer sold the property and he and his family moved back into Lynchburg. Since then the building has been used for a number of businesses, including a machine shop, antique shop, furniture store, gift and grocery store, and restoration of old cars.

ELON STORES, SERVICE STATIONS AND OTHER BUSINESSES

Max Guggenheimer's Store –
Courtesy Max Gugghenheimer Jr.

Customized flour bag from Brightwell's Mill – *Courtesy Max Guggenheimer Jr. & Bonnie Gowen*

C & Y SERVICE STATION/DODD'S SERVICE STATION

Camden and Younger Store with C & Y Service on the right
– *Ruth Foster collection*

At some point in time Bernard Camden and Bruce Younger built the C & Y Service Station a little east of the store building. It had a service bay with a hydraulic lift. The living quarters were upstairs. This was run by Mrs. Gladys Dodd.

This building burned when the Camden and Younger store burned. It was still owned by Bernard Camden and Bruce Younger at the time.

Gladys Dodd with Jimmy Foster outside C & Y Service Station – *Ruth Foster collection*

DODD'S SERVICE STATION

Dodd's Service Station – *Ruth Foster collection*

After the fire which burned the C & Y Service Station, Mr. Camden and Mr. Younger had a new building erected. It was all on one floor with two service bays and living quarters in the back. Not long after the fire, Willie and Gladys Dodd bought the service station.

Max Guggenheimer Jr., and Sue Morris told me how Mrs. Dodd would make them ham sandwiches. Max said one time he requested mayonnaise and mustard on his sandwich. She told him he could have one or the other, but not both. I remember how she would dip ice cream and put it on cones. She kept a container of water close by to put the ice scoop in to clean it and keep from mixing flavors. It tended to be a gathering place for the neighborhood.

When Holcomb and I started dating, he would stop by Mrs. Dodd's and buy a pack of chewing gum before coming to my house. After several Saturdays of making these stops, Mrs. Dodd asked, "Who are you sparking out this way?"

After the death of the Dodds, the property was sold. The building has since been used for several different small businesses.

W. M. HICKS STORE

The store was located on the corner of what is now Route 130/Elon Road and Monacan Park Road. Mr. W. M. "Will" Hicks bought land from Mr. O. P. Morris in 1931. According to some old records, Mr. Hicks was running his store in 1933. He may have been running a store sooner, but we are not sure.

As with most of your country stores, he had quite a variety of merchandise to sell in his store, and he also sold gas.

The living quarters were in the back of the store building. Mr. Hicks raised chickens and sold eggs. He had a long white building a little beyond the

Side view of Hick's Store – *Ruth Foster collection*

ELON STORES, SERVICE STATIONS AND OTHER BUSINESSES

Mrs. Lillian Hicks and Mr. Will Hicks in store – *June Howard*

Very long chicken house beside what is now Monacan Park Road partially hidden on left by shrubs but in plain view to right with Jimmy Foster in foreground – *Ruth Foster collection*

l.–r.: Doris (Morris) Foster, Frances Morris and Nancy Morris beside W. M. Morris store – *Courtesy Doris Foster*

store, beside Bethel/Salt Creek Road, which is now Monacan Park Road, for his chickens.

In April, 1947, Mr. Hicks conveyed property to William Morris. (Actually Mr. Morris and Mr. Hicks made a trade of property). Mr. Morris' property was at the corner of what is now Route 130/Cedar Gate Road.

W. M. MORRIS STORE

After the trade with W. M. Hicks, the store was then known as W. M. Morris store. W. M. (William) Morris was the son of Mr. O. P. Morris who had previously sold the land to Mr. Hicks. He sold the usual groceries, etc. found in a country store, as well as gas.

The living quarters were to the back of the store, and on the front right of the store was a storage room. There was a gold fish pond in the back yard.

Mr. Morris made a number of changes to the front of the building, including removing the front porch and putting a brick facade across the front of the store.

In 1950, Mr. Morris purchased a store on Route 29, near Dixie Airport Road, and sold the store in Elon to Ralph J. Foster.

ELON SELF SERVICE MARKET

Elon Self Service Market

l.–r.: Jimmy Foster and Sonny Roberts inside Elon Self Service Market – *Ruth Foster*

After Ralph Foster acquired the property he renamed it Elon Self Service Market. He lived with his family in the store living area for a while. Later, he and his wife, Ruth, built a brick house behind the store on what is now Monacan Park Road.

In the late 1970s Jimmy Foster, son of Ralph and Ruth, acquired the Elon Self Service Market property.

l.–r.: Scott Nixon and Scott Stinnett in front of old building with new building on the right – *H. R. Nixon*

ELON STORES, SERVICE STATIONS AND OTHER BUSINESSES

COUNTRY CORNER MARKET

After acquiring the Elon Self Service Market and running it for a while, Jimmy decided to build a new and modern building.

In September, 1977, the Country Corner Market was completed and moved into. At that time the old store building was torn down.

In 1985 or 1986 the property was purchased by Howard and Rosemary Hudson. They lived in the house behind the store for a while. They are now the owners of the Wigwam property and live there.

G. J. THOMAS & SONS

G. J. Thomas & Sons store – *Peggy Thomas*   Gerald Thomas inside store – *Peggy Thomas*

Gerald James Thomas and his wife, Mildred, along with their sons, Gerald and N. J., moved to Elon in 1940. In February 1948, Gerald opened a store, G. J. Thomas & Sons. They built the store across from Cedar Gate Road on a lot adjacent to their house.

It was in this store that the last Elon Post Office was located.

The store was closed in 1959 and the family moved to Madison Heights. The building has been used as an antique shop, beauty parlor, and last as a tack shop.

l.-r.: Calvin Burford, N. J. Thomas in G. J. Thomas & Sons store – *Peggy and Jerry Thomas*

ELON ESSO SERVICENTER

Elon Esso Servicenter – *Courtesy Jeffrey Bibb*

This service station was built in 1953, and owned by Wallace Bibb. It was located next door to the G. J. Thomas and Sons store. He ran the business for several years and then sold to Coke Stuart. Glen Campbell purchased the property in the 1960s and gave it the name "Campbell's Texaco" and ran the business until in the 1980s. During the time that he owned it he made additions, including a restaurant, and a hardware store. During the 1980s he sold the business at Elon and purchased a store in Pleasant View.

METZL'S BARBER SHOP

Mr. Rudolf Metzl and his wife, Margarete, moved to Amherst County from Newport News, Virginia, in the late 1940s. They had two children, Robert "Bobby" and Glen. Bobby was born before they came to the United States, and Glen was born in Newport News. The Metzl's were living in Czechoslovakia during some of WWII, and then were able to come to this country.

They purchased a farm on Winesap Road where they raised milk cows and sold milk to a dairy to be processed. Mr. Metzl operated a barber shop in the one-story building next door to Camden and Younger store.

l.–r.: June Rucker and Frances Belk with Metzl's Barber Shop in first floor of one story building in right background. W. M. Hicks Store is in far left background

BERNARD CAMDEN'S CASKET STORAGE

Mr. Bernard Camden was associated with Fauber Funeral Home which later was Virginia Funeral Home. He stored caskets in the basement under the barber shop. In early years, it was more convenient for people to buy caskets locally instead of going to Lynchburg. (On occasion people would barter chickens as well as eggs at Camden and Younger store and the chickens would be kept in the basement until they were sold).

This building burned during the 1949 fire at Camden and Younger store.

Bernard Camden and Mary (Gatewood) Camden with building in left background where he stored caskets in the basement. Camden and Younger store is in right background
– *Ruth Foster collection*

SMALL STORES AND FILLING STATIONS IN ELON AREA

In the 1930s and 1940s, cars did not have very big gas tanks, therefore there were a lot of little gas stations beside the road where they could stop to fill up.

MORRIS FILLING STATION

Earl Morris in front of his filling station *–Mary Foster*

This filling station was built of logs and owned by Earl Morris. There was a rock wall behind it and it was located on the west side of Elon, beside Route 130/Elon Road. It was just beyond his house and to the right of his driveway, almost across from the Presbyterian Manse. He sold items other than gas.

A story is told that he had a drink machine which required coins to get a drink. Some of the boys found that they could press a bottle cap into the linoleum floor and get a slug that would work in the machine and get a drink without having to pay. Needless to say the drink machine was soon removed.

This building is no longer standing.

ROUS AND HICKS COUNRY STORE

This store was a log building located east of Elon just beyond the American Legion/Ruritan Building. It was on the left in the wide space beside the driveway into Cloverdale, the home of W. P. "Buck" and Lena Wills. You can see the gas pump in the picture, and it says Merchandise on the front of the store.

After the building was no longer being used for a business, several families lived there. Bessie and Clayton Moss lived there when they were first married. The last people to live there were Ross and Aubrey Burford. Some years ago the building was moved to the property of Ed and Marita Taylor, and an addition was made to the cabin for some family members to live in.

Rous and Hicks Store with l.–r.: Ruth Harris, Elmer Foster, Ralph Foster, Bobby Morris – *Ruth Foster*

LEE JONES STORE

This store was located east of Elon on a section of old Route 130 that turns to the left onto Horseshoe Bend, the road you get to just before you get to the River Road. (A loop of old Route 130). The store was closed in the late 1940s or early 1950s. The building is no longer standing.

FOSTER'S CASH STORE

Foster's Cash Store showing gas pumps – *Courtesy Helen Connelly*

l.–r. Will Foster, Carolyn Horsley, Clayton Moss at store window – *Courtesy Helen Connelly*

This store was located east of Elon, on the left, just beyond the road named Horseshoe Bend. Joe and Lois Foster built the store in 1947 and the adjacent garage shortly thereafter. They ran the store until they traded properties with Earl and Vernie Wiley in 1955. The

Wileys' ran the store for a while and their son-in-law, Harold Throneburg, operated the garage.

The building is still standing and is now used for apartments.

Lois Foster in store
– Courtesy Lois Foster

COFFEY'S GROCERY STORE AND GAS STATION

According to Joyce (Coffey) Mason and Marita (Loving) Taylor, Robert and Carolena (Mays) Coffey, Joyce's parents, opened a small grocery store and gas station on Route 130/Elon Road in 1932. The building was located at the wide graveled area across from the home of Elmer and Ann Loving. Traveling east, it was on the right just before you head up the hill to the bridge over the railroad tracks.

In 1935, Robert and Carolena moved their business to a small building on Route 29 in Madison Heights, which they later replaced with a larger building.

Store and filling station building after being moved *– H. R. Nixon*

They sold that business to Charlie Camden in 1954, and then later Joe Moss purchased the business. Biscuitville is now located on the site.

After Robert Coffey moved to Madison Heights, Talmadge Coffey and then Lewis Loving ran the little store and gas station, on Elon Road, for a while. Sometime later the building was moved to Monroe and sold.

Robert Coffey in front of Silk Farm Service Station –
Courtesy Joyce Coffey Mason

LEIGH'S BROOM SHOP

In 1949 William Leigh Foster, who was partially blind, opened a one-man broom factory near Elon. He had a newly built store with the sign "Leigh's Broom Shop" with brooms of all sizes hanging at the window.

He was born near Naola and could see well. He had a bad case of measles when he was in the fourth grade which left him almost sightless. He continued his education through grammar school by having books read to him and passing oral examinations given him by the teachers in public school. He then attended the School for the Blind in Staunton for a short while, but he did not like it there. He returned home to work on his father's farm.

In 1948 he attended the Workshop for the Blind at Charlottesville where he learned the trade of making brooms which enabled him to start his own business. The workshop helped by supplying his machines. He helped build his own shop. He bought his supply of broom corn through the school. He sold his brooms at his shop and through some of the stores in the county.

Some years later, he had a business to fill vending machines at various businesses, with a driver to take him from place to place.

He learned to make small items of furniture using electric power tools. He made fern stands and a number of other items.

He also did a beautiful job of putting cane bottoms in chairs. He could weave the herringbone design, which is difficult even for a sighted person.

Leigh Foster – *Courtesy Helen Connelly*

ELON WATER SOURCES

THE COMMUNITY SPRING

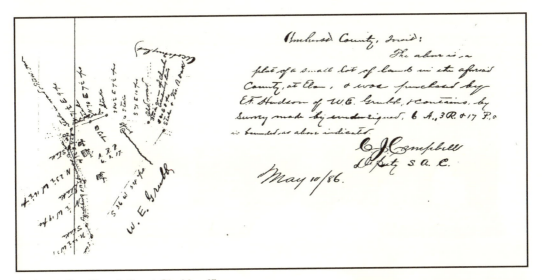

Amherst Co. Circuit Court Clerk's office

I have always heard that the community spring was given to the Elon community by Mr. O. P. Morris, but we have not located any legal documents, so possibly it was just a gentleman's agreement. When I was growing up my father would often say, "A man's word is his bond," and this was true because back then that was usually as effective as a signed document.

Mr. Morris owned most of the property in Elon at one time, and the spring was located on his property. Around 1920, he put water into his house. He later moved to Lynchburg and sold most of his Elon property.

Mr. O. P. Morris – *Mary Foster*

Former O. P. Morris house with his son, Earl Morris, in front – *Mary Foster*

When we moved to Elon, Mr. Bruce Younger and his wife, Miss Lizzie, lived in what had been the residence of Mr. O. P. Morris and his family. The Younger's daughters, Beth and Ann, grew up there. In 1949, Mr. Max Guggenheimer purchased Camden and Younger's store and the Younger's house. The family moved from Lynchburg and lived there for a while.

The pump house for the spring was below the house, and the spring was down near Cedar Gate Road. There was a foot log you could cross to go through the field to Camden and Younger's store. A cement storage tank/reservoir was beside the foot log with an overflow pipe with a steady flow of water, where you could get a drink or catch some water in a container. When we attended Bible school, before Elon Presbyterian Church had the water piped to the church, we would either take cups or cup our hands to get a drink of water.

Most of the houses and stores in the community, as well as the school, had water piped from the spring. At the time we moved to Elon, some of the houses were: Addie Brown, Mrs. Ila Brown, Willie Burford, Bernard Camden, Bruce Younger, Will Hicks, William Morris, Gerald Thomas, Sam Belk, Sherwood Stinnette, the Hunt Club House, Sigmon/Plunk Camden house, and the Presbyterian manse.

With Elon School being at such a high point, if many homes were drawing water, the water pressure at the school would be very low. They could usually get a sufficient amount of water in the kitchen. There was a water fountain in the auditorium, beside the door to the kitchen. Also, there were water fountains and a sink in the vestibule. When the water pressure was very low you couldn't get enough water to drink from the fountains, so

Snooks and Fred Stinnette on spring path with Elon Presbyterian Church in background – *Doris Foster*

we would make paper cups from notebook paper and get water to drink from the spigot at the sink.

Eventually a well was drilled at the school and bath rooms were added.

When Elon Baptist Church added a Sunday school building, bathrooms were installed, with the water coming from the spring. Up to that time, the church had used the outdoor toilets provided for the school.

A lake was built on Graham Creek for a county water supply for this section of the county. It was called Elon Water Works. Later it was named Henry L. Lanum Jr. Water Filtration Plant.

Well drilling equipment – *Jackie Miller Mann*

In 1964, the water lines were extended to Elon and a lot of people tapped on the county system. About that time, Bernard Camden started a subdivision (the first subdivision in the area) on land that he had been using for his apple and peach orchards. People building new homes could tap on to the county water, instead of drilling wells.

Several years ago, Ann and Spence Correll, and Holcomb and I tried to locate the spring. We found the encasement, but crayfish had re-directed the water flow, so it was underground at that point. The ground above where the spring was originally located was marshy. There is still a spring branch, but the foot log is gone.

For historical purposes, Holcomb and I wanted to re-establish a community spring, but the owner of the property would not agree to sell us the small tract of land where the spring is located.

ELON WATER WORKS

Madison Heights Sanitary District Utilities was established in 1936 to serve and provide water and sewage in the southern-most end of the county and primarily to the old Madison Heights area.

In 1955, Elon Water Works was built with a water treatment capacity of 1,000,000 gallons of water, with the lines going as far north as Monroe. The lines went down Dixie Airport and Amelon Roads to the east, and along Route 29 as far as Monroe, and as far west as Harris Creek on Route 130/Elon Road where the water works is located.

In 1964, water lines were extended west to Elon, and north from Monroe to Faulconerville.

The Graham Creek Reservoir was completed by 1969 and had a total storage capacity of 90,000,000 gallons.

In 1979, the water works expanded to 2,000,000 gallons of water per day production capacity.

Henry Lanum Jr., served as superintendent of public utilities for over 30 years. Upon his retirement in 1982, in honor of his decades of dedicated service, Elon Water Works was renamed Henry L. Lanum Jr. Water Filtration Plant.

In 1987, Madison Heights Sanitation District Utilities Department was reorganized and became Amherst County Service Authority.

Due to very dry weather, water lines were laid down Johns Creek Road to the James River in 2002. We now have three water sources: Harris Creek, Graham Creek, and the James River. Water from the James River will only be used in the event that we have a severe drought.

In 2007 the Graham Creek Reservoir was expanded to 232,000,000 gallons of usable water storage.

Dan E. French, director of public utilities, who has served in this capacity since 1982, furnished the above information.

With a public water system and availability of land, a large number of sub-divisions have now been developed in the Elon area, as well as in other areas in the county.

A VILLAGE DIVIDED

From the late 1890s, off and on, there was an Elon Post Office in the village.

By late 1941 when my family moved to Elon there were rural carrier routes, and Mr. Willie Taylor delivered our mail. The newspaper was sent through the mail at that time. In later years with paper carriers, you could get either the morning or evening paper or both delivered to you.

Most of the Elon residents received their mail as Route 1, Madison Heights, Va. In later years we were assigned box numbers, too. The Madison Heights route came up Route 130 all the way to Elon, taking in all the side roads on the way. When the mail carrier got to Cedar Gate Road, he turned and went over the road by Elon Presbyterian Church.

The Agricola Post Office delivered the mail as far down Rt. 130 as Homewood Farms. From the Manse down to Cedar Gate Rd. there was no mail delivery. Most of the people placed mail boxes beside the road, across from the Cedar Gate Road entrance, and had Madison Heights addresses. Later Gerald Thomas built a store and their mailboxes stood beside the road in front of his store.

For many years after Mr. Taylor stopped delivering the mail, a Korean War Veteran, Kendall Bailey was our mail carrier.

During the 1950s after Max Guggenheimer built his new store in Elon, there was an Elon Post Office, again, and it was located in the store. Elon villagers would go there for their mail. After Mr. Guggenheimer closed his store, the post office

Postal Card with date of Sep 25 1903 showing Elon, Va. address

Mr. Willie Taylor – *Courtesy Abbitt Horsley Jr.*

was moved to G. J. Thomas and Sons' store, and remained there until the post office was closed.

In the 1962, a lot of the small post offices were closed. Some of the nearby ones were: Agricola, Knoll, Naola, Pedlar Mills, Pleasant View and Snowden.

At that time, the people from above Cedar Gate Road at Elon started receiving their mail as Rt. 2, Monroe, Virginia. Our son, Alan, who owns the old Manse which is inside the "Elon" sign on the west side of Elon, has mail delivery from Monroe.

The people living on the east end of Elon between the "Elon" signs have mail delivery from Madison Heights.

This creates a situation with the village being divided. Now with the 911 system in effect, we all have street addresses.

Russell Riley, an Elon resident, delivered mail from the Madison Heights post office for many years. By the time he retired, there were so many households that the route was split with a mail carrier added.

For many years, the mail from Monroe post office has been delivered in this area by David Humphreys.

It is very confusing to people corresponding with Elon villagers with the community being divided by having two different mailing addresses. Some don't know whether to show the address as Madison Heights with zip code 24572 or Monroe with zip code 24574.

Sign on west side of Elon with Manse in lower right hand background – *H. R. Nixon*

Sign on east side of Elon – *H. R. Nixon*

THE HOME FRONT DURING WORLD WAR II

During the war a flag would be put in a front window for a family member who was in service. A flag with a red border and a white star in the center indicated that your family member serving in the war was living. If the star was gold, the family member had been killed in service. I remember the flag with a white star hanging in the window of our front door while my brother, James Foster, was in the Navy.

We had blackout times when windows in houses were supposed to be covered with dark shades or curtains, so lights wouldn't shine through, in case an enemy airplane flew over. It was especially important so large cities could not be detected. Watchtowers were built to keep watch for any enemy aircraft that might fly over.

A number of the community ladies took a Virginia State Department of Health Course in home nursing, taught in connection with the National Civilian Defense Program. Upon completion of the course, they received a Home Nursing Certificate. In connection with this class, they rolled bandages. They tore strips from old (well washed) sheets and wound them up for bandages, just like we see gauze wrapped, today.

During the war years with so many of our American men serving in the armed services, it became necessary for the women to step up and work in the factories. I think we all remember the posters showing "Rosie the Riveter," advertising for women to go to work in industry.

My mother went to work when I started school in the fall of 1943. At the time, I wore my hair in long curls. Sometimes my father would comb my hair, getting me ready for school. He would bring the comb down through each individual curl. One day I tried to comb my own hair, but instead of combing down through the curl, I wrapped the hair around the comb and you can imagine how tangled it became. Mother worked with the mess and finally got it straightened out without cutting my hair.

Mother was first employed at Lynchburg Hosiery Mill which was located on Fort Avenue, and they made socks and stockings. To help with the war effort, they made bomb chutes during the war. Therefore, it was difficult for women to purchase stockings at that time because the nylon was being used for items needed by our armed forces. I remember my sister, Eleanor, and her friends, using leg make-up to give color and look as if they were wearing hose. Back then the stockings were made with seams up the back, so you could tell whether they were wearing stockings or not. I have often wondered if they got any warmth from the makeup or if it just gave their legs color. (Even though some nylon stockings were produced in 1946, there weren't enough nylon stockings to satisfy women customers until late in 1947.)

Mother was a very good seamstress, so after she had worked for a while at the Hosiery Mill, she went to work at the tent factory where as the name suggests, they made tents for our military.

The tents were large and the canvas was very heavy, so with the bulk and the heaviness, she had a helper. Her helper, a black lady, lived in Lynchburg, and at this time butter, as well as so many other items, was rationed. Oleomargarine was developed as a substitute for butter. It was white and came with a little packet to mix with it to give it a yellow color. Occasionally mother would take some of her freshly churned butter to her black helper. When she took it home, the natural color was so much better than the oleomargarine with its artificial color, her little boy called it orange butter.

At that time, you didn't have automatic washers and dryers, and there was a need for women working outside the home to have domestic help. Some of mother's helpers were Mary Lee (who sometimes would bring cup cakes or other goodies for me), Nannie Rose, and Aunt Mary Jackson. Our elderly black neighbors were given the courtesy of being called "Aunt" or "Uncle" and then their given name.

The Japanese attack on Pearl Harbor ended the debate about America's entrance into the war. Almost overnight, the economy shifted to war production. Consumer goods now took a back seat to military production as nationwide rationing began almost immediately, in 1942. The first non-food item rationed was rubber. The Japanese had seized plantations in the Dutch East Indies that produced 90% of America's rubber. President Franklin D. Roosevelt called on citizens to help by contributing scrap rubber to be recycled, (old tires, old rubber raincoats, garden hose, rubber shoes, and bathing caps).

Gasoline, fuel oil, tires, shoes, rubber and metal products of any kind as well as butter (as mentioned above), sugar, coffee, meats and fats, processed foods (which included vegetables, fruits, juices and soups) were rationed. At certain times you could buy specific items with your ration stamps.

You were not supposed to tear stamps out of your book before making a pur-

The A, B, C's of Mileage Rationing

Ration Books

Ration Point Values

chase, but you were allowed to detach War Ration Stamp No. 17 from your War Ration Book No. 1 to buy rationed shoes from the Sears, Roebuck and Co. catalog. By the end of the war, rationing limited consumption of almost every product. Most rationing restrictions ended in August 1945, except for sugar rationing which lasted until 1947 in some parts of the country.

Of course people living in the rural areas of the country had cows, hogs, and vegetable gardens, so food was not the problem for them that it was for people who lived in the cities. (I didn't realize until a year or so ago, when I was watching the History Channel on television, that the Japanese had taken over the island where rubber trees grew, and that was one of the reasons it was so important to recycle tires.) Of course, priority of tires was for our military vehicles. New car production was banned beginning January 1, 1942, as former auto plants switched to the production of military vehicles: trucks, jeeps, tanks, etc. Some of the bigger automobiles from the 1930s came with two spare tires, so one was taken to be recycled for military purposes. Automobile owners were reminded that they must register all tires owned by them with the local War Price and Rationing Board before November 22, 1942. The forms were to be obtained from any of the official tire inspectors, and a list was given.

An article appeared in the October 15, 1942 newspaper entitled *Amherst County Shows Its Metal*

"165,000 pounds of it dug up and added to the huge pile of scrap needed for America's war efforts!"

"We are proud of Amherst County's part in answering the call for scrap metal.

"The school children of the county played an important part in the harvest under the able direction of their teachers. The children proved themselves able scrap foragers. They deserve praise as do the members of the local salvage committee, the town officials, the State Highway Department, as directed by one resident engineer, as well as every individual who contributed scrap and who helped in any way to make the intensive drive in the county successful.

"We are urged to continue to save and to search for scrap metal and rubber for as long as we need tanks and guns, we will need the scrap."

There was a U. S. Victory Pulpwood Campaign Committee, and then each county had their own Victory Pulpwood Committee. The goal was met for 1943. It was stated that the need was to produce 14,000,000 cords of wood to meet military and essential requirements in 1944.

People saved newspapers, magazines, tin cans, old tires, and aluminum foil from chewing gum and cigarette wrappers to be recycled. In 1943 instead of Virginia issuing new tags, they issued a small tag for the year 1943 to be placed over the year on the old tags. Before the war was over, some states issued new paper license plates instead of metal. New stoves and refrigerators were not being made at that time, nor were cars and trucks for public use. I remember that my father, Lyle Foster, had his name on at least three lists at car dealers to purchase a new vehicle. It was some time after the war ended before new stoves, refrigerators, or motor vehicles were available to the public.

A number of men were deferred from serving in the armed forces because they could not pass the physical. By the time the war ended, the physical requirements had lessened and they were drafting some who had been rejected earlier, as well as some family men up to 45 years old with several children.

Some of the men with no physical problems were deferred because it was so important to have workers on the farms to raise crops. Some were deferred due to the number of dairy farms where the cows needed to be milked twice a day. Also some were deferred if they were the only son left to work on their family farm.

I remember that people were encouraged to gather milkweed which grew wild, but as a child I was not sure why. From a newspaper article dated September 21, 1944, there was an item: "School Children of America! Help Save our Fathers' Brothers' and Neighbors' Lives By Collecting Milkweed Pods!" For many years the United States had been using kapok, a silky, seed-pod fiber for filling life jackets.

Although the kapok tree which produces kapok grows in many places in the tropics, only in Java were there plantations where large quantities could be obtained. When Japan captured the East Indies our supply was suddenly cut off, and what was already in the United States and on in ships on the way was all that was available. Other things could be used for some articles, but milkweed floss, because it was sufficiently waterproof and buoyant, was found to the best substitute for use in life vests. A satisfactorily filled bag should contain about 800 pods, for which the government paid 20 cents per bag when properly dried.

School children were required to take cod liver oil about once a week. The teacher would give you a spoonful and you would swallow it and then put the used spoon in a dish pan. This was to give us vitamin D to help us stay healthy and prevent rickets.

In a newspaper article dated Oct. 15, 1942, it stated: "The County School Board of

Amherst County ordered the schools of Amherst County to be opened at 10:00 o'clock war time and closed at 4:00 o'clock war time, beginning Monday, October 19, 1942. This time is to remain in force until further order of the board. A. J. CAMDEN, Division Superintendent." Below the article there was this phrase—FOR VICTORY, BUY BONDS—

A newspaper article in April 1945 stated: "Beginning Monday, March 26, public schools in Amherst County will resume the regular schedule, opening at 9 A.M. and closing at 3 P.M. During the winter months the hours were moved so that children living some distance from the highway would not have to leave home before daylight in the morning in order to catch the bus."

People were encouraged to buy war bonds and even the children were encouraged to buy war savings stamps at twenty-five cents each. They were pasted into collections books. Once a book was filled it could be exchanged for a savings bond worth $18.75 or it could be given to be used toward purchasing a jeep, etc. If held for ten years, the bond's value would be $25.00. A Madison Heights School group saved enough stamps to buy several jeeps.

The newspapers were praised for their promotion of war loan drives. In January, 1944, the fourth war loan got under way. "The quota for Amherst County for this drive is $175,000.00 which is more than the last drive; however, we went over the top before, and we will do it again. All that is needed is for the people of this county to get busy and lend every dollar that you can to our government to help the boys on the fighting front"

"The following persons have been named as a County Committee, but more particularly to work in their locality to see that everyone who can purchases a bond: MADISON HEIGHTS: N. M. Worley, Aubrey Wright, E. H. Mays and Munsey Hill; MARGRUDERS: W. T. Thomas Jr.; WRIGHT SHOP: Marion Ernest, John H. Mays, Jimmie Cash and J. R. Story; ELON: B. H. Camden, Roland Lea, D. H. Dillard and Bruce Younger; MONROE: Seth Hicks, H. Clay Robertson and Miss Christine McIvor; PEDLAR MILLS: James W. Davis, Marshall Foster and Will Jones; NAOLA: J. D. Williams, W. L. Bailey Jr., and Mrs. Grey Burford; SNOWDEN: Moses Williams and Harry Wood; PERA: C. M. Ware and C. D. Thornton; PLEASANT VIEW: Mrs. Claude Watts, Mrs. Martha Hudson, Mose Trevey, and J. E. Springs-

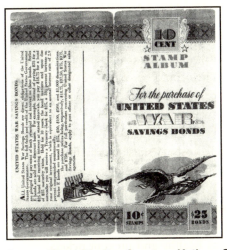 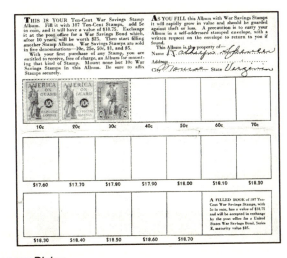

Stamp Album/Book – *Courtesy Kathryn Spencer Pixley*

ton; ALLWOOD: Roy Eubank; LONG MOUNTAIN: Ashby Davis and Ed Davis; ALTO: Hiter Coffey and Frank Coffey; FANCY HILL: F. B. Sandidge, H. P. Mays and B. Clark Campbell; LOWESVILLE: T. W. Cash, Thornton Hite, J. S. Wood and Gordon Woodson; CLIFFORD: Mrs. J. V. Howell, Hope Hudson, John Crawford, Mrs. John Nash, T. S. Williams and Walker Hudson; MAYFLOWER; W. H. Richerson, W. E. Shrader and John T. Shrader; RIVERVILLE: Calvin Mitchell, L. F. Drumheller and J. H. Higginbotham; HICKS: Glen Hicks, Nelson Hicks and Harry Morris; COURT HOUSE: O. B. Ross, chairman, Dr. D. L. Watts, W. H. Carter, J. E. Wood, Paul Grekos, Donald Selvage, Judge Edward Meeks, W. E. Sandidge, A. L. Turner, Camm Drummond, Miss Inez Wood, Mrs. L. V. Parr, Mrs. T. T. Hatcher, Miss Dabney Meeks, Miss Lucille Cox, Mrs. Harriet Sandidge, Mrs. Lillian Livesay and Marie Patteson; TEMPERANCE DISTRICT: Hon. B. Frank Camden, chairman; COURT HOUSE DISTRICT: Hon. W. D. Burford, chairman; PEDLAR DISTRICT: Hon. Dr. E. M. Sandidge, chairman; ELON DISTRICT: Hon. James Weir, Assisted by: W. E. Sandidge, County Clerk, and W. H. Carter, Commonwealth's Attorney; Chairman for all churches: Rev. T. G. Laughon; Chairman for all Schools: Hon. Jordan Camden, Supt. of Schools; Committee in charge of Sweet Briar, Va.: Hon. Don C. Wheaton, and Dr. Lucy Crawford; Chairman of Publicity: Mr. L. H. Shrader."

It was further stated: "You people have been selected because of your ability and willingness to serve your country as statesmen as best you can for the service you are called upon to render. Do your part just as you imagine your girls and boys are doing their part in Italy or the Southwest Pacific, or wherever they may be on foreign soil."

"This is no time to criticize the government. There may be many things we do not like in the setup and we do not like this war. The only way to win is to get out and do our part, all of us working to the same end to bring victory at the earliest possible moment."

In the same newspaper, an article was written by Alfred Percy. The first paragraph was as follows:

"There is safety and security in buying War Bonds. Safety, for some man under fire who may get hold of the superior arms your bonds will buy. There is no doubt about it, as long as we can continue to develop superior weapons there is an added margin of safety for our fighting men [which means] Security, for us here at home. We have got to have security in order to build the weapons to provide the safety for those men fighting to keep us secure here with a reasonable guarantee to them there will be homes to come back to." Mr. Percy went on stating that the fourth war loan drive had started and encouraged people to continue buying war bonds.

THE ELON MILITIA

The Virginia Reserve Militia was organized upon order of the Governor, and the Governor himself was the commanding officer, operating through the Adjutant General's Department.

The Elon Militia was a branch of the Virginia Reserve Militia. This was established for security on the home front. The members were to be prepared in case of enemy attack, or if there were escaped prisoners. Also, the Militia units would be called up in the event of disaster or disorder especially if the Virginia National Guard was being used elsewhere.

Some of the ones who served in the Elon Militia were: Alfred Percy, Capt. Earl Morris Sr., W. P. "Buck" Wills, Rev. Talbot, Bernard Camden, Terrell Stinnette, Ambrose

Some of the Elon Militia: l.–r. front: Earl Morris, Alfred Percy, W. P. "Buck" Wills, 2nd row: H. M. Burford, Raymond Wills, ?, ? Coffey, ?, Bobby Morris, Willie Taylor, Ambrose Shepherd, Houston Morris, ?, Elmer Loving Sr., Terrell Stinnette; back row: l.–r. 4th from right end: Jack Litchford, ?, Buddy Wills, ? – *Mrs. Lena Wills collection*

Shepherd, Fritz Belk, Malcolm Wills, Bobby Morris, Buddy Wills, Elmer Loving Jr., Billy Horton, Broadus Foster, Willie Taylor, H. M. Burford, Landon Humphries, Bobby Ricketts, Charles Singleton, Charlie Davis, Raymond Wills, Glen Coffey, Gerald "Sonny" Thomas, Abbitt Horsley Jr., Demarest Coffey, Sherman Caldwell, Basil "Babe" Caldwell, Hannon Rucker, Dick Stinnette, Walter Turner, Houston Morris, Elmer Loving Sr., Lewis Loving, and Elmer Foster.

Our local militia (Company 105 VRM) would meet once or twice a month, usually at the C & Y Service Station which was run by Mrs. Gladys Dodd. Sometimes they would meet on the front porch of Camden & Younger Store. Their first uniforms were jackets and khaki pants. According to Bobby Morris, they later inherited uniforms from the Virginia National Guard when they got new ones.

Occasionally they would practice marching and drilling on Elon Road on Sunday afternoon. They didn't have to worry about being hit by an automobile because of gas being rationed, and tires being so hard to get. I have been told that one time, one of the sergeants was marching the group down the road from Elon. They kept going, and finally got down to about W. P. "Buck" Wills' house, the sergeant had forgotten the command "To the Rear March," so he stopped and said "Alright boys, turn around and go back."

In April 1945 there was a muster of three Lynchburg area companies of Virginia Reserve Militia, numbering about 150 men, at Shrader Field as part of a State wide review in commemoration of the annual muster in "colonial days." It was a competitive drill, with judges. Capt. Alfred Percy, member of the State Guard Staff and Virginia Reserve Militia, coordinator in charge of training companies in the Lynchburg area, said that Capt. W. P. Wills would be in charge of Company 105 VRM which was our Elon Militia. Virginia Reserve Militia and heads of other company's were named also.

In a conversation with Mrs. Alfred Percy in 1982, she told me about maneuvers they had in Amherst County. Several groups had gotten together to have a mock battle with a lot of the big brass looking through their field glasses (binoculars) at the different groups. They saw a group of the Elon boys eating blackberries when they were supposed to be looking for the enemy. She said this was very upsetting to Mr. Percy, whose father had served in the armed forces in WWI, as well as the other leaders. She said her husband then called them "The Bush Militia."

Some of the maneuvers took place on Mrs. Ladd's property.

The National Guard Unit was activated, and Capt. Alfred Percy went active with them. At that time, W. P. "Buck" Wills was promoted to Capt., Earl Morris Sr. to 1st Lt., Terrell Stinnette to 2nd Lt., and Willie Taylor to Staff Sergeant.

Some of the men, who were in the Militia, later, served on active duty during WWII. The militia disbanded in 1945.

Some of the Elon Militia: l.–r. kneeling: W. P. "Buck" Wills, Earl Morris; 2nd row: Fritz Belk, Raymond Wills, Malcolm Wills, Bobby Morris, Terrell Stinnette; 3rd row: Ambrose Shepherd, Buddy Wills, ?, Elmer Loving Jr., Billy Horton, Broadus Foster; back: ?, Harry Horton, ?, ? Coffey, Willie Taylor – *Mrs. Lena Wills collection*

ELON HONORS WAR VETERANS

This is the headline that was in the May 23, 1946, issue of the *Amherst New-Era Progress*. The article was as follows:

"Between 35 and 40 World War II veterans, each with a guest of his choice, were entertained last Friday night at a banquet in their honor at Elon School by the Elon Baptist and Presbyterian churches, and Mt. Carmel Presbyterian Church.

Rev. S. S. Day, pastor of Amherst Presbyterian Church, was the guest speaker. Rev. G. B. Talbot, pastor of the Elon group of Presbyterian churches welcomed the veterans, and a response was given by Broadus A. Foster, representing the veterans.

Opening prayer was by Rev. R. A. Oliver, pastor of Elon Baptist Church. Rev. E. K. Emurian, pastor of Madison Heights Methodist Church sang several numbers and led group singing.

The banquet table was decorated with white candles and rosebuds, garden flowers and pine completed decoration of the banquet hall.

Approximately 55 veterans of the host churches served the nation during the war. Herbert Thomas Morris lost his life on Guadalcanal in 1942, five were prisoners of war, and six received the Purple Heart for wounds suffered in action.

Members and friends of the congregations who did not attend the banquet came to a social period held afterward."

I am not sure who the six Purple Heart recipients were. The five POW's were: Earl Grey Morris Jr., Elmer Loving Jr., William (Bill) Burch, and brothers Frank Burford and George Burford.

Some others living in the area at the time of WWII who were in service were: Raymond Wills, Jack Litchford, Garland Taylor, Reuben Garrett, Joe Mason, Earl Mason, Bill Tabor, Frank Tabor, John Moss, Preston Moss, Clayton Moss, Daniel Moss, Charles Moss, Gerald Moss, William Moss, Sanford Gowen, John Turman, Gordon Saunders, Fritz Belk, Ed Taylor, H. M. Burford, Glen Coffey, Warren Layne, Buddy Ogden, Raymond Ogden, John Ogden, Dick Stinnette, Sonny McConnell, and Edwin Young.

Veterans who were in attendance, l.–r.: Back row: Broadus Foster, Lloyd Miller, Ed Burch, James Foster, Buddy Camden, Houston Morris, Charlie Camden. Middle: Earl Grey Morris Jr.; Edward (Buddy) Wills, Ernest Burch, Wallace Bibb, Marshall Coffey, Frank Horton, David Oblinger. Front row: Wallace Hicks, T. W. Hicks, Gilbert McGlothlin; Beth Younger; John Paris; Dan Loving; Henry Brown; Elmer Foster. (Not pictured: Elmer H. Loving Jr., Bill Burch, Frank Burford, George Burford – *Ann Correll*

Veterans and guests at banquet: l.–r. around outer edge of table: Daughter of Mary Due and John Paris, John Paris, Mary Due Paris, ?, Billy Layne, Buddy Camden, Elmer Foster, Mrs. Addie Foster, Russell Shelton, Frank Horton, Mrs. Horton, Wallace Hicks or T. W. Hicks, Mrs. Edna Hicks, Rev. Emurian, Mr. Teddy Hicks, Mrs. Talbot, Rev. Talbot, Buddy Schermaker, ?, Mr. Bruce Younger, Beth Younger, Daniel Loving, Dorothy Loving, Lloyd Miller, Aileen Miller, Earl Grey Morris Jr., Monyeene Bibb, James Foster, Doris Morris, Broadus Foster, Mary Foster, Buddy Wills; l.–r. inside edge of table: Mrs. Bibb, Wallace Bibb, Esther Oakes, Ed Burch, Margaret (Dillard) Camden, Charlie Camden, Mrs. Camden "Miss Cutie," ? . ?, ?, Rev. Oliver, Mrs. Marshall Coffey, Marshall Coffey, (3 empty chairs), Helen Burch, Ernest Burch, Daisy (Smith) Oblinger, David Oblinger, Elizabeth Dillard, Mrs. John Dillard, Haywood Ogden? – *Mary Foster*

THE UNWELCOME GUESTS

It was reported in *The News*, Lynchburg, Va., Tuesday morning, Febuary 27, 1945, with the following headline: "Believe German Prisoners Broke Into Monroe Home" "Three men believed to have been German prisoners who escaped from the Danville Prisoner of War Branch camp Sunday broke into the home of George Henry White at Monroe last night shortly before 8 o'clock.

Tucker Eubank, Southern Railway officer, who reported the incident to City police said the men were wearing Army uniform jackets and trousers and that they left some underwear and an overcoat with "PW" printed on each article. He said all the men were bareheaded and appeared to have been men ranging from 20 to 25 years of age. The three prisoners escaped from the Danville camp by cutting wire enclosing the prison grounds."

Their names and descriptions were given in the newspaper.

Mrs. Lloyd Miller's house near Elon was vacant. Since her husband had been shipped overseas, she was living with her parents, Teddy and Edna Hicks, who lived almost within sight of her house. Her daughter, Jackie was about six years old and she had a young baby about six months old. She checked ever so often to make sure everything was all right at her house.

In talking with Mrs. Miller in 1982, she said that when she pulled into the driveway, the prisoners ran out the back door and into the woods. They had gotten rid of their own clothes and were wearing clothes which belonged to Mr. Miller. They were very ill-fitting, so they had pinned them up, belted in the trousers and done various things to make them fit a little better.

When she saw the men running from the house, she went over next door to Mr. Tyler Fulcher's house and asked him to get a gun and shoot them. Mr. Fulcher, being a lawyer, as well as a school principal, told her that since they were not on his property, he could not shoot them. At that time they did not know that they were escaped prisoners, but suspected it. Mr. Fulcher called Mr. Alfred Percy who was in charge of the Militia, at that time, and asked him what to do. An immediate alarm that the men were in the neighborhood was given to members of the Virginia Militia. Lieut. Bird Talbot and Sgt. Bernard Camden were the first to arrive at the Miller home.

Picture of house taken in 2010 – *H. R. Nixon*

They went to search for them. As they were driving down the road they noticed the three men, all in clothes which they had allegedly stolen from the Miller home, walking down the road. They drove up beside the men and they did not attempt to run and surrendered without any trouble. Sgt. Camden held the shotgun on the men as Lieut. Talbot drove to police headquarters.

They had hardly entered the lockup in Lynchburg before they started pulling articles, including pipes, tobacco, flashlights, tooth brushes and wrenches, from their pockets. As one handed over an Army issued flashlight, he exclaimed "From Camp Pickett." The first thing they wanted to know was could they smoke. They then asked for matches and lit their pipes.

One of the items the authorities took from the men was a map of the eastern part of the United States. When asked where he and his companions were headed, Groneck said smilingly: "New York City, that is a big place and I can speak English." He seemed to think if they had reached New York they would have been safe. He said he and his companions were captured in Italy more than eight months ago and that they were members of Hitler's parachute troops.

According to the newspaper, Sgt. L .L. Stanley and Trooper J. H. Barnes arrived at the Lynchburg headquarters and took the men to the Amherst jail. Very little damage had been done to the house. They had napped in the beds, gotten food, ransacked and gotten Mr. Miller's clothes and used the bathroom facilities. They stated that they had been listening to the gramophone (radio) and heard for a while the reports of their escape. One of the prisoners spoke very good English; the other two spoke broken English and German.

Commonwealth Attorney, Walter Carter, said he would probably charge the men with housebreaking and larceny, but that he had not definitely made up his mind. A telegram from a Camp Pickett public relations officer, that night, said that the three men would be returned to military custody.

Later that night, Mrs. Miller had to go to the Amherst Jail to identify Mr. Miller's clothes, and that these were the prisoners. Mr. Tom Torrey, Mr. Bernard Camden, Mr. Bird Talbot, Hazel and O. D. Campbell, and a few others went with her.

In doing further research, I found that there were a number of Prisoner of War

THE UNWELCOME GUESTS

Branch camps under Camp Pickett in that area. When the German and Italian armies were defeated in North Africa in mid-1943, more than 250,000 enemy soldiers were captured. Many of these POW's were brought to the United States to perform farm work and other non-war related jobs as allowed by the Geneva Convention. A total of approximately 6,000 German prisoners were sent to Camp Pickett beginning in January, 1944. The Army built two main camps and nine smaller satellite camps in the nearby counties to house the Germans. The prisoners were employed in a variety of jobs. The majority of POWs at the main camps cut logs and made pulpwood, while most of those in the smaller, outlying camps performed farm work. Some of the prisoners worked in the post hospital's wards and kitchens.

Some of the Camp Pickett satellite camps were: Catawba, Roanoke County; Cumberland, Goochland County; Danville (independent city); Green Bay, Prince Edward County; Radford (independent city); Salem (independent city); Sandy Level, Henry County; and Shelton, Virginia Beach (independent city).

One of the members of the Elon Militia who helped capture the German prisoners was Bernard Camden. He served on the Amherst County board of supervisors for many years.

Bernard Camden – *Collection of Ruth (Harris) Foster*

SOME ELON MILITIA MEMBERS.
See ORGANIZATIONS

l.–r.: Buddy Wills, Terrell Stinnette, Percy Loving, Earl Morris Sr., Elmer Loving Sr., Fritz Belk, Elmer Loving Jr., Broadus Foster, Houston Morris, Ambrose Shepherd – *Collection of Mrs. Lena Wills*

l.–r.: Malcolm Wills, Raymond Wills, Buddy Wills, and their father, W. P. "Buck" Wills – *Collection of Mrs. Lena Wills*

ENTERTAINMENT AND FUND RAISERS

Starting in the early 1900s there was a considerable amount of entertainment sponsored by the Elon Civic Betterment League as a fund raiser. After the Elon Home Demonstration Club was organized, they joined with them in sponsoring fund raiser events.

Elon Horse Shows sponsored by the Elon Civic Betterment League and Elon Home Demonstration Club were held at Homewood Farms, as fund raisers.

FOREWORD

The Elon Horse Show is sponsored by The Elon Civic Betterment League and Home Demonstration Club and proposes:

1. To encourage and promote the intelligent interest of children in horses and horsemanship.

2. To maintain this interest in grown-ups.

3. To provide a time and place for friendly competition among horse owners.

Riding Is More Popular In This Country Today Than Ever Before.

The Elon Horse Show Association wishes to promote the interest of every one in this splendid sport and thus keep Elon abreast of the times along with her sister Communities of the South.

The proceeds from the Horse Show are for the benefit of the Hot Lunch Committee of the Elon Consolidated School.

Foreword in Horse Show program – Courtesy Ann Correll

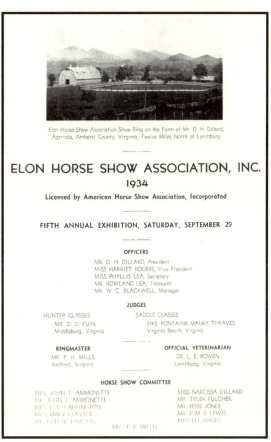

Program with picture and other information – Courtesy Ann Correll

ELON CIVIC BETTERMENT LEAGUE FUND RAISERS

Other fund raisers were: talent shows, minstrels, womanless weddings, beauty contests, and male beauty contests.

On September 29, 1954 the Elon Civic Betterment League sponsored an Aunt Jemima Pancake Supper. Ticket prices for the meal were $0.25 and $0.50. They could be purchased from: Mrs. George Pick, Mrs. Rudolf Metzl, Mrs. Horace Anderson, Mrs. R. E. Ricketts, Mrs. Jerry Stowe, Mrs. Ed Taylor, Mrs. Broadus Foster, Mrs. Wlliam Panzario, Mrs. James A. Hodges, Mrs. Elmer Loving Jr., Mrs. Wallace Bibb or at the Elon stores.

They gave highlights of the past activities of the League from 1913 to 1954:

1913	Organization of the first rural lending library.
1916	Promotion of the first area Pig Club, forerunner of present-day 4H work.
1919	Present library built with funds raised in the community.
1921	Elon School built with combined funds raised in the community and from the School Board.
1945–46	25th Anniversary of building celebrated.
1949–50	Theodora Lea Playground Fund raised money to install the equipment at school. Mr. Rowland Lea and his wife, the late Mrs. Theodora Lea, were among those instrumental in establishing the Elon Civic Betterment League.
1951	Boy Scout troop sponsored.
1954	Possibilities of a future community health center under study.
1944–54	During the past 10 years the league in conjunction with the Elon Home Demonstration Club and with the cooperation of the Amherst County School Board, made improvements and additions including: repainting of school, remodeling of kitchen and installation of electric hot water heater; repainting kitchen and dining room, furniture made by league members; repairing and repainting library; installation of new lights in the classrooms; addition of gravel to grounds; installation of 4 new stoves; and inauguration of hot lunch program.

THE ELON CIVIC BETTERMENT LEAGUE SPONSORED THE FIRST REUNION AT THE ELON SCHOOL IN APRIL 1958, AS A FUND RAISER.

Some former students and others at fund raiser; l.–r. at wall: ? Hudson, Ed Burch, Lewis Keith, James Brown, Houston Morris, ? Hudson; center row: ?, Ed Taylor, Harry Horton, Preston Moss, ? Peters, Earl Grey Morris Jr., Elmer Loving Jr.; front: Pembroke Davis, Gilbert McGlothlin, Preston Moss – *Courtesy Marita Taylor*

ELON AMERICAN LEGION POST 100 FUND RAISERS
LAWN PARTIES

The Elon American Legion Post 100 started holding lawn parties on the lawn of W. P. "Buck" Wills and Lena Wills in the early 1950s and continued having them as fund raisers until in the late 1970s. They had lawn parties for several years before they could start their American Legion building. They continued to have them for many years to pay for the building.

Most of the food was prepared and donated by the people in the community. They would have homemade ice cream that they froze at the American Legion Hall the night before.

An account in the newspaper on August 19, 1959, was as follows:

"Plans are well under way for the annual Lawn Party to be held Saturday, August 22, at 4 P.M. by Elon American Legion members. It will take place on Buck Wills' farm near Elon, joining the Legion property on Elon Road.

According to the chairman of the event, James Brown, the members are 'going out in a big way' to serve an expected crowd of 1500 persons. Country ham and fried chicken will be the highlights of the meal.

The carnival-type sideline will consist of numerous games, plus pony rides for the children.

The main event of the evening, about 8 P.M. will be the announcement of the winner of the Cadillac which has been seen in different parts of the county throughout the past month. This prize is being given by the Legion after its donation by Sullender Chevrolet of Amherst.

The Amherst County High School Band will present special music for the occasion.

'The Legion body, consisting of 75 to 100 men, women and volunteer helpers, await serving all their friends and guests on this special occasion' said Mr. Brown."

They would have games and rides for the children.

Cadillac donated by Sullender Chevrolet with sign advertising American Legion lawn party; see Lawrence Truck Sales Inc. building in left background – *Courtesy Garland Huffman*

Ladies preparing to serve: l.–r. Mrs. Pearl Brown, Mrs. Duff, Margie Litchford, Aileen Miller, Mrs. Eva Burch, ?, Mary Foster, Mrs. Edith Burford

People in serving line. Man wearing glasses: Bernard Camden, ?, ?, Mary Gatewood Camden standing next to food price sign; notice Tobacco Row Mountain in background

Game booths

Harold Jennings with horse and buggy for rides

John Warner and his wife, Elizabeth Taylor – *Amherst New-Era Progress*

Virgil Coleman, Queena Stovall, John Warner – *Amherst New-Era Progress*

A lot of people would come from Lynchburg, not only for the good home cooked food, but for the nice drive and view of the mountains.

On election years a lot of politicians would attend the lawn party to campaign. The Republican Party in Amherst County was instrumental in having John Warner and Elizabeth Taylor come to the lawn party in 1978.

John Warner was running for the United States Senate. He wore an American Legion overseas cap, which made it difficult to pick him out from the local Legion members in the crowd.

After everybody had eaten they would play Bingo until all the donated prizes had been won. Of course people kept playing because they knew the money was all staying in the community.

MINSTRELS

For a number of years the American Legion sponsored minstrels.

People who participated in the May 18, 1956, minstrel, as well as the chorus line were: Ran Wood, June Bibb, Mary Harper Thomasson, Jay Arnold, Charlie Beard, Donnie Craven, Jannetta Snyder, Garland Huffman, W. W. Winnia, James M. Brown, Houston Morris, Robert Hodges, Harold Jennings, M. B. Younger, Elmer Loving, Elmer Foster, Harry Horton, Buck Wills, Lyle Foster, Clayton Moss, Buddy Wills, Emery Ranson, Roberly Loving, Fred

ENTERTAINMENT AND FUND RAISERS

Chorus line for minstrel circa 1954: l.–r. Shirley Brown, Sandra Coffey, Vera Loving, Florence Foster, Helen Jean Carroll, Carolyn Horsley, Rebecca Dawson, Sylvia Loving, Marita Taylor, Margaret Camden – Lynchburg *News & Advance*

Chorus line for Minstrel May 18, 1956, l.–r.: Betty Gowen, Carolyn Thompson, Nancy Gowen, Sylvia Loving, Rebecca Dawson, Barbara Clarkson, Vera Loving, Bertha Stowe – Lynchburg *News & Advance*

l.–r.: James Brown, Dan Loving, Bennie Paris, Edward Taylor, Broadus Foster – Lynchburg *News & Advance*

Harris, Mayo Crist, Margaret Martin, John Odgen, Ralph Foster, Charlie Camden, Earl G. Morris Jr., Virginia Tibbs, Bob Burford, Sam Burford, Monyeene Wood, Shirley Brown, Dot Williamson, Virginia Allen, Ella Brown, Florence Foster, Earl Wiley Jr., Rhonda Davis, Russell Franklin, Dennis Tankersley, Broadus Foster, Melvin Bailess, Russell Franklin, Wilma Jennings, Frank Williamson, Hubert Shrader, Dan Loving, Edward Taylor, Wallace Bibb, Bobby Morris, Spence Correll, Jack Litchford, Sherman Caldwell, Raymond Ogden, Addie Brown, T. W. Hicks, Billy Bailess, Earl Morris Sr., Buddy Camden, Benny Paris, Ray Coffey.

"MINSTREL MEN AT ELON"

The ADVANCE, Lynchburg, Va., Thursday, April 23, 1957, stated:

"James Brown, left, makes point as four other end men for annual minstrel show at Elon School Friday night look on. Left to right: Dan Loving, Bennie Paris, Edward Taylor and Broadus Foster. Elon American Legion Post 100 is sponsoring the event, which will start at 8 o'clock."

There were a number of acts, as well as jokes, solos, duets, and group singing.

THE ELON AMERICAN LEGION SWIMMING POOL CLUB

A "Swimming Pool Queen of 1962" contest was held on July 14th, 1962 at 7:30 P. M. at the Elon American Legion Pool. Music was furnished by the group "Suzanne And The Ramrods" which consisted of: Suzanne Duffield, Ronald Dave, Johnny Rigsby and "Pinky" Ramey. A group of swimming pool club members presented a "Water Ballet" directed by Joanne and Dick Ricketts.

The "Winners of 1961" presented cups to the "Queens of 1962." Winners of 1961 were: Gay Allcock, 4–6 age group; Ann Massie, 7–9 age group; Terry Jean Wells, 10–12 age group; Linda Foster, 13–15 age group; Becky Brooks, 16–18 age group; and Jean Ogden Ballard 19 and over group.

ELON RURITAN CLUB

They made apple butter for several years which was very interesting to people who had never seen this done before. It was a good fund raiser.

They have sponsored pancake meals for many years. They have sponsored yard sales at the American Legion/ Ruritan Club building. For many years they have had a food booth at the Apple Harvest Festival.

TALENT SHOWS

A number of talent shows were given at Elon School as fund raisers. There would be solos, duets and quartets. Also, they would be a group of people playing different instruments which was very entertaining. I am not sure if Mr. Hicks and Dot (Brown) Mason ever participated in any talent shows, but they did play their instruments together at times.

Dot (Brown) Mason and Mr. T. W. "Teddy" Hicks – *Courtesy: Jackie (Miller) Mann*

RECREATION/GAMES

BASEBALL

Elon Baseball Team – 1924: l.–r. back row: Carl Ramsey, Buck Wills, H. P. Camden, Howard Watts, Ashby Wills, Ambrose Page ?, Chip Ramsey; front row: Jack Martin, Bruce Younger, James Ballowe, Austin Salmon?, Bill Salmon?, Dick Wills – *Courtesy Ann Correll*

Over the years there have been baseball teams. Often times they would get up a Sunday afternoon game, and play on Mrs. Ladd's field which was up the hill behind the store located on the corner of what was then Salt Creek Road (now

Monacan Park Road) and Route 130/Elon Road.

Jerry Thomas, who grew up at Elon, went on to play professional baseball. He played in the St. Louis, Los Angeles, and New York organizations. After that he served as a baseball coach at Amherst County High School for three years. In 1995 he retired from Lynchburg College where he had been a baseball coach for twenty-seven years. At recess time at Elon Elementary we would sometimes play ball. Of course, the high schools had baseball teams.

Over the years boys and girls from the area have been involved in playing baseball and softball.

l.–r.: W. T. "Tucker" Eubank, Lyle Foster, John Woodroof judging jousting tournament

JOUSTING TOURNAMENTS

I attended a jousting tournament on the Mays farm located near Pleasant View on what is now Puppy Creek Road. The horseback rider would try to catch all the rings that were hanging down. The judges were to see if the riders caught all the rings. Someone had to hang the rings after each rider had gone through. Smaller rings were hung after each round of competition. At the end of the tournament the winner received a trophy.

Lyle Foster with grandson, Bill Foster, and grey fox – *Courtesy Connie Foster*

FOX HUNTING

From early years in the country, fox hunting was a big sport, as it was in England. Before the days of automobiles, hunters would ride their horses and follow the baying of the hounds to hear the fox chase, and maybe see the fox. There were fewer red foxes than grey foxes. At times the fox would be treed (he would climb a tree to get away), and at other times he would go into a den. On occasion my father would get the fox out of his den and put him on a chain in the barn, where he would be fed.

After a period of time the fox would be turned loose, and shortly thereafter the foxhounds would be released. This helped train them to hunt foxes. If he transported the dogs someplace and turned them out, if they all didn't come back before he had to go back home, he would blow his hunting horn. If they still didn't show up he would leave his jacket or another item belonging to him. He would go back later and the dog or dogs would be waiting for him there.

My father bred and raised Trigg foxhounds. He had a dog lot with quite a large dog house. It was about the size of a small two-room house with a covered porch across the front. There were two tiers of dog beds inside. The fenced lot extended down into the woods and down to a spring. He built a spring box to catch water, making it easier for the dogs to drink. One time he purchased a dog from Mississippi and had him shipped by train. A number of his dogs had pedigrees.

Over the years my father attended bench shows and field trials. In 1939 he attended the Piedmont Foxhunters Association in Lynchburg where one of his dogs won a silver coffee server, silver cup and ribbons. In later years he belonged to the James River Foxhunters Association, which was organized in about 1945 according to Earl Carson. His dogs won trophies and ribbons.

Lyle Foster training dog for bench show competition – *Florence Foster Nixon*

After there were so many deer, the dogs would chase them sometimes. One time my father had to go to the Boonsboro area in Lynchburg to pick up a dog which had swum across the river chasing a deer. The dogs wore collars with my father's name, address and telephone number.

Some years before he died, my father got rid of his hounds and stopped fox hunting, due to the woven wire fences on people's property and the increase of the deer population.

Leaving with dogs and horse to go on fox hunt or drag hunt – *Sweet Briar College Riding Center collection*

DRAG HUNTS

They would have drag hunts where someone would drag a cloth that had the scent of a fox. Later the dogs would be turned loose. The horseback riders would follow the hounds as they followed the fox scent.

At times some of the Sweet Briar students would come to Homewood Farms and participate in the hunt, along with Mr. Dillard,

Sweet Briar students on drag hunt 1952 – *Sweet Briar College Riding Center collection*

David Hugh Dillard on horse – *Courtesy of Narcissa Basten*

With deer, l.–r.: Lyle Foster, James Marshall Brown, Houston Morris, Bruce Younger; kneeling: Nehemiah Tucker – *Florence Nixon collection*

Miss Phyllis Lea, Althea Smiley, and Lyle Foster, who would also be riding horses and wearing riding gear.

The Hunt Club property got its name because of the foxhounds being kept there. At different times Mr. David Hugh Dillard, Mr. C. G. Patterson and others would have foxhounds on the property with someone living in the Hunt Club house to feed and take care of them.

DEER HUNTING

There had been no deer in this area of Amherst County for many years. Deer were brought in and after their population grew, hunting was allowed. On the west side of the Southern Railway tracks the hunting season for deer was very short. The season for hunting was a little longer on the east side of the tracks. Even then you could only kill the bucks (male deer). The deer pictured was killed by Lyle Foster in 1951,

RECREATION/GAMES

the first year deer hunting was allowed in this area. He had the head mounted, the hooves made into a coat/hat rack, and the hide tanned.

In recent years the hunting season has been extended to a longer time, and at certain times hunters are allowed to shoot doe (female deer).

The deer have gotten so over-populated in this area of the county that they cause many car accidents, and are a real nuisance. Also they eat flowers, vegetable gardens, fruit, bark from trees, and do other damage.

FISHING

The Indians and early settlers trapped and caught fish as part of their food supply. Fishing is now a sport. Fishermen look forward to Trout season. Sometimes special bait is used to catch different kinds of fish. Some people fish from the bank of a river, creek or lake, and others fish from boats. Contest are sometimes held with trophies and large amounts of money being awarded.

CROQUET

Playing croquet was a big thing in the 1940s and early 1950s. Some people even had croquet courts. My sister, Eleanor, and a number of her friends would play croquet in our yard at night after having worked during the day. They had light bulbs in some of the trees to give light, and they tied a piece of white cloth on the top of the wickets to be able to see them.

Early croquet player – *Ruth Foster collection*

TENNIS/BASKETBALL COURT

The new Elon School was built and the old school which stood at the top of the hill was torn down. A nice fenced in area was built with basketball goals and pavement marked for a tennis court which our youth enjoyed for a number of years. There began to be a problem with people coming in from other areas and not taking care of the equipment. The fence and basketball goals were removed. It is now used as a parking lot.

ELON COMMUNITY POOL

The building of the pool was started in 1957 and completed in 1958.

A bathhouse with rest rooms was built in the 1960s. Before that people had to go up the hill to the American Legion Hall building to use the facilities. The pool continues to be a source of recreation and enjoyment for the community pool members.

Elon Community Pool – 1964

ELON VILLAGE LIBRARY

Mrs. Aileen Miller watching Mary Ellen and Susanne on the merry-go-round – *Courtesy Jackie Miller Mann*

This was a source to get books to read. Also during the 1940s the boys would play marbles on the dirt out from the front of the library. The girls would at times play hop scotch in the same general area. Later a merry-go-round was placed in the front of the library.

WEE TEE PLAYGROUNDS

Wee Tee Playgrounds – *Monelison*

This was a putt-putt/minature golf course, described as Carpet Golf. At one time it was owned and operated by Charlie and Margaret Camden. It was located at the corner of Route 130/Elon Road and Route 29. It was across Elon Road from Buck's Place, almost in the present location of the Good Will Industries store.

BUCK'S PLACE

This was located across Elon Road from Wee Tee Playgrounds at the corner of Route 29. It was a dance hall, and was off limits for me when I was growing up. After it closed as Buck's Place, Parkway Restaurant was there for a while. Since then the building has been renovated and used by several banks. A few years ago, BB&T built a new bank on the site.

Buck's Place in left background. Note 3-lane highway – *Courtesy Nancy Marion*

LITTLE ELMO'S PLACE

Little Elmo's Place was long building in left background; Martin's Store in right background – *Courtesy Nancy Marion*

This was another dance hall which was located beside Amelon Road, diagonally across Route 29 from Buck's Place. This was also off limits for me. After that there was a service station on the corner of Amelon Road and Route 29 with Lawrence Trucking Company behind that. A Sheetz business is now located on the site.

Martin's Store was run as a grocery store by the Martin's until a few years ago. The building is now used for a furniture business.

AMHERST DRIVE-IN THEATRE

The Amherst drive-in theatre opened in April 1952, and was located up Route 29 north of the intersection of Route 130/Elon Road and Route 29. On the right, under the sign, you can see Buck's Place after it was renovated for a bank.

You could attach the speaker to the side of your vehicle, and there was a button to adjust the sound.

Speaker box posts; screen in left background; and concession stand in right background – *Amherst County Museum and Historical Society collection*

Sign for Amherst drive-in theatre – *Amherst County Museum and Historical Society collection*

OTHER THEATRES, ETC.

Theatres in Lynchburg were mostly on Main Street and they were: Academy, Paramount, Isis, and Trenton, later named Warner. Fort Early Theatre was near the corner triangle where Fort Avenue and Memorial Avenue meet. The Harrison, a black theatre, was located on Fifth Street. Harvey's Drive-In was located up from the corner of Wards Road and Candlers Mountain Road where there is a shopping center with Kroger's.

DRIVE-IN EATING PLACES
BILL'S BARN

Bill's Barn – *Courtesy Jack Martin*

This was a popular hang-out especially for the Madison Heights teenagers. It was located near the 29 Grill, but on the opposite side of Route 29.

The menu was shaped like a barn with a lean-to. Dinners ranged from $3.75 for New York sirloin strip with french fries, salad, rolls, and coffee to $1.25 for hamburger steak with french fries, rolls, coffee. Ice cream was $ 0.15 and extra coffee was $0.10. Sandwiches ranged from steak $0.85, lettuce, bacon, tomato $0.45, ham $0.40, to grilled cheese $0.30. French fries were $0.25, soft drinks (with food) $0.10, soft drinks (only) $0.15 and a milk shake was $0.30.

Bill's Barn on far left with 29 Grill on far right – *Courtesy Jack Martin*

HOLLINS MILL DRIVE-IN

Hollins Mill Drive-In was located on Hollins Mill Road a little beyond the dam that was used for the Hollins Mill. If you continued up the hill you came out on Bedford Avenue. Car hops came to your car to take your order. They would bring your food on a tray that could be attached to the side of your car with the window down.

Lendy's Big Boy Restaurant in left background with a Big Boy holding a hamburger at entrance beside Pure Station which is now location of Arby's – *Courtesy Nancy Marion*

SOUTHERNER DRIVE-IN

The Southerner was located on Wards Road in Lynchburg, just beyond the K-Mart shopping center.

LENDY'S BIG BOY DRIVE-IN

Lendy's Big Boy drive-in was built later than the other drive-ins. It was located where La Carreta Mexican restaurant is now in Seminole Shopping Center.

There was a speaker for you to call your order in and then a car hop would bring your tray with food and attach it to your car.

GAMES

Some of the games we played, other than ones already named were: drop the handkerchief, farmer in the dell, sling the statue, red rover, tag, kick-the-can, "mother, may I?," hide and seek, foot races, horse shoes, jump rope, and Andy over.

At Easter there would be Easter egg hunts. You would boil hen eggs, dye them, and sometimes decorate them. You would usually have an Easter egg hunt at church and then still hunt eggs with your cousins over the Easter week-end. The egg shells were usually in bad shape by the time you finished playing with them.

SLEIGH/SLED RIDING

We used to have several snows a winter and the young people would get together and go sleigh riding, especially during the war years when gas was rationed. There were lots of hills in and around Elon to ride down. My sons liked going down the Fairfax's hill.

AREAS FOR PICNICS, WIENER ROASTS AND HAY RIDES

In the *New Era–Progress* dated April 21, 1949, it had the headline "Two Picnic Areas in County Ready." The article told about the State Highway Department making picnic areas ready for the spring and summer motoring season.

Amherst Wayside was located on Route 60, six miles east of Amherst Courthouse with shelter, toilets, water, picnic tables, fireplaces and recreation grounds with a custodian in charge. I remember having church picnics. The church youth went there and had wiener roasts. We would use straightened coat hangers to roast our wieners at the fireplace. Only picnic tables are there now.

Long Mountain Wayside, sixteen miles west of Amherst Courthouse on Route 60 had picnic tables. They used to have Easter sunrise services. I remember going there at least once.

Some other places we had church picnics were Miller Park in Lynchburg. In some of the later years we went to Eagle Eyrie. Also, we would have church ice cream socials, and watermelon feasts on the lawn of some of the members of the church.

Eating watermelon: l.–r. back: Ruth Horsley, Thelma Smith, Alvin Smith, Bessie Moss, Clayton, Moss, Abbitt Horsley; front: Mr. Fleming Taylor, Mrs. Lillian Taylor, Jean Sutherland – *Courtesy Abbitt Horsley Jr., and his wife, Carolyn.*

Front to back: Ann Younger, Frances Belk, James Brown beside C & Y Service Station – *Courtesy Ann Younger*

BLUE RIDGE PARKWAY

You travel west on Route 130/Elon Road for approximately twelve miles from Elon to an entrance to the Blue Ridge Parkway. Once you turn on the Parkway, if you go east (to the right) there are picnic tables and the Otter Creek Restaurant and Campground. If you go west (to the left) you are not far from a Ranger Station where there are picnic tables, and a restored canal lock. You are in Amherst County until you cross the bridge over the James River.

COUNTY FAIR

Sometime after WWII was over and gas was more plentiful, we would attend the Amherst County Fair. The county schools would be closed for the day for school children to be able to go. I don't know about other areas, but for us from the Elon area, Mr. Hannon Rucker would drive his bus. He would pick us up just like he did for a regular day of school and then take us to the fair for the day. I remember in particular the swings that we rode. They had a Ferris wheel, but I never cared to ride that. Of course there were booths where you could pay to play games, and receive a small prize.

They had canned goods, needlework items, different farm products, and animals that were judged and winners would receive ribbons.

By the early 1950s the local counties combined their efforts and had a farm show at the Lynchburg Stadium, for a few years.

BIRTHDAY PARTIES ATTENDED IN 1940S

We attended a birthday party for Nancy Morris at her house when the family lived in the house at the corner of Route 130 and Cedar Gate Road.

Some years later we attended a birthday party for Norman Throneburg at his house on Cedar Gate Road. The picture was taken in the dining room.

l.–r. front: Earl Collins Wiley, Barbara Ann Wiley, Talmadge Foster Jr., Nancy Carol Morris; 2nd row: Ivan Wiley, Eleanor Wills, Florence Foster; 3rd row: Fred Stinnette, Snooks Stinnette, James Marshall Brown, Wade Talbot, Charles Wills, Nancy Wills; center back: Gordon Foster – *Courtesy Doris Foster*

l.–r.: Helen Foster, Eleanor Wills, Florence Foster, Norman Throneburg, Charles Wills, Earl Collins Wiley Jr., Sylvia Kaye Wiley – *Courtesy Throneburg family*

HAPPENINGS AND ACCIDENTS IN AND NEAR ELON

TRAIN ENGINEER BURIED NEAR ELON

We have heard that the engineer of the Old 97 which derailed in Danville, Va., was buried near Elon. Later, we found out from someone who had visited his gravesite that Engineer Broady was buried in Saltville, Va.

Robert Floyd let us have a copy of a newspaper article that further cleared this up.

On February 12, 1906, according to a newspaper article in the *Washington Post*, a Southern Passenger Train (Southern express train No 34) was passing through the yards in Greensboro, N.C., and ran into an open switch and crashed into a shifting engine. Three men were killed outright and a fourth died in two hours. None of the passengers were injured, and the train was not damaged. Another engine and crew were provided, and the train which had not been damaged in any way was soon heading north.

Engineer Owen Norvell resided in Monroe and his body was shipped back by train.

Last year, Holcomb and I located his grave and the graves of other Norvell family members, near Elon.

AIRPLANE CRASH AT ELON

There was a fighter plane trainer crash just below Elon during World War II. The pilot was on a training mission and had flown from the Preston Glenn Airport in Lynchburg. (At one time the airport was controlled by the Navy and another time by the Army during WWII).

According to conversations with Mr. Calvin Falwell and Jerry Thomas, when the engine cut off the pilot rode the airplane on down.

Elmer Foster with Mr. Dillard's fence and field in background
– *Courtesy Mary Foster*

The airplane came down over Mr. David Hugh Dillard's field on the north side of Route 130/Elon Road and went through his fence and crossed the road through another fence onto property owned by Talmadge and Florence (Horton) Foster. This was approximately where the house is now across from the entrance to the Mason's farm, now Nottaway subdivision. He was only slightly injured and was able to walk away from the accident scene. According to Jerry Thomas he was later in another crash and did not survive.

We were allowed to walk down from Elon Elementary School to see the accident scene while the airplane was still there.

AIRPLANE CRASHES ON TOBACCO ROW MOUNTAIN

Sherman "Sherry" Caldwell told me about several airplane crashes on Tobacco Row Mountain during WWII. Sherry told me about one time, in the spring, when he was plowing new corn, he heard an airplane sputtering and then saw it crash. He said there were two people in the airplane and they walked away from the crash scene.

Tommy Burford also said that he knew about several crashes. Apparently the terrain at Tobacco Row Mountain was a good training area for military pilots.

YOSIE ROSE ACCIDENT

In November, 1948, Yosie Rose and Emma Massie, along with two other black girls were waiting for the school bus beside Route 130/Elon Road (near what is now the entrance to Hunter's Ridge subdivision) when someone stopped a vehicle in the road and was talking to them. Apparently a vehicle was coming from the other direction when a car came along. In order to avoid a head on collision, the driver of the car unfortunately hit two of them with the result being the death of Yosie, and injuries to Emma. Yosie is buried in Mt. Sinai Baptist Church Cemetery.

STEPHEN ERNEST EWERS ACCIDENT

On February 11, 1950, Stephen Ewers was found unconscious and near death in a ditch after a hit-and-run accident, beside Route 130/Elon Road in Elon on Sunday morning, about twelve hours after being struck. According to the investigating officers, he had been last seen at about seven o'clock Saturday night when he left an Elon general store operated by G. J. Thomas. He was found 125 yards west of the store so police thought he was struck shortly after leaving the store, and lay there bleeding. He died on February 20, 1950, and was buried in Bethany Methodist Church Cemetery. I remember going by the spot where he was found, and seeing where he had a great blood loss.

ACCIDENT AT WINESAP RAILROAD CROSSING

A headline from the Daily Advance, Lynchburg, Saturday, May 26, 1962 read:
"DANGEROUS CROSSING CLOSED"

"Dangerous Winesap Road crossing was closed today and traffic routed over the new $111,000 bridge. The closing ended a long battle by Amherst County residents and State Highway Department officials to eliminate the death trap where two young girls were killed when struck by a Southern Railway Co. train in 1956. Construction will continue on the bridge and approach roads, but traffic no longer will have to cross the tracks near the Monroe yards."

Nancy (Hicks) Murphy was killed in the accident, and Nancy McIvor, who had severe burns, lived for a few weeks.

There was a poor sight distance for vehicles crossing the railroad tracks.

CAMDEN AND YOUNGER STORE FIRE

See ELON STORES,
SERVICE STATIONS AND OTHER BUSINESSES.

Camden and Younger Store, C & Y Service Station, Barber Shop building burning; Lyle Foster is in light colored pants and Max Guggenheimer is in light colored shirt and pants – Lynchburg *News & Advance*

BOMB SCARE AT ELON SCHOOL

Alan Nixon told me about the bomb scare they had in 1965 at old Elon School. The children were taken over to Elon Baptist Church while the school was being searched. No bomb was found. When students returned to the school the piano in the auditorium had been completely disassembled in the search for the bomb.

HALLOWEEN PRANK

Sherman "Sherry" Caldwell told me about one Halloween, Garne Brown, a black man, had been working on a wagon in Mr. John Sigmon's blacksmith shop. Some of the boys did some disassembling and put the wagon up on the roof of the shop and reassembled it. He said Garne Brown was really surprised when he saw it on his way to work.

l.–r.: H. P. "Plunk" Camden, Ambrose Page, Bernard Camden, Jim Horton – one of the buildings in left background was probably Mr. Sigmon's blacksmith Shop; old Camden and Younger store in background on far right – *Courtesy Ruth Foster*

Frances and Nancy Morris with Mr. John Sigmon's house in right background – *Courtesy Doris Foster*

SOME ELON PEOPLE

RIDING RICKSHAW

Mr. Robert Taylor in rickshaw – *Collection of Edna Foster*

Garland Taylor made a career with the military and traveled overseas. At one of his duty stations, he purchased a rickshaw. The American Legion members borrowed it to use at their lawn party, as a fund raiser. You paid for someone to pedal the bicycle and give you a ride in the rickshaw.

UNCLE HARRY WILLIAMS

Uncle Harry Williams lived in a house over in the woods from Mary and Broadus Foster's house. He would plow gardens for people.

Uncle Harry Williams with his mule – *Courtesy Ann Correll*

SOME YOUNG PEOPLE IN THE LATE 1930S OR EARLY 1940S:

l.–r.: back: Hoge Smith, Broadus Foster, Russell Foster, Bea Shepherd; 3rd row: Earl Mason; 2nd row: Ruth Smith, Mildred Camden; front: Irene (Foster) Shepherd, ?, Margaret Smith, ?, Eleanor Duff, Mary (Morris) Foster, Ruth Watts, Jean Dillard, Virginia Smith – *Courtesy of Mary Foster.*

THOMAS BROTHERS IN KNICKERS

l.–r.: N. J. Thomas and Gerald "Jerry" Thomas – *Courtesy Peggy and Jerry Thomas*

Could it be that even at this young age Jerry was hoping to play baseball professionally, and then coach baseball until his retirement?

SOME MEN WHO ATTENDED A DINNER IN 1940S

l.–r.: front: Walter P. Wills, Gerald Thomas, Harold Jennings, Edwin M. Shepherd, Elmer H. Loving Jr.; 2nd row: Robert Young, Will M. Hicks, Earl Grey Morris Jr., Henry Brown, Early B. Coffey, Ervin Carver, Will W. Dodd; 3rd row: Carl Dewey Simmons, Mr. Torode, Spence Correll, ?, Melvin Bailess, Edwin Wetmore, Terrell Stinnette; 4th row: Frank Wills Sr., Addie M. Brown, M. Bruce Younger, Samuel E. Belk, Rev. Graham Gilmer, Elmer Hill Loving Sr., Henry Horton, Ashby Brown; standing: Lloyd M. Miller, Ted W. Hicks Jr., Harold Throneburg, Ambrose Shepherd, Ted W. Hicks Sr., Houston Morris, Glenn Coffey, Malcolm Wills, Robert P. Morris, Russell Shelton, Fritz Belk, Lewis Higginbotham, Bernard H. Camden, W. Percy Loving, Earl G. Morris Sr. – *Courtesy of Ann Correll*

ELON PRESBYTERIAN CHURCH CIRCA 1943

Some have been identified: Howard Shelton, Elmer Loving Sr., Mrs. Guy Lewis, Mrs. Evelyn Mason, Mrs. Lizzie Younger, Teddy Hicks, Joe Mason, Vera Loving, George Talbot, Nancy Wills, Wade Talbot, Sylvia Loving, June Wills, Jenny Morris, Betty Jean Coffey, Helen Jean Loving, Connie Stinnette, Nancy Morris, ? Layne, Aubrey Smith, Mr. Bird Talbot, Sam Belk, Mrs. Annie Morris, Mrs. Elmer Loving Sr., Percy Loving, Earl Morris Sr., Ed Shepherd, Glenn Coffey, Ethel Dawson, Cathlene Horton, Frances Belk, Mrs. Vera Wills, Barbara Wills, Lena Hudson (holding baby), Daisy Smith Oblinger, Marilyn Burch, Lois Burch, Esther Oakes, Houston Morris, Ambrose Shepherd, Irene Shepherd, Addie Brown, Bobby Morris, Fritz Belk, Rufus Coffey, Malcolm Wills, Russell Shelton, Billy Layne, Bruce Younger, Tom Burch, Bernard Camden, Ruth Harris, Helen Brown, Mrs. "Cutie" Camden, Charlotte Burford, Vernell Morris, Doris Oakes, Marita Loving, Terrell Stinnette, Alex Morris, Willie Burford, Robey Ewers, Lloyd Miller, Aileen Miller, Marie Harris, Mrs. Ed Shepherd, Beth Younger, Margie Litchford, Mrs. Eva Harris, Lena Burch, Mrs. T. W. Hicks Sr., Mrs. Early Coffey, Mrs. Gladys Dodd, Mrs. Daisy Smith, Dorothy Loving, Shirley Loving – *Courtesy of Ann Correll.*

SOME ELON PRESBYTERIAN CHURCH PEOPLE

l.–r.: Mitzi Thomas, Naomi King, Winnie Dodd, Barry Tucker, Virginia Roberts – *Collection of Ruth Foster*

HOME DEMONSTRATION CLUB

l.–r.: Ethel Pick, Pearl Brown, Edith Foster, Mrs. Lizzie Younger, Mrs. Addie Foster, Alma Brown – *Courtesy of Ann Correll*

LUNCH IN DILLARD'S PACK SHED

l.–r. end and back: Mrs. Will Hicks, Ann Loving, Mrs. Sam Belk, Helen Rucker, Mrs. Walter Dawson, Mrs. Alex Morris, Ruth Foster; front: Mrs. Guy Lewis, ?, Aileen Correll, Mrs. Bruce Younger, ?, Mrs. Bernard Camden, June Bibb – *Courtesy of Ann Correll or Ann Loving*

MEETING IN AUDITORIUM IN OLD ELON SCHOOL

l.–r. standing: ?, Ed Taylor, Randall Layne, ?, Bernard Camden, Jack Thomas, Seated: Phyllis Lea, Joanne Ricketts – *Courtesy of Marita Taylor*

ELON BAPTIST CHURCH SUNDAY SCHOOL SUPERINTENDENT

Taken in old sanctuary: Broadus Foster served as superintendent for over 40 years – *Courtesy of Mary Foster*

SUNDAY SCHOOL CLASSES AT ELON BAPTIST CHURCH

Taken in 1950s: l.–r. from wall: 1st row: Catherine Martin, Glenna Langley; 2nd row: Barbara Wiley Stinnette, Snooks Stinnette, Carolyn Horsley; 3rd row: ?, Dot Brown Mason, ? Goins; back row: Buddy Langley, ?, Ruth Langley, Gordon Foster

SOME ELON PEOPLE

Taken in 1960s, l.–r.: Dottie Davis, Melody Boydoh, ? , Timmy Sigmon, Jeanette Branch, Clara Tiller, Debbie Massie, Tommy Massie, Lisa Ross, Regina Coleman

Taken in early 1970s, l.–r.: standing: ?, Sitting: Scottie Throneburg, Nancy Foster, Cheryl Connelly, ? , Jackie Huffman, ? , ? , Kim Davis, ?, Vicky Campbell, ? , ? , Sara Harris; back row: Dot Mason, ? , ? , Carrie Williamson

W.M.U. MISSION STUDY
l.–r. back: Massie Foster, Lois Foster; 3rd row: Doris Tyree, ? , Maggie Massie, Connie Foster; 2nd row: Gloria Throneburg, Ruby Williams, ?, Barbara Stinnette; front: Mary Foster, Doris Foster, Florence Nixon, Mary Marks

LADIES ATTENDING W.M.U. MISSION STUDY

Mrs. Mary Marks, a member of Madison Heights Baptist Church came to Elon to teach our W. M. U. Mission Study Book. Sometimes we had a covered dish meal and then had the mission study. Sometimes instead of a meal we would serve refreshments after the study.

ELON BAPTIST CHURCH BIBLE SCHOOL CLASS – 1951

Mrs. Shumaker in window; l.–r. back: Carol Langley, Ronnie Foster, Billy Bailess, ?, ?, ?, ?, Nancy Green, holding flag, Talmadge Foster Jr.; front: Tommy Joe Foster, Doug Inge, ?, "Sissy" Inge, Carl Ray Davis, Robert Moss, Linda Bailess, Walter Pick, Linda Gaye Foster, ? , Sylvia Kaye Wiley, Freda Davis in front of Sylvia Kaye

ELON BAPTIST CHURCH WOMEN'S SUNDAY SCHOOL CLASS
Taken in front of old Sunday School building at furnace room; l.–r. back: Connie Foster, Doris Tyree, Opal Eubank, Lois Foster, Mary Moss, Ethel Pick, Martha Moss; front: Cecil Foster, Lurleen Wallace holding Joe Wallace, Mrs. Melvin Bailess, Gloria Throneburg, Doris Foster, Edith Gowen holding Ellen Gowen

GROUND BREAKING FOR NEW ELON BAPTIST CHURCH SCANTUARY IN 1963
Doris Foster, Gwen Campbell, Broadus Foster, Billy Johnson, Boyd Tyree, James Foster, Holcomb Nixon, Abbitt Horsley Sr., Charlie Vail, Rev. Eugene Campbell

CHOIR PRACTICE IN OLD ELON BAPTIST CHURCH
l.–r. back: Melvin Bailess, Robey Ewers, Broadus Foster, Pete Elliott, Billy Bailess; front: ?, ?, Dossie Elliott, Edith Gowen, Ethel Dawson Pick – *Courtesy of Helen Connelly*

ELON SCHOOL CHILDREN

l.–r. back: Harold Stinnette, Barbara Ogden; 3rd row: William Watts, ?, ?, ?; 2nd row: Dorothy Blanks; front: Florence Foster, Barbara McGlothlin – *Courtesy of Helen Connelly*

l.–r. back: William Watts, ?, ?, ?, Wayne Watts, ?; 2nd row: Frances Paris, Patsy Stowe, Barbara Wills, ?, front: Ray Watts – *Courtesy of Helen Connelly*

THE DAMERON HOUSE

Photo by H. R. Nixon

This house was located on what is now Monacan Park Road, near the entrance to Salt Creek Road. It was struck by lightning and destroyed by fire in the 1980s. The house was last lived in by Robert and Mildred Young.

A Civil War story was told by Mr. Will Dameron for the Elon Home Demonstration Club Scrap Book. The story was as follows:

"My mother, Emma Dameron, and my grandmother, Mrs. George H. Dameron, were standing on my grandmother's porch when they heard galloping horses. They looked up the road and saw a troop of Yankee cavalrymen. The horses leaped the yard fence and pulled to a halt in front of the house. Within a moment Yankees were all over the house and there was nothing to stop them. A few minutes later, another horse leaped the fence and stopped in front of the house. The Yankee officer dismounted and approached grandmother with his hat in hand and asked permission to call his men out of the house. My grandmother very readily granted him permission to do so.

The soldiers were lined up, and the sergeant instructed to collect from them whatever they had removed from the house. When this was done, he asked grandma to see if anything was missing. He then asked if she could furnish him and his men with something to eat, since it was near nightfall. She told him she could give them cabbage, fat meat, potatoes, cornbread and milk. He exclaimed, 'that is plenty good.' Grandma called the cook, who had taken to the tall timbers, and had her prepare supper, which she served the men on their tin plates. After this, she had the cook prepare a supper of fried chicken, hot biscuits, etc. for the Yankee officer who ate at the family table.

During the meal the Yankee officer asked Grandma if her husband was in the Confederate Army and expressed hope that he wasn't at home or else he would have to make him a prisoner of war. Grandmother's reply was, 'not if I see him first!' She then added that he was away from home.

Grandma assigned the officer to a bedroom upstairs and his troopers to a hayloft in the stable.

Next morning the cook served a breakfast of bacon and eggs to the troopers and the officer enjoyed a more genteel breakfast with grandmother and her two children, Charlie and Emma, my mother.

He offered her an order on the government to pay for the food and lodging, but she refused it."

DAVID HUGH DILLARD

He was best known in the Elon area for his impressive home "The Shelter" and his ownership of Homewood Farms and Orchards, and the many other properties he owned in Elon and the surrounding area. He also owned Oak Park Farm, which was a dairy farm.

Mr. Dillard was born in Campbell County. He began working at age 16 for the Old Dominion Box Co., and eventually became president and owner of the business. His wife was the former Leonora Rosa van Gelder.

He served as a member of the board of directors of Craddock-Terry Shoe Corp., Lynchburg National Bank and Trust Co., Lynchburg Livestock Market, Quality Dairy Products, Inc., Lynchburg Bottled Gas Co., Fidelity National Bank, and Dillard Paper Co. He was a member of number of other boards and councils.

The Fine Arts Center at Lynchburg College was named in honor of Mr. and Mrs. Dillard. He also contributed much toward the establishment of the Lynchburg Fine Arts Center, and the construction of Lynchburg General Hospital.

He was widely known as a Lynchburg industrialist, businessman and philanthropist. He died at age 80, on January 21, 1970, after a long illness.

Mr. David Hugh Dillard – *Courtesy of Narcissa Basten*

Mr. and Mrs. Dillard when he received an award from the James River Club in 1964 – *Courtesy of Narcissa Basten*

HOMEWOOD FARMS

Buildings on Homewood Farms, l.–r.: horse barn, calf barn, grainary, dairy barn with silos. Note orchards in left and right background – *Courtesy Spence and Ann Correll*

Homewood Farms horse barn – *Courtesy Lou Basten*

He raised horses for riding and also for racing with a rider on a sulky. Several horse-pony shows were held at Homewood Farms. Usually one of the local clubs would have a concession stand as a fund raiser. The shows were held in the field just up from the horse barn, between the barn and Route 130.

An item in the *Amherst New-Era Progress* dated Sept. 4, 1947, stated that: "The Woodbrook Stables Fall Horse and Pony Show will be held at Homewood Farms, Elon, beginning Sunday at 2 P.M. Admission is free, and the public is cordially invited to attend."

There was a picture showing Toni Tappman on "Button" owned by Althea S. Moseley of Agricola. "Both the rider, a student of Mrs. Moseley, and the horse will take part in the Sunday horse show at Homewood Farms."

Some of the other riders listed were: Susan Bailey, Judy Kessler, Billy Leggett, Tucker Knight, Teddy Harper, Nancy Potts, Barbara Keefer, Mary Tappman, Goode Robinson, Mary Spence Pollard, Anne Gerhardt, Lloyd Haskins, Owen Harper, Betsy Potts, Verne Keefer, Mary Katherine Burton and Elizabeth Christian.

The riders under eight years of age were listed as follows: Jimmy Watts, Julia Ayers, Dunbar Haskins, Ann Martin, Bobby Echlebaum, Marcia Tappman, and Jane Baber.

HOMEWOOD FARMS DAIRY

A Virginia Guernsey Breeders' Association Annual Field Day was held at Homewood Farms on Aug. 10, 1954. The program gave a history of Homewood Farms.

"Homewood Farms Dairy was started by Mrs. Ella Dillard, mother of the present owner, David Hugh Dillard, about 1925. The Dairy began with one barn, a pure-bred Guernsey bull, and about a dozen grade cows.

Homewood Farms dairy barn – *Courtesy Spence and Ann Corrrell*

Homewood Farms dairy barn - interior – *Courtesy Spence and Ann Correll*

Mrs. Ella Dillard taken at Pedlar Farm – *Courtesy Shirley Brown Franklin*

By the early thirties, the operation had grown beyond the capacities of Mrs. Dillard who then sold it to her son, David Hugh, and bought the farm of her birthplace at Pedlar Mills, Virginia." [This was lower Pedlar Farm. In later years it was purchased by the Malige family].

"Registered Guernsey cows were bought from time to time, and Mr. Dillard always used registered Guernsey bulls. He bought a herd of mostly registered Guernseys in Alabama in 1941, and since that time the grades have gradually been replaced with registered cows bred and raised on the farm."

"The last of the grade cows were sold in the early spring of 1953. The present Homewood herd consists of about 150 head, of which about 70 are milking cows and four herd sires. We are doing both D.H. I.A. and A.R. testing. Every cow has been classified as to type."

"Homewood Farms also consists of about 250 Hereford cattle, Hampshire hogs, and 150 acres of apple orchard."

They further stated at Field Day:

"OUR PROGRAM

We are endeavoring to develop a sound farming and breeding program applicable to any farmer-breeder. We believe in sound economical production and reproduction.

Our entire herd is milked three times a day. All are milked by machine. All are fed according to production and condition.

Production records are kept and studied carefully on each cow, especially on a year after year basis. We believe in a good average production rather than a few individual high records. Our D.H.I.A. average for the past seven years on sixty cows is 9051 lbs. milk and 462 lbs. fat. Individual A. R. records have their place too.

We try to produce all our grain, hay, silage, and pasture, believing that home grown feeds are superior and most economical.

Homewood Farms milk house – *Courtesy Spence and Ann Correll*

We believe in raising our replacements and rigid culling. We grow and sell bulls only from the best cows.

We are constantly on guard against disease. Every cow in the herd has been calfhood vaccinated against bangs. The entire herd is blood tested and T. B. tested annually. We are constantly seeking new methods of mastitis control and of other diseases."

OAK PARK FARM

Oak Park Farm was located a mile from Route 29 on Route 130/ Elon Road at Kings Road.

A tenant house stood just to the left of the entrance to Oak Park Farm, facing Route 130. It was torn down some time after 1957.

Since Dillard Road was built, Kings Road goes off that road, and the entrance to Oak Park Farm is from Route 130/Elon Road and Mitchell Bell Road.

Oak Park Farm was a dairy farm, and feed crops were raised there.

Tenant house beside road to Oak Park Farm
– *Courtesy Spence and Ann Correll*

Oak Park Farm dairy barn with calf barn on right behind dairy barn – *Courtesy Spence and Ann Correll*

Mr. Sam Camden was the farm manager. He was completely deaf but could read lips very well. Occasionally he would come to our house at Elon to visit. My father would try his best to be heard, and would yell, which only made matters worse, because it distorted his lips. Mr. Camden said he could understand me much better because when I talked I looked directly at him and talked in a normal voice.

In the early 1950s Mr. Dillard built the Quality Dairy on Oakley Avenue in Lynchburg. It was incorporated as Quality Dairy Products, Inc. The milk from Homewood Farms dairy and Oak Park Farm dairy was sent there to be processed. At that time the bottled milk and other dairy products were sold with the Quality Dairy brand name.

They had a counter on the first floor where you could order a serving of ice cream or a milk shake. You could also buy half gallons, etc. of ice cream to take with you.

Oak Park Farm dairy barn and feed room – *Courtesy Spence and Ann Correll*

A nice community room was upstairs at the Quality Dairy, which was used for meetings, parties, bridal showers, and baby showers. Since there was no charge to use the room, for refreshments you would serve ice cream in some form along with other items. It was especially nice to have this room available, because the only other place for such events was at the Seminole Trail Club House in Madison Heights. Most homes could not accommodate the number of people you wanted to invite. This was in the days before churches had social halls, and the Elon American Legion Hall had not been built.

The Oak Park Farm was originally owned by a King family. My father would occasionally go down to that farm. He would say "I am going down to the old King place." I was very young and I thought he was going to see a king. From my story books, I could imagine an old king sitting on his throne when he got there.

The Oak Park Farm was sold after Mr. Dillard's death, and Mitchell Bell Foundry was operated on a portion of the property. The roadside development is mainly residential. Over the years the lower part of the farm has been used for the manufacture of brick. Old Virginia Brick Co. is currently located there.

Some of Mr. Dillard's property that was sold on Monacan Park Road and John's Creek Road are now Homewood Estates subdivisions. Some of his other properties that are now subdivisions and mentioned in other stories are Homewood Bounds, Hunt Club, some lots on Elon Road in front of Wigwam property. Some of the property adjoins Camden Drive at the end of the street. Two streets on John's Creek Road near Route 130/Elon Road: Scarborough Fair, and Ridgeview Lane are located on what was Dillard property.

HOMEWOOD FARM ORCHARDS

See ORCHARDS story.

THE MIRACLE ON CEDAR GATE ROAD

It was the amazing story of Frank "Dick" J. Wills' recovery from an unusual back injury that was reported in *The News* on October 10, 1954.

In 1941, Mr. Wills, an employee of a paper mill, was cleaning out a digester. A fellow workman turned on a high-pressure stream of water. It knocked him into some pipes.

He suffered great discomfort in his back. A doctor told him that some muscles and tendons had been torn. After a few days he went back to work, but in a few months he had to quit his job because of the acute pain. Physicians diagnosed that he had arthritis of the spine.

The pain became almost unbearable, and then his legs became paralyzed. They kept him dosed with sedatives for years. The debts mounted from doctors and hospital bills.

After two years, Mrs. Wills said they had to find some way to pay their bills. They had twenty-three milk cows, so every time they needed more money they would sell a cow. In not too long a time all of the cows had been sold, but one. Mrs. Wills said, "We kept the kickin'nest cow of them all, "Old Spot," but she gave the most milk.

Mrs. Wills did all the milking. Dick used to ask her why she took so long in the barn just to milk one cow. She knelt out there every night praying for his recovery and knew that her prayers would be answered.

Mr. Wills would lapse into despondent moods and tell Mrs. Wills "I will never walk again". She would tell him "Sure you will. In five years you'll be as good as new". But when five years had passed and he was still paralyzed, he became more and more depressed, but she never gave up hope.

After selling off all their livestock except one cow, they found they had to sell a 58 acre farm they owned. When the proceeds from this was gone, their one alternative was to go on relief.

Mr. Wills said that he didn't know what they would have done without such kind neighbors as they had in Elon. They were always doing things with gifts of money and food. Every time he had to go to the hospital in Charlottesville, a neighbor would drive him.

Many times it was his pastor from the Presbyterian Church.

The turning point came after more than 7 years of agony. A neurosurgeon removed the tenth vertebra and two discs from his spine.

After that he had to live in a heavy cast and all kinds of braces, but the excruciating pain began gradually to slack off. Then one day he was able to sit up in bed. A few days later he had his feet dangling over the side, but when he tried to stand up, his legs crumpled up under him like jelly. he thought he was still paralyzed.

Mrs. Wills said she kept on praying every night. One day she and their oldest son persuaded Dick to stand between them and try to move his legs as though he were walking. They kept this up for days. Finally, with the help of a cane, he was able to hobble about.

About the spring of 1951, Mr. Wills felt well enough physically to set out about seeking some kind of employment. The Amherst County Welfare Department put him in touch with Mrs. Kate Cobb, State Employment Service counselor.

Those 10 years in bed did something to him inside. He didn't realize it until he went out to apply for an overhead crane job. Even though he was up and walking around, he felt like he had really lost his balance.

Mrs. Willis said that when he came home from his job-hunting expeditions he kept reporting gloomily, "well, I didn't get it". She told him to leave his cane at home when he went out that maybe that spoiled his chances. He left his cane at home and he did get a job.

Mrs. Wills remark was "If ever there was a miracle, it happened right here on Cedar Gate Road".

Mr. Wills stated "Even when I was offered a good job, I was afraid to accept it. My confidence was all shot. At 47 I thought I was all washed up."

When he was interviewed just leaving his job as overhead crane operator in Montague-Betts steel yards, you would never have believed that he was listed as a handicapped worker. He came clambering agilely down an iron ladder leading from the swaying cab of his crane, almost a hundred feet in the air.

"A little more than three years ago" he asserted, "I stood in this very spot, looked up the iron ladder at that cab and figured I'd never make it. After 10 years flat on my back I wasn't used to looking down from high places. It made me nervous just thinking about it".

He worked many years and then retired from Montague-Betts. Mrs. Wills worked at a garment factory, and later worked and retired from General Electric.

l.–r. Front row: son, Charles Wills, Mrs. Lula Wills, Frank "Dick" Wills; and son, Frank Wills Jr., back row: Barbara Ann Wills, daughter, Eleanor Wills; and daughter-in-law, Betty WIlls. – *Lynchburg News Photo*

QUEENA STOVALL AND TRIPLE OAKS SCHOOLS

According to the booklet printed for the display of *Queena Stovall Reflections Of A Country Life* at the Daura Gallery at Lynchburg College January 19–April 12, 2009, Queena Stovall was born in rural Campbell County, Virginia, on December 20, 1887, and was one of twelve children. Her parents were James Spotswood Dillard and Ella Nathan Woodroof.

She was christened Emma Serena, but her paternal grandmother nicknamed her "little Queena" after some in the family couldn't pronounce the name Serena.

In 1894, the family moved to the city of Lynchburg, where Queena and her siblings attended public school. After her father's death, just three years later, her mother opened up their large house to boarders.

After leaving high school, she took a job as a secretary for a buggy business. At age eighteen she married the owner, Jonathan Breckenridge "Brack" Stovall. When the buggy business failed due to the emerging popularity of automobiles, the Stovalls moved to Amherst County, near Elon. The farm, known as the Wigwam, faced the Blue Ridge Mountains and this is where she spent the remainder of her life, raising a family and eventually painting scenes of life in the rural world.

I asked Annie Laurie Stovall Bunts about the original part of the Wigwam since I had

Wigwam – 1957 – *Ann and Spence Correll*

heard Mr. Easley Edmunds talk about it. She said she didn't really know much about it except the Edmunds family had bought it from a Judd family, and that her uncle, David Hugh Dillard, bought the property from Mr. Edmunds. Mr. Edmunds talked about coming to Elon when he was young and staying at the house. Apparently they used the original house as a hunt lodge. The addition was made sometime after the Stovall family moved in. The Wigwam is now owned by Howard and Rosemary Hudson.

In 1974, forty-one of her paintings were on exhibit at the Dillard Fine Arts Center at Lynchburg College, named for her brother, David Hugh Dillard, and his wife, Rosa Van Gelder Dillard. This exhibition later traveled to the Abbey Aldrich Rockefeller Folk Art Center in Williamsburg, Virginia, where it was the first solo exhibition for a living woman artist, and the exhibition also traveled to the Fenimore House Museum of the New York State Historical Association in Cooperstown, New York. (I have a copy of the program from Cooperstown with "End of the Line" pictured on the front, given to me by her daughter Annie Laurie Bunts when we were working at the same law firm).

During the period January 19–April 12, 2009, thirty-one of her paintings were on display in the Daura Gallery at the Dillard Fine Arts Center at Lynchburg College.

The "Cabin on Triple Oaks Farm" has been one of her most popular paintings. This was actually used as a school house. According to Annie Laurie Bunts, Triple Oaks Farm was owned by the Longs, and Miss Fannie Long was in charge of the Triple Oaks School. Annie Laurie said she attended the school for a short while, and that it had two rooms. The one main big room, and the little room on the left, facing the building. She said the small children, (kindergarten and first grade) were in the little room, and she couldn't remember the teacher's name. She said Miss Fannie Long taught the class in the big room which had the grammar school grades. They did not teach any high school classes there.

Triple Oaks Preparatory School was also run by the Longs. Both of the Triple Oaks schools were located on their property on Elon Road. This is now "Hans Hill" subdivision property.

Painting of Cabin on Triple Oaks Farm

Triple Oaks School used in her painting – *H. R. Nixon*

Triple Oaks Preparatory School and students as follows: Mrs. John Long, at post, with Carl Whitlock, teacher. Students are: Armistead Long, Chris Winfree, Freeland Kinner, Ben Ammonette, Fred Guthrie, Alfred Percy, D. A. Langhorne, John Craddock, Maynard Campbell, Randolph Harrison, Robert Winfree, and Roy Carrington, NOT PICTURED: Billy Wilson Edmunds, Ed Ivey, Nat Catlette, Alex Mosby, and Victor Wood, photographer – *Courtesy of Nancy Marion*

VIEWS OF ELON AND AREAS ON ROUTE 130 IN 1930S AND 1940S

There were a number of rock quarries near Elon. Two were on Route 130/Elon Road above Woodruff's Pie Shop, on the right before you go through the cut of the mountain to Agricola.

There was also a quarry on Mistover Mansion Road, and another one located between Graham Creek and Harris Creek, across from the Henry L. Lanum Jr. Water Filtration Plant.

The view is of Earl Morris' orchard with his house on the right. Wallace Bibb's Esso Station was built on the property in the center background. The tack shop would be on the left and Campbell's Food Store in the center (which at one time was Elon Esso) with many additions.

Mr. Bruce Younger's barn is in the right foreground. You can see the old, old Elon school in the left background which is located on what is now Cedar Gate Road. Some houses were built beside the road years ago, but the big field in the background did not have any houses until it was developed as a section of Hunt Club subdivision.

Talmadge Foster Jr., and Nancy Morris – *Courtesy Doris Foster*

View from behind Camden and Younger store with Cedar Gate Road in background – *Courtesy Ann Correll*

Field in the background of picture with Linda Foster is now the Route 130/Elon Road section of the Hunt Club subdivision.

Linda Foster – *Courtesy Mary Foster*

Bernard Camden's peach orchard – *Jack Litchford*

Race track – *H. R. Nixon*

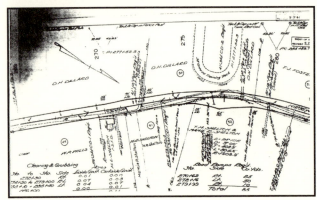

Drawing of race training track – *VDOT Highway Plan*

The view is of Mr. Camden's peach orchard when it was in full bloom. You can see the corner of Mary and Broadus Foster's house in the right background. It is now Camden's subdivision on Camden Drive.

Located to the right of the driveway to the Wigwam was the race track. According to Melvin Bailess, on February 20, 1990, the horses were housed in barns at the race track. The horses were kept and trained by Mr. Kaiden (sp.) from Russia. He said there were four black men who worked with him and stayed in quarters at the barn. The horses were trained pulling two-wheel sullys. The horses never raced at Elon, but were taken to race tracks in Goshen, N. Y. and other places for racing.

He said that sometimes they would hurry and finish the milking at Dillard's Dairy on Homewood Farms so they could go down and see the horses run on the race track just before they left to go to Goshen, N. Y. He said the horses would go around the track about twice and then when they reached a certain turn they would really go fast, without the driver even touching the reins, they were so well trained.

In the early 1950s the horses were taken to Goshen, N. Y. to race. One of the horses was badly hurt and, with the races being rigged, Mr. Dillard decided to sell his race horses.

The race track tract is now owned by Lloyd and Vickie Jennings. They built a home at the back of the field.

The property with houses on the right of Route 130/Elon Road, just beyond the Wigwam was owned by Mr. Dillard.

VIEWS OF ELON AND AREAS ON ROUTE 130 IN 1930S AND 1940S

According to Bobby Morris, a lot of convicts were used in hard-surfacing the road to Elon. The small house on the left as you head east up the hill from the water filtration plant, a short distance before you get to the Hans Hill entrance on the right, was where the superintendent lived. Early Coffey and his family lived there in the late 1940s and early 1950s.

One-lane bridge over railroad tracks – *Courtesy: Nancy Marion*

This was a one-lane bridge on Route 130/Elon Road over the Southern Railway tracks. You can see that for traffic heading east, the approach to the bridge had a sharp curve just before you got to the bridge. A driver would almost be on the bridge before he could see if a vehicle heading west was approaching from the other side. Over the years, there were quite a number of automobile accidents.

The present two-lane bridge was built in 1952 just north of the original bridge.

Present bridge over Norfolk -Southern railroad tracks looking east – *H. R. Nixon*

Present bridge over Norfolk-Southern railroad tracks looking west – *H. R. Nixon*

135

MT. SINAI BAPTIST CHURCH

This is a church located on a loop of old Rt. 130, now Mt. Sinai Road.

The church was organized in 1925 and the first church was a wooden frame building. In 1971 this building was torn down and replaced by a brick building. There are large black-topped parking areas on both sides of the church.

A large cemetery is off from the parking lot to the left of the church.

Mt. Sinai Baptist Church – *H. R. Nixon*

AGRICOLA/MT. TABOR

During the Civil War when the Gilmer map was prepared, the community was named Mt. Tabor, which is the name of the church. Later, with there being so many crops grown there, it was named Agricola when Mr. Parks McDaniel Rucker, got the name out of a Latin book.

MT. TABOR UNITED METHODIST CHURCH

Mt. Tabor United Methodist Church – *H. R. Nixon*

According to an article written by Pansye Franklin Anderson in 1999, Mt. Tabor United Methodist Church was built in the early 1800s from brick fired on the property. One acre from the Cheatwood Farm was deeded for Mt. Tabor Church. Over the years the church has been modernized with electricity, heat pump, and stained glass windows. It is still an active Methodist church.

MT. TABOR/AGRICOLA SCHOOL

Mt. Tabor School, which was a private school, was erected near the church. Early Keith records show that some family members attended Mt. Tabor School in the 1850s.

It is thought that Agricola School was erected sometime in the late 1800s as a one-room school serving five grades. In 1890 there were 90 schools listed in Amherst County, all private. In the years 1918–1923, Agricola School was operated by the Amherst Public School System.

Agricola School – *H. R. Nixon*

The building was converted into a dwelling in the late 1920s, and additional rooms were added to the original structure.

B. C. FRANKLIN'S STORE

B. C. Franklin's store – *H. R. Nixon*

Pot-bellied stove

Burks and Grace Franklin had a house, store, service station, and post office. When road improvements took some of the curves out of Route 130, the business was no longer beside the main road. During 1942–43, prison labor accomplished the feat of moving the store, service station, and post office from its original site to its location on Route 130/Elon Road with the Franklins and the Virginia Department of Highways sharing the cost equally.

They continued to live in the house that was at the site of the original store. In 1951, due to Mr. Franklin's declining health, they built living quarters onto the store. The store was heated with a pot-bellied stove, as were churches, schools, and other public buildings during that period of time.

The Agricola post office was located in the store for years, and remained there until 1962, when it was closed, as were so many of the small post offices.

WINDY HILL FARM

A large farm at Agricola was owned by the Davis family. The Davises first purchased 300 acres known as Cheatwood Farm, in 1918, and later a portion of the Perrow property was inherited by Ruth Wood Davis. Through the years of the depression more parcels of land were purchased, and eventually the farm contained more than twelve hundred acres. At that time the Davis family resided and worked in Atlanta, Georgia.

The Davis family named their property "Circle View Farm" and for many years spent only summers there. Eventually James Wood Davis and his wife, Corinne B. Davis took up residence at Circle View Farm where he raised cattle. He served as a state senator for many years.

In 1975, the entire property was sold to Keene C. Brown who specialized in Black Angus cattle. In 1986, the property was purchased by Louis and Helen Loving Nelson, who sold part of the tract to Cloudcroft, Inc. A subdivision named "Cloudcroft" was established across the road, a little beyond Mt. Tabor Church.

Cloudcroft sold the house plot and other acreage to Carolyn Folkers in 1996. She named the property "Windy Hill Farm" and operates it as a horse farm.

ALLWOOD AREA

BUFFALO SPRINGS HOTEL

The Buffalo Springs Hotel and sulphur springs were located on Buffalo Springs Turnpike, near Allwood. The resort was not far from Forks of Buffalo and Route 60.

According to research and a paper written by Eddie Myers in 1976: Around the turn of the century, the resort consisted of a series of small cabins. Several decades later a hotel was built. Mary L. Myers purchased the property in 1907, and built a second hotel to replace the one which, earlier, had been destroyed by fire. She reopened the resort and rented it to visitors for about ten years. Since that time, the property has remained in the Myers and Turner families.

Before the use of canals and railroads, many travelers would stop at Buffalo Springs on their way to larger resorts, such as Warm Springs, Hot Springs, and White Sulphur Springs.

Buffalo Springs Hotel – *Eugenia Myers collection*

Buffalo Springs Hotel – *Eugenia Myers collection*

They arrived at Buffalo Springs by way of stagecoach on the Buffalo Springs Turnpike. The turnpike began at the River Road that led up the James from Lynchburg and continued to Elon, Pedlar Mills, Pleasant View, and on to Route 60.

The resort was so popular that advertisements were placed in the Lynchburg papers in the 1850s giving the departure times of the stagecoach. Apparently some of the hotel guests were from the Lynchburg area. In 1837, there was mention of the Lynchburg–Buffalo Springs Turnpike Company. For many years, the road that led to Buffalo Springs was State Route 635. With the 911 emergency system put into place in Amherst County, in recent years, it is again known as the Buffalo Springs Turnpike.

The hotel was closed in about 1920, and the building served as a private home for a number of people, including Mr. and Mrs. John Whitmore, and Mr. and Mrs. Emmett Sale. Highway construction workers occupied the building when Route 60 was being built in the 1930s.

The eighteen-room hotel has greatly deteriorated since being last lived in, but it is still standing. Also, the wall and roof that once covered the sulphur spring have fallen to the ground.

Gazebo which was built over the sulphur springs – *Eugenia Myers collection*

DAVIS' STORE

Davis' Store – *H. R. Nixon*

One of the early owners of this store was Bennett Harris. His wife was Sadie (Camden) Harris, who moved to Elon sometime after his death. There have been other owners also.

This store has been owned by Warren and Eleanor Davis since 1950, and is located on the corner of Buffalo Springs Turnpike and Chinquapin Road, in Allwood. It is a general store with groceries and gas pumps.

Mr. Davis stayed busy with farming and raising cattle, so Mrs. Davis was usually running the store.

Mrs. Davis in store in 1992 – *H. R. Nixon*

PINEY HILL BAPTIST CHURCH

Piney Hill Baptist Church in 1992

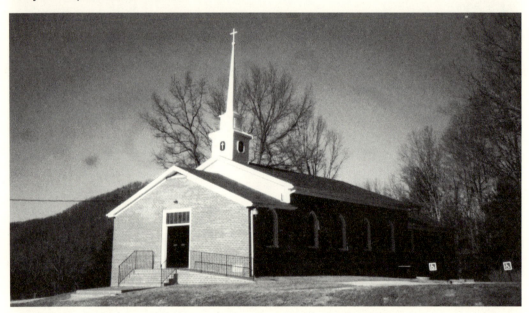

Present Piney Hill Baptist Church

This church was founded in 1847 and over the years has been at different locations with different names. In 1929, the property was purchased where the church now stands on Route 636/Slapp Creek Road at Allwood.

Improvements have been made to the grounds, and additions and improvements have been made to the church. In 2003 the church was remodeled and at that time the outside of the church was bricked.

EL BETHEL CHURCH

El Bethel Church – *H. R. Nixon*

El Bethel Church was founded in 1837 as a part of the Mt. Pleasants Methodist charge. One of the pastors, then called circuit riders, was the Rev. Pitt Woodroof. The church was much larger than it is today. The present church building was erected in 1930 after the old structure was torn down; much of that lumber was used for the new building.

Old El Bethel Church in 1920s – *Ruth Foster collection*

Due to such a few active members, the church closed in 1988. In 1998, the Pedlar Ruritan Club adopted the restoration of the church as a project for the betterment of the community.

The El Bethel Community Association is now in possession of the building, along with its well-kept cemetery which is still used.

Allwood School – *H. R. Nixon*

ALLWOOD SCHOOL

This two-room school with grades 1–7 had a hallway and a stage. It was located over to the side and down from El Bethel Church.

The children would go down under the hill to Mr. Henderson's spring to get water and bring it back to the school. Later Mr. Henderson had a well, so they got water from that.

The school closed around 1920, and after that the students attended Pleasant View School. The property is now owned by Todd Camden.

BETHEL/SALT CREEK

According to Sherrie and William McLeRoy in their book: *More Passages: A New History Of Amherst County, Virginia*, Nicholas Davies and his son, Henry Landon Davies, established the town of Bethel in 1775. This was at the point of where Salt Creek flows into the James River. They even placed an ad in the *Virginia Gazette*, but it failed to develop, due to the Revolutionary War. They did build Davies' Lower Ferry.

Next to Madison, the largest tobacco warehouse was at Davies' Lower Ferry. In 1799 Henry Davies built a tobacco station inspection/warehouse. Davies and his partner, Thomas Cocke of Bedford, applied for a town charter for Bethel, which was granted in December, 1801. They built a flour mill at Bethel with a dam located above the town on Salt Creek. Only the dam survives today.

Mill dam on Salt Creek – *H. R. Nixon*

Later a second tobacco warehouse was built, and with the ferry, and then the construction of the James River and Kanawha Canal (with the 'Bethell Lock'), they could handle large quantities of cargo. The town passed out of the Davies family, and later owners built a tavern, lumber house, stable for the canal animals, and several houses. The death of the canal in the 1870s killed the town, even though the ferry (later called Abert Ferry) continued to be operated until in the 1930s. (You can still see the tow rope attached to trees between Monacan Park and Salt Creek).

The 1888 Lynchburg City Directory showed that there was a post office at Salt Creek. Also listed at Salt Creek (which was their mailing address) were: magistrate, A. C. Rucker; druggists: Charles Buchanan and Robert Thompson; foundry and machine shops: George Wright; general merchants, E. F. Hudson; hotels: D. H. Hawks; land agents, R. G. Scott; saw mills: R. G. Scott; millwrights, D. W. Wash; physicians: W. B. Roberts, and E. W. Scott; principal farmers: Edward Fletcher, R. G. Scott, Ambrose C. Rucker, George H. Dameron, W. Tinsley, John J. Old, J. T. Plunkett, M. Wright, Clarence Dearing, Jane Dearing, Mattie Blanchard, David Tees, John Moorman, William R. Terry, and John Dameron.

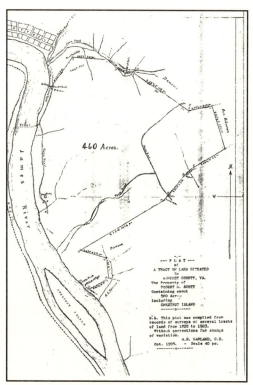

Plat drawn in 1905, compiled from records of surveys of several tracts of land from 1820 to 1903 which shows lots for Bethel

The next pictures were in the Elon Home Demonstration Scrap Book which was prepared in the 1960s.

This building housed the old post office and store which was built by a Mr. Berry, and later operated by young Bob Scott. Mr. Andrew Watts was operating the store and post office at the time it burned. He rebuilt a short distance up the river at Salt Creek.

In a letter received from E. Crawley Williams Jr., of Covington, Va. dated Feb. 21, 1983, he stated: "My grandfather, Andrew Mitchell Watts ran

Old store and post office at Salt Creek – *Elon Home Demonstration Club Scrap Book*

Rebuilt store and post office – This is the building Mrs. Mary Fannie Woodruff went to as a girl to get mail and groceries – *Elon Home Demonstration Club Scrap Book*

the mill, post office, and store at Salt Creek from about 1920 until his death about 1932, after which my grandmother, Lenna Watts and my mother's youngest sister, Elizabeth Watts, ran the complex until Elizabeth's marriage to my father about 1935. All was shut down at this time. Since then the mill was washed away, the store collapsed, and the home burned—nothing remains on the old site but ruins."

"It has always been my understanding that Bethel was located roughly ½ mile down the James River from Salt Creek. Prior to moving to Salt Creek, my grandparents ran a post office and store at that location. The store burned and they moved to Salt Creek and built a new one. The foundation of their old home at Bethel still remains between the road and the river, just upstream from the cabins located at the lower end of the property. I believe my grandparents moved to Bethel about 1908 from Pleasant View."

The home belonged to Andrew Watts and was located just across Salt Creek from where the store, cabins, and one old building (tavern or wash house?) were located. In later years, his daughter, Katherine Elizabeth Watts Williams, would stay there for a portion of the summer. It was struck by lightning in the 1970s, and burned to the ground. She was a distant relative, and my father used to go there and fish from her dock.

I was originally told that the remaining building was a tavern. In recent years I have been told that it was a wash house. Whatever it was used for, it is the only old building still standing today. In November, 2003, a fire was set which burned all the cabins. Some of them have been replaced and are used in the summer.

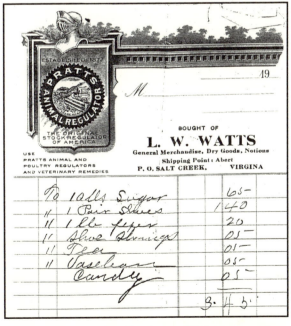

Copy of bill head after Mrs. Lenna Watts was running store, showing: P. O. Salt Creek, Virginia, and Shipping Point: Abert

Andrew Watts home – *Elon Home Demonstration Club Scrap Book*

Remaining old building at Salt Creek – *H. R. Nixon*

RIVERVIEW/MONACAN PARK

Riverview was a large plantation on the James River owned by Robert "Bob" Scott. It was located a little below Bethel/Salt Creek. Some sources say the Mansion house was built in the late 1700s and some say it was built in 1810. It was a very large house. He and his family and slaves farmed the land and had easy access to the river for ferrying purposes.

In earlier times when it was used as a resort, boarders would offload from the train on the Bedford side of the river and be ferried across the river by means of a small steam stern wheeler. It is said that at one time a bowling alley was operated in the building.

Riverview in its early days – *Courtesy Family of R. C. Scott*

In 1936 Coke Stuart and his wife purchased Riverview and ran it as a food and lodging resort.

According to *Lynchburg Magazine* for January-February, 1973, giving an account of the dedication of Monacan Park, the site of the park was purchased in 1968 by Appalachian Power Company. Due to the hazardous condition of the abandoned house, they decided that it should be torn down. You can still see the remains of a rock wall. They built a picnic area with a shelter, comfort stations, charcoal grills, parking facilities for cars and boat trailers. They leased it to Amherst County on a no-charge basis. In return the County agreed to maintain and police the property. A boat ramp and dock were developed by the Virginia Commission of Game and Inland Fisheries. It was named Monacan Park for the

Riverview as it looked in later years – *Courtesy Lynchburg Magazine*

Monacan Indians who were the first people in this area.

The first launching of the first replica of the Amherst County bateau into James River was from the boat ramp at Monacan Park in May 1986. It was named the *Anthony Rucker* for an Amherst native who, along with his brother, Benjamin, originated the James River batteau in 1775.

In 1991, Joe Hobbs talked about the old house which stood at what is now Monacan Park. He said his Burks grandparents rented the house from Coke Stuart and lived there for a while in the late 1930s. When the railroad men were working across the river changing the railroad ties, his grandmother would send sandwiches and buttermilk over to them for lunch. Some of the grandchildren would take the food over in a boat. Of course, she got paid for the food.

He also said that in the morning they used to drive the cows across to the little island (Chestnut Island). The cows would have to swim part way. They would then have to get them back over in the evening for milking.

Joe said his grandmother had a riding horse that had rubbed a place on its side. When she put some ointment on it, apparently it burned or stung and the horse started kicking and stomped her, and she could not get away. She died as a result of her injuries.

The Abert Ferry and village of Bethel/Salt Creek were up the river, just a little ways from what is now Monacan Park. (See Bethel/Salt Creek story with copy of plat showing lots at Bethel, and Scott property with Chestnut Island which can be seen from Monacan Park.) It also shows Vault Hill which is a cemetery with a rock wall, where some early settlers are buried. An Indian cemetery has been established beside the rock wall.

First launching of Amherst Co. Bateau in 1986 – *H. R. Nixon*

BURFORD AND BURFORD'S MILL

Burford was one of the earlier settlements located in what is now the Monroe area, and it is shown on Gilmer's Civil War map.

The only original building still standing is the house that was the home of Mr. Sylvester M. Burford, who was born in 1825 and died in 1892. Burford's chapel was built in 1869, and Sylvester Burford is buried in the cemetery. One-quarter of a mile from the house was Burford's Station, where the depot, post office, and general store were located. A wheel and blacksmith shop was located directly across the road from the house, and Burford's school was a short distance from the house on the same side of the road. An undertaking business was located near the school, at the entrance to what is now "Winridge Bed and Breakfast."

Burford house now owned by Wills family – *H. R. Nixon*

Thompson/Dawson home, now Winridge Bed and Breakfast – *H. R. Nixon*

In a deed made in 1872, S. L. Burford conveyed to A. L. Burford property known as "Burford's Mill." The mill race and dam for Burford's Mill were located on Harris Creek, northeast of the present bridge on what is now Winesap Road. The mill was located on the south side of the old bridge. Later it was Danny Peyton's Mill. It is thought that the mill ceased operations in the early 1920s. Sometime after the mill closed, the mill wheel was disassembled and used at Hollins Mill in Lynchburg.

The name "Burford" was later changed to "Winesap" because of the great quanity of winesap apples hauled to the Burford Depot for shipment.

Winesap Station taken in 1919 – Southern Ties *magazine*

CEDAR GATE FARM/ LAUREL CLIFF

The home known today as Laurel Cliff, is located on what is now named Laurel Cliff Road, which is between Cedar Gate Road and High Peak Road.

The property was known as the Zack D. Tinsley house place, and in 1883 was sold by his wife, Mary L. Tinsley, and daughter, Mary S. Warner, and her husband, John W. Warner, to Charles S. Thackston. It was described as being situated on the north side of the road from McIvor Station to Bethel and on the west side of what is known as Ambler's Mill Road, and contained a little over 298 acres.

In 1896 the property was sold at public auction. In 1905 the property was purchased by H. Don Scott.

Scott was the physician for the Southern Railroad and was nicknamed "the railroad doctor." He owned the home when it was a log cabin with a weatherboard wing attached. Their main home was in Lynchburg, and they used the home in Amherst County in the summer. He and his wife, Eva Davies Scott, raised three sons: David P. Scott, Stuart D. Scott, and Samuel B. Scott. He grew up at "Riverview" which was the Scott home located at what is now Monacan Park. His sister, Florence Scott, married Alfred Dearing and they lived at what is now named "Speed-the-Plow." After the death of Mr. Dearing she married Oscar Watts.

In 1936 Mr. A. N. (Abe) Campbell purchased from J. M. Stinnette, property which adjoined Ruckers' Fruit Farm, Dr. H. Don Scott's Estate and B. H. Ewers lines. In 1941 he purchased an additional tract of land containing about

Dr. H. Don Scott

Mr. Abe Campbell – *Florence Foster Nixon*

102 acres near Elon post office, from W. W. and Bessie V. Burch.

In June, 1946, David Scott and his wife conveyed 304 acres that had been the property of Dr. Scott to Mr. Campbell.

Mr. Campbell lived in the Tinsley house, called the "House Place" in an earlier deed. His office was in a little building near the house. Sometime later he moved into the house on the Stinnette tract which he had purchased in 1936, and had his office in that house. The driveway for the Stinnette house went off what is now Phyllis Lea Road. It was a large two-story house with porches across the front. The house has now been torn down, and the road to the site where the house stood has been closed. Mr. Campbell was a bridge builder and Tommy and Russell Burford visited him.

Mr. Campbell liked to fox hunt and became a good friend of the family of Lyle Foster, and visited our home and ate meals numerous times. We moved to Elon in 1941 and on a few occasions he brought me little frilly dresses and would bring boxes of stick candy. We visited his home a few times, and I remember he had a polar bear rug in his living room.

On June 10, 1947, Mr. Campbell sold his property which he called "Cedar Gate Farm" to Frank Stone Loyd, containing 781.5 acres, more or less.

Ten days later Mr. Campbell purchased property in Campbell County from the estate of the late Carter Glass. This property, consisting of about 318 acres, was known as "Montview Farm" and is now the site of Liberty University. My family visited Mr. Campbell after he moved to the Carter Glass property. Mr. Campbell died in 1950. A portion of the large house lived in by the Carter Glass family and Mr. Campbell was used as an office by Jerry Falwell.

Stinnette house with Leroy and Brenda Humphries in front – *Courtesy Brenda (Humphries) Staton*

Most of the renovations to the Tinsley/Scott house were made by Frank Loyd. He added the green house, bricked the façade, added a formal living room, and office. Also, he renovated the inside of the house, which now has 11 rooms. He acquired several other farms and consolidated them into one large dairy farm which he named "Laurel Cliff." He used to travel through Cedar Gate Road

House before the porch was enclosed – *Courtesy Brenda (Humphries) Staton*

and Elon Road. Sometime after he moved into the Laurel Cliff house, the road was improved and, he traveled on the Bethany Church road (now High Peak Rd.) to get to Route 29.

Mr. Loyd was a very wealthy man and he owned a private railroad car. In early years it was stored on a siding in the Southern Railroad yards at Monroe. According to Robert Floyd, due to vandalism in later years, he stored it on tracks at the Montview yard in Lynchburg.

Laurel Cliff was operated as a dairy farm, but in later years, Mr. Loyd spent most of his time in Hawaii leaving the farm to be operated by his farm manager, Archie Humphries. He would have the farm manager and his wife, Vernell, fly to California to discuss the business of running the farm. The Humphries family moved into the Laurel Cliff house and remained there until the property was sold.

According to Tommy Burford, prior to selling Laurel Cliff Farm, Mr. Loyd purchased property on Archer Mountain in Nelson County and had a large contemporary house, and hot house built there. He had a mile long driveway and had no telephone, and he used generators. In about 1964 there was a big snow storm. The snow was so heavy that the roof of the hot house caved in where he had fruit trees, including lemons, limes, etc., as well as thousands of orchids. He rode a tractor to the intersection of Rt. 29 and Rt. 6 to call for help. He continued to spend some of his time in Hawaii, where he also owned property.

In June 1969 Mr. Loyd sold the Laurel Cliff Farm property, containing 1,329 acres to the Flippin family. Later he died in Hawaii and was buried in Spring Hill Cemetery in Lynchburg.

In 1982 the Flippin family formed F. F. Associates, Ltd. and purchased property from some of the other owners. After that, additional remodeling was done to the house and an upstairs porch was enclosed. Some of the old window glass remains in the house.

In 2006 they sold the property to Richard A. Carrington III and the Oceanus Group Corp. Since that time cattle are again being raised on the property, and the dairy barns have been painted.

In 2008, the property was put back on the market for sale.

Frank Loyd's private railroad car – *Courtesy Roy Evans*

Overview of Monroe Railroad yards, with Loyd's railroad car on a siding

CHESTNUT GROVE BAPTIST CHURCH AND AREA

Mrs. Mary Fannie (Burton) Woodruff lives on Elon Road between the village of Elon and Agricola. She grew up near Salt Creek, and remembers going to Mr. Watts' store to make purchases and to pick up her family's mail.

Mrs. Woodruff's deceased husband, James Earl Woodruff, was the son of Walter Woodruff, and the grandson of Wyatt Woodruff.

Wyatt Woodruff's blacksmith shop was located on what is today the corner of Route 130/Elon Road and East Peach Road. He had worked in the shop for Mr. Thomas Townley, and later purchased the shop with money he had earned while working for Mr. Townley. This was the same Mr. Townley who owned the Townley Tan Yard. The tan yard was located off what is now Mistover Mansion Road which you get to shortly before you get to East Peach Road and it is shown on the Gilmer Map.

Mrs. Woodruff ran Woodruff's Store for about 30 years, where they sold groceries as well as gas. She closed the store in 1982. It remained closed, except for about two years when it was run by her son-in-law as a fish market.

In 1998 one of her daughters, Angie Woodruff Scott, re-opened the business as more of a deli-type store. She named it Woodruff's Café and Pie Shop. She serves sandwiches, hot dogs, barbeque, and other foods. Sometimes her special for the day is homemade soup, or pinto beans and corn bread. She makes delicious salads and pies. Mrs. Woodruff makes wonderful fried fruit pies. Angie takes orders for her homemade pies, chicken salad, and other items for take-out as well.

Remains of Townley Tan Yard chimney – *Elon Home Demonstration Club Scrapbook*

CHESTNUT GROVE BAPTIST CHURCH

Chestnut Grove Baptist Church is located just a little ways down East Peach Road from the Café and Pie Shop.

Mrs. Woodruff took her first music lessons from a Mr. Slaughter who lived in the community. As a young teenager, she played the piano some for church. Later she played the organ,

Chestnut Grove Baptist Church – *H. R. Nixon*

Mrs. Woodruff playing the church organ – *H. R. Nixon*

and has served as organist at Chestnut Grove for over 70 years and continues in that capacity. Mrs. Woodruff will be 94 years old later this year (2010).

Organized in September 1866, the congregation met in a tobacco house on Mr. Townsley's farm. In November 1866 of that year they moved into a log school house near where the present church is located. In 1872 they purchased one acre of land from Mr. Townsley to build a church.

Some of the lumber was hauled on the old packet boat from Lynchburg, and five trees were purchased from Mr. Ned Fletcher who lived where Mrs. Ella Dillard later lived. (The house was located on "Killy Kranky Farm" later named "Homewood Farms.")

The church was made of planks straight up and down. Some years later, because the church membership had grown so much, they sold the building to the public school board. They built a new church, and in 1886 they began to worship in the present building. Shortly thereafter they bought some additional land. Over the years some additions have been made to the building, and the outside was bricked. There is a cemetery behind the area where the Chestnut Grove School stood.

CHESTNUT GROVE SCHOOL

This was a two-room school located just above Chestnut Grove Baptist Church. In later years only one room was used for grades 1-6. After completing the sixth grade, students attended the Madison Heights Negro School located on Colony Road and graduated from there. They did not have indoor plumbing. They brought water from a spring above the school which was on the property of Walter Woodruff. The school closed in the early 1960s, and the church used the building for dinners, etc. until it was torn down a few years later.

Chestnut Grove School – *Tyler Fulcher's Booklet*

HIGH PEAK ROAD AREA

WATTS "OLD MOUNTAIN HOME"

A portion of Morris Orchards is located near the corner of High Peak Road and Ambrose Rucker Road. The old Watts House and most of the orchards are on Ambrose Rucker Road. The oldest part of the house has chimneys made of homemade brick of native clay, as well as its original plaster walls and old glass in the windows. The floors are wide pine boards over hand-hewn beams.

The front hall was covered with maple board flooring in the 1950s, made from trees harvested from the mountain. Additional improvements have been made in recent years.

Wattses and their descendants have always occupied the house. It is currently owned by Scott and Judy Barnes and family. It is now known as Morris Orchard due to marriages between the Watts and Morris families. (See ORCHARDS).

Watts "Old Mountain Home" circa 1837 – *Judy and Scott Barnes*

Old Watts house at Morris Orchard 1992 – *Judy and Scott Barnes*

WATTS' STORE

Mr. Rufus Watts and his wife, Lela, ran Watts store which was located at the corner of what is now High Peak Road and Ambrose Rucker Road. Their living quarters were behind the store, in the same building. The store was closed in the late 1960s.

R. R. Watts store – *Courtesy of Ken and Vickie (Richeson) Englund*

Lela Watts and Rufus Watts in store – *Courtesy of Ken and Vickie (Richeson) Englund*

WATTS' MILL

Mr. Watts also ran a gasoline powered mill and ground corn. This building was located on High Peak Road near the store building.

Watts' grist mill showing High Peak in distance on right – *Courtesy Ken and Vickie (Richeson) Englund*

Current Watts' grist mill building – *H. R. Nixon*

BETHANY UNITED METHODIST CHURCH

In the spring of 1886 Samuel L. Watts and his wife, Nora, deeded one acre of land to trustees of Bethany Church to be used for building a place of worship. Many of the members in the neighborhood helped with the actual building, as well as with the funds. On October 16, 1885, the church was dedicated by Dr. John Hannon.

According to Mrs. Dorothy (Kent) Harvey, at one time there were six Methodist churches in their charge, with one preacher. They were: Bethany, Centenary, Monroe, Mt. Tabor, Pleasants Chapel, and Smyrna. At that time, the Methodist parsonage was located next door to the home of Miss Christine McIvor who later married a Smith.

Centenary and Pleasants Chapel have been closed for many years and the buildings no longer exist. Mt. Tabor and Smyrna share a minister; Bethany and Sardis share a minister; and Monroe has a full-time minister.

Old Bethany United Methodist Church

Current Bethany United Methodist Church – *H. R. Nixon*

CASH'S MILL

This mill was earlier known as Ambler's Mill. Some deeds recorded for the area, mention locations near Ambler's Mill, etc. The mill was located on Harris Creek on what is now High Peak Road, and not far from Bethany United Methodist Church. There is a mill wheel standing in the general vicinity of where the mill was located.

William Cash was a miller at Galts Mill until he bought the Ambler Mill in 1879. From that time it was known as Cash's Mill. The mill was operated until 1933 when the dam broke. Mr. Cash also operated a saw mill and grocery store at the same site as the mill.

Cash's Mill – *Courtesy of Mrs. Dorothy (Kent) Harvey*

l.–r.: Mr. Marvin S. Cash Sr. and ? at Cash's Mill – *Courtesy Marvin S. Cash Jr.*

LONG'S/TAYLOR'S MILL

According to a story written by Garland Branch, Long's Mill was a two-story building situated along Graham Creek beside the bridge on Rt. 130/Elon Road which crosses the creek. Graham Creek which runs into Harris Creek and then into the James River, at one time twisted its way beside Rt. 130/Elon Road before its course was altered.

The two-story house located to the left side of the mill was the home of the miller and his family. Built before the Civil War with wooden pegs instead of nails, it is now covered with aluminum siding. The main road which ran in front of the house, was often traveled by horses and carriages on their way to Lynchburg from Elon. A deed of conveyance in 1885 to John C. Long refers to the mill dam. In 1905 C. W. Taylor, F. L. Taylor, P. G. Taylor, and Robert W. Taylor bought property which included the mill.

The area surrounding the mill was one of activity. Less than 100 yards from the mill was a rock quarry from which rock was taken and used in buildings and later used as gravel for

Long's Mill showing water wheel – *Courtesy Nancy Marion.*

roads. Opposite the mill where the filtration plant is now located, was a barn where the miller kept a few cows, horses, and some pigs. Mrs. Thelma Smith stated, "I remember the large yard surrounding the mill where we children often played. There was a cherry tree in front of the mill where we gathered cherries when they were ripe. Behind the mill was a large garden where we often had to work in the summer."

Even though Long's Mill did not have an ordinary, it was still the social center for the area. Men often gathered at the mill to exchange tall tales. Children ran across the small timber bridge with the several cats who lived there, while Matt or Fleming Taylor measured out one gallon of grain from each customer's bushel. Standing in aprons covered with flour, they could feel the grain with the tips of their thumbs and fingers and know if the mill was running at the best speed, and if the stones were set at the proper distances.

The mill was torn down in 1940 when the road was changed. The mill stones are located beside the driveway at the miller's house, now the home of Garland Taylor.

Thelma (Taylor) Smith with mill in background
– Courtesy Abbitt Horsley Jr.

Taylor house occupied by Garland Taylor

MADISON HEIGHTS HIGH SCHOOL

Madison Heights Elementary and Madison Heights High Schools

To complete their education, students who had attended Elon Elementary, Monroe Elementary and Pleasant View Elementary schools went on to Madison Heights High School. At that time school buses were privately owned. Mr. Rucker would pick up Elon students and then meet the Camden and Younger bus for the high school students to transfer to that bus.

Camden and Younger's bus with l.–r. James Brown and Gordon Foster in bus

The Camden and Younger's bus would then head to W. P. Martin's store, picking up high school students on the way down Route 130, for them to transfer to Clyde Clements' bus to go on to the high school.

Students beside Camden and Younger's bus – l.–r. front: June Rucker, Frances Morris, Addie Brown (bus driver), Eleanor Foster, Betty Harris, Beth Younger, Edith Hudson; back: Bobby Morris, Jack Litchford, ?, Cathlene Horton

Joyce and Janice Brown, and the Higginbotham children who also lived near Martin's Store would ride the bus to Elon School. Of course, other students for Elon were picked up on the way back up 130.

Tyler Fulcher, who had served as principal at Elon, went to Madison Heights as principal in the early 1940s.

When I was in the seventh grade at Madison Heights High School we still had to make a bus transfer at Martin's Store. By the fall of 1951 we rode directly to the high school.

Tyler Fulcher 1964 – *Courtesy Helen Walutes*

Students making the bus transfer, l.–r.: Betty Harris, ?, Doris Morris, June Bibb, Eleanor Foster – *Courtesy Doris Foster*

GLEE CLUB – 1952

l.–r. Front: Mrs. East, Carolyn McIvor, Martha Brizendine, June Young, Carolyn Horsley, Corrine Tyree, Jean Shaner, Nancy Johnson, Jean Tyree, Judy Moss; Row 2: Evelyn Davis, Connie Stinnette, Barbara Wiley, Joan Harper, Joyce Bryant, June Simmons, Margaret Franklin, Marie Wood, Lynn Wright, Wanda Moss, Shirley Dean, Rosalie Burford; Row 3: Pete Newcomb, Richard Cash, Harold Pugh, Terry Staton, James Davis, Donald Wilkerson, Withers Whitehead, Richard "Dick" Nichols; Back Row: Homer Massie, Lawrence Cooper, Jimmy Steuart, James Story, Mack Dews, Richard Blount, Arnold Ewers, Kenneth "Bibbie" Layne, Roger Sanders, George Wilkerson – *Jimmie Ray collection*

BEAUTY CONTEST AND SENIOR SING – 1954

l.–r. Front: Patsy Bryant, Florence Foster, Delores Maze, Lydia Hudson, Nancy Wills, Shelby Floyd, Betty Jo Amiss, Loretta Sanders, Marie Nuckols, Nancy Neblett, Janet Craven, Hazel Patterson, Celia Loving, Joyce Steuart; Row 2: Myrtle Campbell, Shirley Floyd, Betty Garrett, Shirley Riley, Jackie Miller, Rose White, Joyce Tyree, Marie Blunke, Lois Tomlin, Doris Jennings, Dorothy Carson, Phyllis Norberg, Bonnie Banton, Joyce Coffey; Row 3: Louis Tomlin, Lloyd Cash, Jerome Cooper, Robert Baldree, Donald McCraw, Calvin Phelps, Preston Bryant, R. E. Traylor, Soule Purvis, Withers Whitehead, Mary Lou Kidd, Shirley Ragland, Donna Thacker, Nellie Turner, Gerry McCraw, Kathryn Spencer, Charles "Buck" Gillispie; Back Row: Holcomb Nixon, T. D. Thornton, Jack Pettyjohn, Hilton Maddox, Gene Goff, Freddie Coffey, Pete Peters, J. T. Banton, Paul Goff, George "Buck" Adcock, Joe Gallagher, Thomas Manley, Buck Caldwell, Gene Allen, Kenneth "Bibbie" Layne – *Jimmie Ray collection*

SENIOR CLASS OF 1954

The Senior class of 1954 was the first graduating class from Madison Heights High School to take an overnight school trip.

l.-r. Front: Hazel Patterson, Joyce Tyree, Janet Craven, Gene Rhea Allen, Sherwood Caldwell, Joyce Coffey, Bonnie Banton, Patsy Bryant, Carolyn McIvor, Betty Jo Amiss, Thomas Manley, Kenneth "Bibbie" Layne; Row 2: Mrs. Mary Pettyjohn, Donna Thacker, Shirley Floyd, Hazel Maddox, Lois Tomlin, Myrtle Campbell, Paul Goff, Winfred Bryant, Miss Virginia McPherson; Row 3: Marie Nuckols, Marie Blunke, Loretta Sanders, Marie White, Nellie Turner, Joan Harper, Doris Jennings, Annie Mae Hicks, Joyce Steuart, George Creasey, Dorothy Carson, R. E. Traylor, Calvin Phelps, Jerome Cooper; Row 4: Betty Garrett, Betty Gallo, Shirley Curd, Delores Maze, Shirley Riley, Nancy Neblett, Florence Foster, Celia Loving, Gerry McCraw, Kathryn Spencer, Phyllis Norberg, George "Buck" Adcock, Donald McCraw, Billy Ogden, Robert Riner; Back: Robert Baldree, Lloyd Cash, Louis Tomlin, Robin Staton, Soule Purvis, Donnie Simmons, Preston Bryant, Holcomb Nixon, Jack Pettyjohn, Joe Gallagher, T. D. Thornton, Pete Peters, Gene Goff, Charles "Buck" Gillispie – *Jimmie Ray collection*

SOME OF THE GRADUATING CLASS OF 1956 ON SENIOR TRIP

Miss Virginia McPherson, class sponsor – *Courtesy Jean Turner*

Joyce Woodroof and Becky Thornton – *Courtesy Jean Turner*

l.–r.: Earl Collins Wiley Jr., Junior Turner, Bobby Pugh, Rhonda Davis, Russell Franklin – *Courtesy Jean Turner*

McIVOR STATION AND AREA

One of the older settlements which preceded the establishment of Monroe was located at McIvor Station, and it is shown on the Gilmer Civil War map.

McIVOR STATION

McIvor Station – *Roy McIvor*

McIvor sign beside railroad tracks – *H. R. Nixon*

Apparently the first McIvor in this area was Christopher McIvor who was nicknamed "Old Kit." It is said he was born in 1805 on a boat coming to America. He married Liza Halsey and had either five or six children. He owned hundreds of acres of land, some of which he purchased in 1843. His land adjoined Spring Garden, now owned by sons of Mr. and Mrs. W. W. Harper.

Sometime after the Monroe Station was built, the McIvor Station was closed. There is still a McIvor sign beside the railroad tracks. Looking south, from the sign, you can see the Five Forks Road Bridge in the background.

SPRING GARDEN HOUSE

Jessie Adams obtained the Spring Garden estate in 1863. He had tenants and also ran a store and post office at McIvor's Depot.

The remains of his colonial home are north of Monroe on a hill overlooking vast acreage which was once part of the farm. Robert Tait obtained it in 1893, and it was sometimes called the Tait Place. When it was sold in 1921 by Robert Tait, it was advertised as a 700 acre estate with mansion, manager's house, servants' quarters, fruit trees and large gardens with boxwoods. According to Richard Harper the property was purchased by the Harper family in the 1940s.

Spring Garden House – *Harper family*

Children riding cart at Spring Garden – *Harper family*

MONROE, VIRGINIA

On November 15, 1856, about 13 acres of Kit McIvor's and about six acres of G. Poindexter's land were condemned for the use of the Lynchburg extension of the Orange and Alexandria Railroad. This was probably the date of the first tracks through the Monroe area. The single track line ran from Alexandria through Orange and Charlottesville to a point on the north bank of the James River. At that point the cargo was loaded on mule wagons and carried down the River Road to Lynchburg. In January, 1860, the tracks finally reached Lynchburg.

Gilmer's Civil War map shows McIvor Station and it also shows Burford. According to the Home Demonstration Club's *History of Monroe, Virginia* apparently by the 1870s there was a station at Coolwell. At one time there was a station at Burford which was later named Winesap.

The Southern Railroad was incorporated in Virginia by an act of Legislature on February 20, 1894. They took over the line known as the Virginia Midland Railroad, which was the Orange and Alexandria Railroad during the Civil War.

According to an article written for the *Ties* magazine by E. R. Conner, III, a Charlottesville newspaper, dated January 1, 1897 stated that "The Southern Railway has quietly purchased a large tract of land at Cool Well, a station on that road in Amherst County eight miles north of Lynchburg, for the purpose of erecting shops for the Virginia Midland Division of that road (officially, Southern's First Division main line from Alexander to Danville) and concentrating the repair work at that point... The purchase includes fifty acres right at the station comprising a level plateau, which will be covered by the workshops."

When the community was first founded they had a post office named Potts.

Not long after that, they decided to give the area the name "Monroe" which was the middle name of James Monroe Watts, a Confederate veteran of Company E, Second Virginia Calvary. The yard was built in the territory between the passing tracks of McIvor and Burford stations. Although the yard at Monroe was relatively level, Coolwell Hill just to the north so impeded the progress of full-tonnage Washington Division freights, during the steam era, that yard engines frequently pushed these trains from Monroe to Coolwell. Both stations became important pulpwood loading points.

The yard opened in July, 1897. All trains north and southbound stopped at the new divisional terminus on the Southern Railway. About twenty engines were kept at Monroe all the time, and engines were changed on all trains. The roundhouse had not been built, so engines were stored on radial tracks. A boxcar mounted on a foundation housed the first telegraph office.

The first station was built in 1898–99. In the early picture at left, there is only one set of tracks. Between 1912–1914 when the double tracks were laid and the yard at Monroe enlarged, the station was moved on rollers, several yards north of its original location and was used until 1949.

In 1907, a railroad Y. M. C. A. building was erected west of the tracks for its employees. It had a library, reading rooms, and a lunch counter, as well as apartments. It was replaced by the Sands and Company Hotel in 1936, which was a brick building near the station. The Y. M. C. A. was torn down.

In the foreground you can see a new bridge being built over Watts Creek. The houses on the left were company houses. Carrie Mays lived in one of the houses and taught music. One of the houses was later used as a pool hall. Beyond the houses you can see the tipple, water tank, and station. In the right background was Lillie Jones' big house; just back of that was the Gouldthorpe house; and back of that was Bryant's boarding house.

First Monroe Station – *Southern* Ties *magazine*

Y. M. C. A. building with water tank in right background – Credit: *S.R.H.S., B. F. Roberts collection – Courtesy Macon Andrews*

Sands and Company Hotel which replaced Y. M. C. A. in 1936 with edge of Monroe Post Office building on right – *Taken by Mildred Purvis in 1940*

Early 1900s – Taken by Frank L. Cash, photographer, Monroe, Va. – *Courtesy Dorothy Harvey*

MONROE, VIRGINIA

Monroe Post Office with edge of hotel on left – *Taken by Mildred Purvis in 1940*

Monroe in 1912 showing J. J. Kelly boarding house on the left – *Courtesy Edith Martin Foster Picture was owned by her father, James Martin*

Water system plant - pump house showing top of round house in background – *Taken by Mildred Purvis in 1940*

Water treatment plant – chemical building showing round house in right background – *Taken by Mildred Purvis in 1940*

In 1912, Mrs. O. I. Peyton moved to Monroe from Hurt, Virginia, and took over the J. J. Kelley boarding house. The hand bell Mrs. Peyton used to call her boarders to meals was used for many years by Miss Christine McIvor as the principal of Monroe School. In later years the bell was returned to Mrs. Peyton who used it during her last illness to call her daughter, Mrs. Roy Spencer.

The water system plant was built during 1918–1919 and all put into service in early 1919. A sedimentation basin and coagulating system fed two 100,000 gallon steel water storage tanks, which in turn supplied the various railroad facilities at Monroe. Harris Creek usually ran muddy, and the untreated water that the Southern had originally pumped from the stream caused many boilers to foam. Some of the pumping and treatment machinery was operational by December, 1918.

In its heyday Monroe supported both a turntable and a wye track. The former was ninety feet long, and rotated in front of the eighteen-stall roundhouse on the west side of the tracks. The latter was also on the west side, and somewhat to the south of the roundhouse.

Often, cattle, pigs and other animals were shipped by rail. They had to be unloaded every 28 hours (or 36 hours with the shippers' approval) for at least 5 hours to be rested, watered and fed.

In 1949 the new Monroe Station was built and the old one torn down.

According to the "Memories of the Southern Railroad at Monroe, Virginia" which was in the Monroe United Methodist Church, Railroad Community Recipes, "In the 1940s, 28 passenger trains and 40 freights were scheduled every 24 hours. Cars were reshuffled, locomotives were refueled, engines and cars repaired and all trains were inspected while their crews checked in at the yard office.

Southern Railroad Water Works Reservoir; l.–r.: Jimmy Drumheller and Bruce Purvis with company houses in background – *Taken by Mildred Purvis in 1940*

Southern Railroad Water Works Reservoir showing dam in foreground – *Taken by Mildred Purvis in 1940*

Circa 1919, Monroe yards with wooden tipple and water tanks on right, and railroad station in left background – Notice there were at least six sets of tracks

"During World Wars I and II, troop trains stopped for soldiers to exercise or get food. Private cars of wealthy and well-known people sometimes came through. Franklin D. Roosevelt's funeral train also passed through with soldiers stationed along the tracks in respect.

"Diesel engines began replacing steam engines, and the need for frequent refueling ceased. Diesels were a great improvement for railroading but the beginning of the end of Monroe.

"By 1952, half the roundhouse had been torn down and the turntable removed. The coal chute was removed in 1953. The post office moved to Route 29 in 1965 and to another location a little further north in 2001. The Monroe yard closed in 1985. Sands & Company store was torn down in 1985, and the yard office and hotel destroyed in 1991.

"There is a single track going through the yard, no buildings are left, only an occasional train goes through; none stop. The people and events live only in our memories."

Circa 1920, Monroe yards with roundhouse and water tanks

Coaling trestle

Water tanks and coaling tower – *Taken by Mildred Purvis in 1940*

Round house in left background – *Taken by Mildred Purvis in 1940*

View of back of buildings – *Taken by Mildred Purvis in 1940*

Stock pens at Monroe yard – *Courtesy Beverly Taylor Hamlett*

Old Monroe Station on left with new station under construction on right – *Courtesy: The News and Advance*

New Monroe Station

Steam engine and tender with: l.–r. Robert L. Sales, Engineer; Frank Purvis, Yard Master; Don Smith; R. C. Mayo; Harry McGuire; Gene McIvor; Frank Inge; Russell Stinnett – *Courtesy of Bob Sales*

Monroe rail yards – *Taken by Bob Owens in February, 1966*

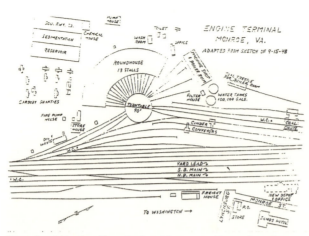

Abandoned fuel tanks at Monroe in 1990 – *H. R. Nixon*

Sketch of Engine Terminal at Monroe – *From* Southern Ties magazine

Taken in April, 1990, showing station on left and hotel on right with windows boarded up – *H. R. Nixon*

Taken in December, 1991, after station and hotel demolished in summer of 1991 – *H. R. Nixon*

There was a one-lane steel truss bridge over the railroad tracks on Cedar Gate Road. The approach to the bridge from the west was very steep and dangerous. This steel truss bridge was torn down in 1990 and replaced by a two-lane concrete bridge which was completed in 1991.

One-lane steel truss bridge taken in April 1990, looking north – *H. R. Nixon*

Two-lane concrete bridge taken in *December 1991, looking north* – *H. R. Nixon*

MONROE CHURCHES AND SCHOOLS

FIRST BAPTIST CHURCH OF MONROE

The church was organized in 1898 as the Monroe Baptist Church. Worship services were held on the second floor of the Southern Railroad Depot until a house of worship was built in 1899. This building burned down some time later and church members used the Odd Fellows hall until 1920 when a new building was erected.

In 1937 the name of the church was changed to First Baptist Church. The church membership grew, and there was a need of more classrooms and facilities. The new sanctuary was dedicated in 1957.

In 1978, the white frame building which was part of the church built in 1920, was torn down to make room for a new brick educational building which was dedicated in 1979. The Sanctuary was renovated in 1989 and some repairs were made to some older areas of the church.

Monroe Baptist Church – *Taken by Mildred Purvis in 1940*

Present First Baptist Church of Monroe – *H. R. Nixon*

MONROE BAPTIST CHURCH

Monroe Baptist Church – *H. R. Nixon*

Monroe Baptist Church was founded in 1920. The church was housed in a log cabin near the present building on Route 29 north in Monroe. The present church was constructed in 1922 by Rev. R. G. Butcher. The church had oil lamps, a pot-belly stove, and two toilets. Church services were held on the first and third Sunday. Deacon Silas Turner traveled by horse and wagon. He would arrive at church early, fire up the pot-bellied stove, ring the church bell, and light the oil lamps when needed.

Few structural renovations have been made. There is no water nor bathrooms, and the same pews and windows are in the church.

MONROE PRESBYTERIAN CHURCH

Monroe Presbyterian Church – *Taken by Mildred Purvis in 1940*

Monroe Presbyterian Church was located over the hill from First Baptist Church of Monroe. The church was organized in 1917 and a building was completed the following year. Later when the field was divided, Monroe Church remained with Amherst Court House. In 1931, the Presbytery regrouped the fields in Amherst and Nelson Counties with the result that Monroe Church was placed in the Elon group (Elon, Mt. Carmel, and Monroe) where it remained. The church closed during WWII due to low attendance, and the building is no longer standing.

NEW HOPE CHURCH

New Hope Church was the main Methodist Church in the community before the area was given the Monroe name. It was located on Winesap Road a short distance from Route 29. There is an old cemetery near where the church building stood. The age of the church is not known, but in 1856, a brick building was on the site. Soon after that one corner fell in and the building was condemned. The brick building was replaced by a frame one which burned during the Civil War. This was replaced by another frame structure. In the 1920s New Hope merged with Monroe Methodist church. The building was sold in 1931 and torn down.

BURFORD'S CHAPEL

Burford's Chapel was located on Winesap road just west of the railroad near Winesap Crossing. There is an old cemetery near where the church building stood. The chapel was built, probably after the Civil War, by Sylvester Burford. In the 1880s a day school was taught in the church building. The church remained a preaching charge until 1926, at which time it merged with Monroe Methodist Church. At that time, the building was sold. It is no longer standing.

MONROE UNITED METHODIST CHURCH

As far back as 1859 the county was divided into the Amherst charge and West Amherst charge. According to the *The History Of Monroe, Virginia*, prepared by the Monroe Home Demonstration Club Monroe in 1961, the Methodist Church was officially organized in 1907. A frame building was erected on Cedar Gate Road soon thereafter. Previously religious services had been held in the reading room of the Southern Depot, and later in the Baptist Church. In 1913 the Monroe charge consisted of Monroe, Bethany, New Hope, Smyna, and Burford's Chapel. In January 1921, the members voted to construct a brick church on the site of the frame building, and it was completed in 1922.

Early Monroe Methodist Church – *Taken by Mildred Purvis in 1940*

In 1956, the congregation began considering the need for adequate facilities and in January, 1957, they purchased a lot from Judson McIvor consisting of about five acres. On March 12, 1967, the third church building in the congregations' history was dedicated. The 450 pound bell was removed from the old church and installed in the cupola of the new building.

Present Monroe United Methodist Church – *H. R. Nixon*

MONROE CHURCH OF GOD

According to Edna Jackson Cronin, the Monroe Church of God dates back into the mid-1920s. Services were conducted in the Odd Fellows Hall, prior to the construction of their church. In early 1928 the little one-room frame building was erected and stood on brick pillars.

Changes and renovations have been made over the years with the major changes being made in the 1950s with a basement added and partitions for expansion of the Sunday school department. Also, the sanctuary was enlarged; new pews and organ were purchased, and a furnace was installed.

Early Monroe Church of God – *Courtesy of Edna Jackson Cronin*

Present Monroe Church of God – *Courtesy of Edna Jackson Cronin*

In the 1980s, improvements were made to the sanctuary; a new fellowship hall was added, and the parking lot was enlarged. A new facility was completed in 1996, and the steeple from the original building was removed and placed on the new building.

MONROE AREA SCHOOLS

In the early days before the area was given the name of "Monroe," the education of the children was mostly a private affair. Some of the neighbors would get together and build a small school house, and then hire a teacher. One is said to have been built in the bottom south of the Poindexter house around 1856.

Another school was held in the 1880s in the Burford's Chapel. Later the school was moved to a cabin on the Fairfax property. In time a one room log school was built on the road near Winesap Station, across Winesap Road from the Thompson Place.

In 1883, Robert Ridgeway deeded land to the Amherst County School Board and a large one-room building was erected. It was called Brushwood Academy.

Land was bought from Albert Watts and Rothwood School was built on Route 657 east of Route 29. This was a one-room school. Later another room was built so that the first four grades were taught in one room and the upper grades in another.

Around 1910, the population had grown so that it was necessary to build a larger school. Land was obtained by trading the old school for a new site owned by J. C. Ford. This four-room school was built with two rooms down and two rooms upstairs on the corner of Route 29 and Route 657. This school had two years of high school. As the enrollment grew, the Old Fellows hall was rented and the first two years of high school were taught there until they were transferred to Madison Heights in 1923. A two-room addition was also built behind the school which was used for the first and second grades. That school was converted into a dwelling.

Monroe Elementary School built in 1935 – *From Tyler Fulcher's Booklet.*

There was an African American school in a log cabin on Winesap Road known as the Lewis Watts School. Later Coolwell School was built.

In 1935 a new Monroe Elementary School was built. It had eight classrooms and a 300 seat auditorium, office, first aid room, and lunchroom. The classes went through 7th grade. Miss Christine McIvor was the principal for many years and also taught 7th grade.

After that, students attended Madison Heights High School or Amherst High School. Monroe was a dividing place as to which high school you attended. It depended on where you lived.

The school closed in 1982 and the elementary students were assigned to Elon, Amelon and Amherst Elementary schools. The faculty and staff underwent similar re-assignments. The building was then used as Monroe Education Center.

Miss Christine McIvor – *Courtesy Carolyn McIvor Dews*

MONROE STORES AND BUSINESSES

Some early stores were: Southern Express Company; Smoot's grocery store, later occupied by C. E. McIvor; Ernest Cash's general repair shop, and Bryant's boarding house with meals at twenty cents, and lodging for night twenty cents.

SANDS & COMPANY STORE

The Sands & Company Hotel stood up the hill from this store. The Monroe Post Office was the first building down from the hotel with the Sands & Company store next to that.

Sands & Company Monroe Store with Herman "Bucky" Bibb standing on porch – *Taken by Mildred Purvis in 1940*

Seth Hicks store – *Taken by Mildred Purvis in 1940*

l.–r.: Monroe Bank, Judson McIvor's store, Henry Clay Robertson's Store, car in left foreground is in front of Seth Hicks' Store – *Taken by Mildred Purvis in 1940*

Taken in early 1900s: C. E. McIvor's store on left, and Bell building is on right

SETH HICKS STORE

Seth Hicks' store was located on the left side of the street that turned beside Sands & Company store.

BANK OF MONROE

It stood on the street one block back from the Sands & Company store. The bank was organized around 1914 and built on this site. In 1926 the bank was liquidated and reorganized with a different cashier. In May, 1929, the Bank of Monroe was closed and a receiver authorized by the State Corporation Commission. Later the bank was reopened as a branch of the Commercial Trust and Savings Bank of Lynchburg, and operated until about 1933–34. The depositors regained most of their savings, but the stockholders lost all of their investments.

MCIVOR'S STORE AND ROBERTSON'S STORE

Chris McIvor owned C. E. McIvor's store. Later it was owned and run by his son, Judson McIvor. Next to it was a store owned by Chris McIvor's mother, Mrs. Bell. In 1919 this was being run by Ed Hudson. In August of that year it was taken over by the W. T. Thomas Co. which was a partnership of W. T. Thomas and H. Clay Robertson. In 1921 they bought the property from Mrs. Bell's estate and operated the store until 1951. The building was torn down around 1956.

MONROE AIR OBSERVATION TOWER

This 35-foot observation tower was built during World War II beside Route 29 on property owned by Judson McIvor. It was used by the Ground Observer Corps for spotting airplanes. Monroe United Methodist Church is now located there.

Judson McIvor standing at left of Monroe Air Observation Tower – Amherst New-Era Progress

SOME MONROE PEOPLE

R. DON FLOYD

The *Richmond Times-Dispatch*, Monday, October 19, 1970 showed the picture at right in their newspaper. The caption read, "R. Don Floyd of Monroe Prepares to Spear Ring at Jousting Tournament. Floyd Appeared for Tournament Parade Dressed in Authentic Armor."

To generations of Amherst High School fans, Don Floyd will always be "the Lancer."

He personified the high school mascot by donning a suit of armor and riding his favorite Arabian horse, "Billy the Gray,' at football games. He was an active member of the Booster's Club for many years.

Don Floyd, known to many as "the Lancer," has served as an ideal role model for youngsters
– Courtesy **Richmond Times Dispatch**

The 1973 Amethyst was dedicated to Mr. Floyd and beneath his picture it said "A Living Symbol of Amherst Spirit."

He went to work in Southern Railroad's roundhouse in Monroe when he was 18. His four brothers also went to the railroad to work. He worked mostly on steam engines and saw diesels start into more service. He spent most of his time in the roundhouse doing what he called "easy work" but had to prove he could still do his job after losing his leg to infection in 1940. He didn't learn to ride a horse until he was 44 years old, after he had his left leg amputated below the knee.

Mr. Floyd won two state jousting titles and continued to ride in tournaments until he was 81 years old, setting a Virginia record.

He continued working as a machinist and mechanic until he retired in 1955. His chil-

R. Don Floyd of Monroe – *Courtesy* Amherst New-Era Progress

dren are: R. D. Floyd Jr., Preston Floyd, and Shelby Staples.

Don Floyd called figures at local square dances and he liked to dance as well. He had a clay croquet court in his backyard. The other court was at "Miss Christine's" house.

He served as riding program director at the Y. M. C. A. Camp Bibee at Buggs Island for 15 years until it closed in 1975. He would take Billy along with ten other horses to the camp to teach riding to the boys. In earlier years when my oldest son, Alan, attended the camp they had two-week sessions. By the time the camp closed the name had been changed to Camp Rochichi, and when my youngest son, Scott, attended the camp they had one-week sessions.

MONROE BASEBALL TEAM

l.–r. back row: ?, Joe Tyree, Samuel Pettyjohn, Perry Ramsey, Lewis Vaughan, Frank Stinnett; center row: Howard Watts, James Vaughan, Charlie Ramsey; Bat boy: Donald Gorrell – *Courtesy Kathryn Pixley*

MONROE HOME DEMONSTRATION CLUB

l.–r. standing: Mrs. Wade, Mrs. Brizendine, Mrs. Ramsey, Mrs. Bruner, Mrs. Owens, Mrs. Burks, Mrs. McIvor, Mrs. Wilsher, Mrs. Hume, Mrs. Beasley; seated: Bea Mills, Marion Spencer, Ellen Thomas. Taken at their Christmas party between 1953 and 1957. – *Courtesy Kathryn Pixley.*

OTHER PEOPLE

l.–r.: Janie Cash, Winnie Bryant, Eunice Ramsey, Ethel Morris, Alice Spencer, Helen Owens; 2nd row: Mrs. Tom Gaines (?), Mrs. Stinnett, Mrs. Bill Adams, Annie Mae Franklin, Sallie Eubanks; children: Erma Adams, Bob Owens, Jean Owens, T. Eubanks – *Courtesy Kathryn Pixley*

Seated at well with well pump handle in background; l.–r.: Shelby Floyd, Jo Anne McDonald, Celia Loving – *Courtesy Celia Richeson*

Sophomore picnic at Bedford Lake; l.–r.: Jack Pettyjohn, Littleberry Hicks, Holcomb Nixon, Carolyn McIvor – *Courtesy Kathryn Pixley.*

Headed to Mrs. Pettyjohn's house for graduation party: l.–r. back: Hilton Maddox, T. D. Thornton, Celia Loving, Jack Pettyjohn; front: Kathryn Spencer, Holcomb Nixon – *Courtesy Kathryn Pixley*

NANCY ANDERSON'S BIRTHDAY PARTY ON CEDAR GATE ROAD
l.–r. back: ?, Kathryn Spencer; 3rd row: ?, Carolyn McIvor, Sally Best, Barbara Floyd, Frances Best; 2nd row: ? Hollinsworth, Harriette Sales, ?, O. B. Inge, Kelly Watson; seated: Nancy McIvor, Jerry Seeds holding Emily Gay Seeds, Nancy Anderson – *Courtesy Kathryn Pixley*

TOM THUMB WEDDING

Some children from the Monroe community performed in a Tom Thumb Wedding at Monroe Methodist Church on Cedar Gate Road in about 1947.

Seated on front row, l.–r.: Benny Hicks, ?, Nancy Johnson, Barbara Floyd; back row: Everett Norman, Jack Pettyjohn, Littleberry Hicks, Dewey Curd; 4th row: Buddy Bibb, ?, Audrey Connelly, Ida Gwynn Graybeal, ?, Paul Campbell, preacher; Harriette Sales, Shirley Curd, Shirley Connelly, Nancy McIvor, Jenny Lind Smith, Franklin Nuckols; 3rd row: Betty Anderson, Emily Gay Seeds, Stewart Shaner, ? ; 2nd row, standing on floor: Ann Overstreet, Bob Purvis; front: bride; Nancy Anderson; groom: Dennis Tankersley – *Courtesy Kathryn Pixley.*

THE MONACAN INDIANS

Apparently there have been tribes of Indians living in this area for hundreds of years. Evidence of Indians living or traveling through this area has been discovered. Over the years, In plowing ground near small streams, just below Elon, a lot of arrowheads and some other items have been found.

In the early 1900s an Episcopal mission program was started for the Indians at Bear Mountain. Unfortunately, for many years they were not allowed to attend the white schools, and they didn't want to attend the black schools. After a school was built for them, it went only through the seventh grade. By 1946, Amherst County was providing teachers for the Bear Mountain mission school. The Indian Mission School at the foot of Bear Mountain is a registered National Historic Landmark.

In early years they hunted and fished in the area for their food. Many orchards were started in the Elon area and around the Tobacco Row Mountain; this gave employment to many people, including the Monacans.

A small chapel was built and consecration services took place in 1908. In 1930 a fire destroyed the church and a new St. Paul's Mission Church was built.

In the 1940s the Elon Presbyterian Church built an Indian Mission on Cedar Gate Road, near what is now the intersection of Cedar Gate Road and Laurel Cliff Road. Church services were held there on certain Sunday afternoons. The building is no longer standing. It was torn down some time after April, 1987. There is a well-kept area with several marked graves near where it stood.

The Indian Mission School which now houses the Museum –
Tyler Fulcher's Booklet

Indian Mission on Cedar Gate Road – *Ann Correll*

In 1970 St. Paul's Mission purchased a five acre parcel, and in about 1980 a parish hall was added to the mission.

St. Paul's Mission began holding its annual Homecoming Reunion and Bazaar in 1969, an event that is still enjoyed yearly in October and attended by many county residents. They serve a meal and have lots of crafts for sale.

For some years, the Monacan Indians have held a Powwow in May. At first they had them at the Sedalia Center in Bedford County. For a number of years they have been in Elon at the Albert Farm, formerly Homewood Farms. They have members of tribes from throughout the United States who attend.

Usually on Friday they have educational programs with demonstrations for school children. On Saturday and Sunday, the focus is usually on dance demonstrations, sale of crafts, and food.

Nearly all the orchards are gone, but with the educational opportunities now available, the Monacans, as well as others, are qualified to be employed in many fields of work. (This information came from the *Amherst County Virginia Heritage* 1761–1999 book, and personal knowledge).

St. Paul's Mission Church – *H. R. Nixon*

NAOLA AND AREA

CENTENARY METHODIST CHURCH

Centenary Methodist Church – *Bill Dawson collection*

According to information from Josephine Bailey Woods, land was deeded for the church by Daniel E. and Judith L. Bailey in 1881. This church was located on the north side of what is now Route 130, a short distance from Corner Stone Baptist Church. After serving the community for almost 100 years, the last church service was held in December, 1976. The building was torn down about two years later. The property now belongs to the Centenary Burial Association.

CORNER STONE BAPTIST CHURCH

Old Corner Stone Baptist Church which burned in 1973

It is known that a Baptist Church was built in 1848 on a one-acre lot donated by Mr. Nicholas Waugh. In 1853 the church was named "Corner Stone," and it was used until it was replaced with a new building in 1922. This building served the congregation until July 26, 1973, when the building was struck by lightning and destroyed by fire.

Corner Stone Baptist Church – *H. R. Nixon*

A new cinder block building was erected on the same site and was dedicated in 1975. The cinder block building was bricked at a later date.

NAOLA SCHOOL

Naola Grade School was built on two acres of land deeded from Isabella Woods in 1917. It was located on the south side of Route 130 between Centenary and Corner Stone Churches.

In about 1930, after school was out for the day, the teachers were burning trash, leaves, etc., and the school caught fire and burned. John Williams who owned the store nearby let them have classes in his grist mill building while the school was being rebuilt. The school went through the ninth grade. For further education some of the students boarded at Pleasant View so they could attend Pleasant View High School and graduate.

FLOYD'S STORE

Frank C. Floyd in front of Floyd's Store and Naola Post Office – *Courtesy Ruth Floyd*

In 1951, Frank C. Floyd had a store built on Route 130/Elon Road, a little west of Minor's Branch Road.

After the Williams' Store was closed, Mr. Floyd had the post office in his store until the Naola Post Office was closed. Since his death, there have been several owners. At this time the store is not being operated.

WILLIAMS' STORE

As early as 1894 there is a recorded history of a store at Naola. There was a deed ".....conveying unto J. A. Meriwether the said firm of Rucker and Oglesby consisting of the stock of goods, furniture and appurtenances used in the store, in the storehouse at Naola." This store was run by Ed Williams. Later John D. Williams built a store where he also had the post office. His wife, Eleanor, helped him.

Williams Store – *H. R. Nixon*

This store was located across Minor's Branch Road from the earlier store. After his death, the family moved into Lynchburg and later the property was sold. The store stayed vacant for many years, and burned in 2001.

WILLIAMS' GRIST MILL

Williams Mill – *H. R. Nixon*

The mill was located on Minor's Branch Road and run by James "Jim" Williams. The gasoline-powered mill was beside his driveway. He just ground corn at this mill, and it closed in the 1930s. The mill building was dismantled in the 1990s.

There was a store on the opposite side of the driveway which was usually run by his wife, Mrs. Lelia Williams.

IVY HILL BAPTIST CHURCH

Rev. M. D. Mays stated in 2004, that Ivy Hill Baptist Church was one hundred and nineteen years old.

A few years after slavery, a small group of African Americans from the Naola, Virginia, community saw the need for a place of their own to worship. In 1865, after much consideration and prayer, they agreed to meet and organized a church which was named the Ivy Hill Baptist Church of Naola, Virginia.

The founding fathers united their resources and energies and built the first structure. In 1919, the church purchased land from the government and built a second structure in a more convenient location. Since that time, the church has been completely remodeled.

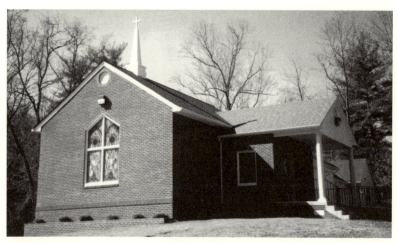

Ivy Hill Baptist Church – *H. R. Nixon*

In 1982, the present pastor, Dr. M. D. Mays was elected. In 2004 he had served the church for twenty-two years.

The ministry focus of Ivy Hill is a commitment to fulfill the mandate of the Great Commission that's recorded in St. Matthew 28:1-20. The church stands as a beacon light within the Naola community. This church is located on Waugh's Ferry Road. See *Amherst County Heritage Book*, Vol. II for list of former pastors, and complete history.

IVY HILL SCHOOL

This school was located up Elon Road/Route 130 west on what is now Waugh's Ferry Road, between what are now McCray and Mosby properties. It was built on land which had been owned by Mrs. Isabell "Belle" Woods, mother of Ashby Woods, Pembroke Woods, and Mrs. Ruth (Woods) Davis.

The original one-room school was a frame structure built in the early 1900s. It burned sometime in the late 1920s or early 1930s. It was replaced by a cinder block structure. That school was closed in the late 1950s or early 1960s.

Most of the one-and two-room schools in the county, as well as Elon Elementary which was a much larger school, had pot-bellied stoves in each room to keep them warm. The teachers in the smaller schools were required to start the fire in the stoves. Larger schools like Elon had a janitor who would start the fires. The teacher and students would have to take care of adding coal or wood during the day.

Ivy Hill School – *Tyler Fulcher Booklet*

Children putting coal in stove

FOSTER HOME PLACE

The home of William Archie Foster and Sallie Walthall Foster was near Naola and located off the road leading to Pearch. The farm was purchased from Aubrey and Lilly Taylor Coleman. The original house was built of logs. An addition was made and the house had two stories. They raised their family there and then sold the farm in 1946 and moved to Elon.

Foster Home Place – *Judy Martin*

TAYLOR HOME

John Taylor and Laura Jenkins Taylor built their house in 1908. It was located off the road leading to Pearch, near Naola, on a portion of Midway Farm which had been purchased from Dr. William Scott's estate. It was a two-story L-shaped house with eight rooms and two long halls. Each room

Taylor home – *Judy Martin*

was 15 feet by 15 feet. The interior doors were painted by a German to give them a wood grain look. The front porch of the house was facing the James River. It is still owned by the Taylor family.

OLD JENNINGS HOME AT NAOLA

According to Margaret G. "Peggy" Myers, this house at one time called Clover Dale, is typical of many old Amherst County dwellings in that it began as a log cabin and gradually expanded. Four families have owned the house, and each has made additions.

Isham Davis acquired the land from his father's will in 1789 and built the log portion at that time. His father, Nathaniel Davis, had held the original land patent and willed that area to be divided between two of his sons, Isham and James. Isham sold his 418 acre section of land to Josiah Ellis Sr., in 1807.

Mr. Ellis held the land until his death in 1810. The land was then divided between his sons. The eldest son, John, inherited 218¾ acres on Maple Creek. John married in 1816 and wrote his brother in 1817 that he was remodeling the house for his new bride. At that time the two-story log-frame addition to the north was erected. The half story of the earliest section was likely raised around 1822. In 1854 after his mother's death, Charles I. Ellis inherited the house from John's estate. The house and about 446 acres of land remained in the Ellis family until

Clover Dale/Old Jennings house – *Margaret G. Myers*

it was sold as part of a court settlement in 1779.

At that time, the house and land were bought jointly by the John W. Jennings family. In 1880 the father gave his interest to his sons, Matthew and John. Matthew received the portion with the house, and shortly thereafter, a kitchen ell was added. The house remained in the family until after the death of his youngest daughter, Emma Grey Jennings Burford in 1968.

Henry S. Myers, III, and Margaret G. Myers bought the house from Mrs. Burford's estate in 1973. In 1976 after replacing the kitchen with a two-story addition, the family moved into the house. Over the years they have added two porches. They continue to live in the old house.

SWISHER/WARE HOME

This house was built on a land grant previously given to Nathaniel Davis, who divided this land between two of his sons. The part earmarked for Robert Davis went to Robert's son, then his grand-daughter, then his great-grand-daughters before it was sold in 1878.

Confederate veteran Daniel Swisher of Rockbridge County and his wife bought the land and built the typical four-over-four farmhouse around 1880. After the Swisher couple died, their estate sold the property. The house and land changed ownership several times in the first half of the 20th century, from the Swishers to a Mr. Turner, to Val Hudson and then to his son. World War II veteran, Owen Ware and his wife, Mabel Mitchell Ware, bought the property from Henry Hudson around 1950. They remodeled the house and gradually added a number of outbuildings, including a large barn. They named their farm "Vic-o-Bel Stables." The property is now owned by Henry S. Myers, III, and Margaret Gilmer Myers, who furnished the above information.

Old Swisher home – *Courtesy of Pamela M. Taylor*

ORCHARDS

In the Elon area and around the Tobacco Row Mountain area there were quite a number of apple and peach orchards. They employed a lot of workers, some year round, and additional ones during the busy season of picking, grading, etc. A large number of Monacan Indians worked, especially in the mountain orchards. Housing was provided by the owners for some of the workers. Some of the orchards were very big where they raised large quantities of fruit to sell, and there were a lot of family orchards with only a few trees for family use. In the early days of the county, a lot of apples were shipped by train from the Burford Station. Years later with so many Winesap apples being shipped the name was changed to Winesap Station.

LARGE ORCHARDS BETWEEN ELON AND HIGH PEAK ROAD

BERNARD CAMDEN'S ORCHARD

This orchard was located in Elon on property that is now Camden's subdivision on Camden Drive. There was a tenant house on the property also. He kept his tractors and spray equipment in a long shed near Camden and Younger's Store. Any grading of fruit was done in that building also.

HOMEWOOD FARMS ORCHARD

Mr. D. H. Dillard had a number of orchards. Some of the fruit trees were at the packing shed area and he had other orchards also. The packing shed is located on Rt. 130/Elon Road

Building on left was used for equipment and grading
– *Ruth Foster collection*

a little beyond Elon. There were several tenant houses at this orchard. There were also five houses built as tenant houses in "Happy Hollow" located beside Rt. 130/Elon Road. Some

Early Packing Shed

New Packing Shed built in vicinity of the old one–now Rock Hill – *H. R. Nixon*

Interior of Packing Shed: l. back to front: Marita Taylor, Catherine Sigmon, Mrs. Annie Sigmon across from Catherine Sigmon – *Courtesy Lynchburg News and Advance*

were rented to people who had no connection to the farm or orchards. The houses are no longer standing. The property was bought by the May family who started the Homewood Bounds subdivision. Scott Nixon, his wife Jacqueline, and their sons, Dylan, Dakota, and Drake live in the subdivision.

MISTOVER ORCHARD

The packing shed and orchards were owned by Mr. Scott. They were located a little beyond Elon on what is now Mistover Mansion Road.

SPEED-THE-PLOW ORCHARD

Speed-the-Plow Packing Shed with workers – *Courtesy Nancy Marion*

Mr. Rowland Lea was part owner of the Montrose Fruit Company. Later he was the owner of Speed-the-Plow. This orchard was located on the Ambrose Rucker Road as you head around the mountain from Elon. Later his nephew, Philip Girling, and his wife Mary "Mae" Girling, moved to Speed-the-Plow and operated the orchards. Some years ago the packing shed was destroyed by fire. Rowland Girling and his wife, Lori, now own the property and have a bed and breakfast in the Speed-the-Plow mansion house.

MONTROSE ORCHARD

The lower part of the packing shed was made of rock. The main house at Montrose Orchard was built of rock.

The orchard was located on what is now Route 806/Montrose Road. Mr. Aronovitch was the owner, and his son-in-law, Mr. Kessler, operated the orchard for him.

Montrose Orchard Packing Shed – *H. R. Nixon*

House at Montrose Orchard – *H. R. Nixon*

The property was purchased by Wallace and June Bibb in 1960, according to their son, Jeffery Bibb. They operated the orchard until in the 1970s. At that time they sold most of the property to Mr. W. D. "Bill" McCraw, who developed it into a housing subdivision. Wallace and June built a house on a portion of the property they had retained.

l.–r.: Terrell Stinnette, William Rose, Bernard Rose with spraying equipment; house on right – *Courtsey Ethel Dawson Pick*

W. M. Dawson's Packing Shed – H. R. Nixon

W. M. DAWSON ORCHARD

The orchard and packing shed owned by W. M. Dawson were located on the right side of Ambrose Rucker Road, just beyond Route 806/Montrose Road, with the large family farmhouse nearby.

After Mr. Dawson's death, his son-in-law, Terrell Stinnette, operated the orchard. The family sold the orchard in 1960, but Terrell and Ruby Stinnette kept the farmhouse and some acreage around the house. They then moved into their home in Elon.

A. M. SHEPHERD'S ORCHARD

This orchard and packing shed were located on the left side of Ambrose Rucker Road, almost directly across the road from W. M. Dawson's Orchard. A. M. Shepherd and Mr. Dawson were brothers-in-law, having married sisters. It is reported that A. M. Shepherd's son "Shep" gave property to one of his Monacan Indian employees.

A.M. Shepherd's Packing Shed – H. R. Nixon

Orchardists: standing l.–r. O. B. Ross, Philip Girling, ?, Ambrose "Shep" Shepherd, (?) two VPI staff, Charlie Drake; with baskets of apples, Hannon and Harry Rucker – *Collection of May Rucker*

Rucker Brothers' Packing Shed – *H. R. Nixon*

Picking apples – Hannon Rucker on ground; Harry Rucker on ladder – *Collection of May Rucker*

RUCKER BROTHERS' ORCHARD

Rucker Brothers' Orchard was owned by Hannon and Harry Rucker. The orchard and packing shed were located on the right side of Ambrose Rucker Road. This packing shed is just up the hill, a little beyond Shepherd's packing shed.

William Morris orchard with Bobby Morris on mule and Manse in distant background
– *Doris Foster*

l.–r.: Hannon Rucker, Mrs. Lena Morris, Senator Harry Byrd – *Collection of May Rucker*

Morris Orchards Packing Shed – *H. R. Nixon*

MORRIS ORCHARDS

The packing shed is located on Ambrose Rucker Road, just a little ways back from the intersection of Ambrose Rucker Road and High Peak Road. After the death of her husband, Harry Morris, Mrs. Lena Morris managed the farm and orchard.

This is the only orchard in this immediate area that is still an active business. It is now operated by Mrs. Morris' grandson and his wife, Scott and Judy Barnes, and their son, Will. They have diversified, with other products, not just apples and peaches. You can pick your own blackberries, blueberries and raspberries. Also in the summer they have fresh vegetables, cantaloupes and watermelons, supplied by local growers.

ORCHARDS

l.–r. Mrs. Elmer (Helen) Loving Sr.; Mrs. Elmer (Ann) Loving Jr.; Mr. Percy Loving making making apple butter for family use – *Courtesy of Ann Loving*

Tom and Addie Foster with orchard in background – *Mary Foster*

In the fall they make apple cider, for which there is a great demand, using very up-to-date equipment. They make apple butter at least once in the fall. Also, Judy makes delicious apple donuts, and fresh apple cakes.

They grow pumpkins on the property to sell, as well as Christmas trees.

SMALL ORCHARDS BETWEEN ELON AND HIGH PEAK ROAD

THRONEBURG (Roy), MASSIE (Ira, I. D. and Homer), WATTS (Oscar Watts/Frank Burford), WATTS' STORE (Rufus), WATTS' (Donald), and SUNSIDE FARM (Watts/Burford). They did not have large packing sheds, but sold fruit commercially.

FAMILY FRUIT ORCHARDS

Over the years, a lot of families had small home orchards for their own use, and sometimes they sold some of their fruit. Some families with fruit orchards in Elon were: Alex Morris, Earl Morris, William Morris, Dick Wills, Tom Foster, and others.

MAKING APPLE BUTTER

In about 1970, members of the Elon Ruritan Club made apple butter to sell to raise funds for club projects. The location for making the apple butter was beside the Homewood Farms (now Rock Hill) packing shed. The first year or two they used wood as fuel to cook the apples in a huge copper kettle. Later they used a bottled gas burner to cook the apple butter. They used about 14 bushels of apples to make 100 quarts of apple butter.

A lot of people came to purchase apples at the packing shed, and then stayed and observed the process of the apple butter being made.

APPLE HARVEST FESTIVAL

The Elon Ruritan Club members started making apple butter beside the Homewood Farms/Rock Hill packing shed. In 1971 the Elon Home Demonstration Club had the idea of selling arts and crafts. The first year they used a small building behind the Homewood Farms/Rock Hill packing shed for display and selling as the Amherst County Apple Harvest Arts and Crafts Festival.

l.–r. Ann (Younger) Correll, Maggie (Brown) Floyd, Arlene (Brown) Jennings – *Ann Correll*

The next year the festival was held at the American Legion Hall Post 100 in Elon, which (according to Helen Feagans) was a picturesque setting at the foot of Tobacco Row Mountain, with many orchards nearby.

The festival continued to be held at Elon for several years, until there were so many arts and crafts for display and for sale that more space was needed. Additional space was needed also to accommodate the large number of people who attended, as well as for parking, so the Festival was moved to Monelison Junior High School.

A number of Ruritan Clubs and other organizations had booths which helped them with fund raising for their projects.

After a number of years, the Apple Harvest Arts and Crafts Festival moved to Amherst County High School. This continues to be a fall event in the county, usually on the third weekend in October.

l.–r. Ann (Younger) Correll – *Ann Correll*

PEARCH FERRY AND PEARCH STATION

Pearch Station circa 1920 – *Courtesy C&O Historical Society*

As early as 1867, permission was granted for a ferry to be run across the James River. The Pearch Ferry was located a short distance above the mouth of the Pedlar River. For many years, people and horse-drawn wagons used this ferry to ride to and from the train, and to pick up and deliver merchandise.

The Chesapeake & Ohio Railroad built a station on the Bedford side of the James River and was in charge of the Pearch Ferry. There was a small building on the Amherst County side of the river.

Ferry boat loaded with horses and wagons, and a small boat with passengers on the left, headed toward Amherst County side of river – *Bill Dawson's collection*

Ferry boat on Amherst County side of river with Pearch Station in distant background – *Bill Dawson's collection*

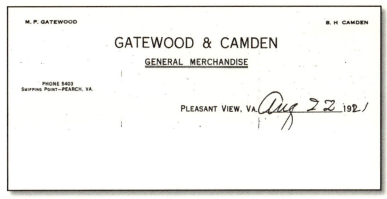

Copy of letterhead

People from Allwood, Pleasant View, Pedlar Mills, and other areas would order merchandise with Pearch being the shipping point, as evidenced by an old business letterhead dated Aug 22, 1921.

One time the cable broke and the ferry went over the Pearch dam. The people were able to get off, and the horses were cut loose, with no loss of life.

The ferry was operated until in the 1930s. Sometime after that the railroad removed the large station and replaced it with a way station.

It was not easy for people from Allwood, Pleasant View, Pera, Pedlar Mills and other areas to travel to the Pearch Ferry. According to a conversation I had with Owen Ware in March 1992, before Route 130/Elon Road was extended with the bridge being built over Pedlar River and completed in 1948, there were several ways to get to the ferry area without going all the way down to what today is East Pearch Road. One was the road at the end of the bridge on Route 635 (now Buffalo Springs Turnpike) which parallels Pedlar River all the way down to the James River. Another way was to go on Minor's Branch Road and then travel down what is now Volley Hudson Road to the river. (At present, neither of these roads gives public access to the James River). Another way was to go on what is now Dancing Creek Road and go to the right when you get to Oak Grove Church (the left would take you to Pedlar Mills) and continue until you got to what is now Pera Road, take that road and then go to what is now West Pearch Road. Of course, people from Allwood and Pleasant View could just get on Pera Road and go to the road leading to Snowden, and go back down to West Pearch Road.

Way station – *Mrs. Arrington*

Covered bridge on Route 635 over Pedlar River heading to Pedlar Mills – *Courtesy Elizabeth Dillard Ogden*

Covered bridge in process of being removed – *Courtesy Pedlar Mills Home Demonstration Club Scrap Book*

Remainder of covered bridge with replacement bridge on lower right – *Courtesy Pedlar Mills Home Demonstration Club Scrap Book*

Bridge over Pedlar River on Route 130/Elon Road which was built in 1948 making it much easier to travel to Pearch, Naola, and Snowden – *H. R. Nixon*

PEARCH SCHOOL AND AREA

Pearch School – *Courtesy Louise (Oliver) Berg*

In a telephone conversation with Louise (Oliver) Berg in October 2006, she shared location of Pearch School and other information about the area.

This one-room school was located across from what is now 2400 West Pearch Road. (The school was closed in 1936, and later the building burned). Louise's brother walked to school a little ahead of the others so he could build a fire in the stove. They would take a pail to a spring on Mr. Mitchell's property to get water for the school. They had only one dipper from which they drank. (This was common practice at that time, often homes had only one dipper for drinking water from a bucket). Some of the teachers were: Agnes (Brown) Rowbotham, Dorothy (Johnson) Arthur, Dorothy Eubank, and Beulah Steele.

Louise attended Pearch School for grades 1–6. For the seventh grade, Louise's father drove her and her sister, as well as some neighboring children, to Elon Elementary School. Tyler Fulcher was the principal at that time, and she remembers being in school with Opal Taylor and Margaret Dillard.

For grades 8–11 she and her sister, and some of the Mitchell and Horton families would walk from home (which was near Route 130/Elon Road) to the Pearch Ferry on James River. Mr. Oliver, her father, had built two row boats for them to row across the river at Pearch. From there they would walk down to Holcomb Rock where they would catch the school bus and ride seven miles to Boonsboro High School. They would arrive back home at about five o'clock and still have to do their chores. She did this for four years, until she graduated from high school. One year, during this time, she had perfect attendance.

She remembers cleaning and filling oil lamps before electricity got to their area.

Occasionally they would attend church at Naola, but they usually attended the Adventist Church in Lynchburg. Her father would drive their car down to Pearch Ferry and take the car across on the ferry.

There were some old iron mines on her family's property. Her parents warned them not to play near the mines, fearing that they might fall in. (See information about mines, below).

THE VIRGINIA NAIL AND IRON WORKS

One of the mines – *H. R. Nixon*

A plat of record in the Campbell County Clerk's Office shows "Plat of a tract of land containing 67 acres (from which is be deducted 5 acres condemned for the J.R. and K (James River and Kanawha Canal) situated in Campbell Co., Va. and an island in Amherst Co. PROPERTY OF THE VIRGINIA NAIL AND IRON WORKS." This was platted from a description in deed from James River Steel Manufacturing and Mining Company made in 1880. The nail works went into receivership in 1893, according to Douglas MacLeod. Oriskany, a producer of pig iron, was the next company at the foundry site until 1917.

The iron ore was dug from the mines on what is now West Pearch Road and placed in carts which were taken down to where they were ferried across the river. *The Upper James Atlas* shows the location of the cable where the loaded carts were placed on the ferry. The iron ore eventually reached the site of what today is known as Reusens.

E. J. Lavino purchased the property and produced ferromanganese until the 1960s. In the late evenings when they dumped the slag, you could see a red glow from that direction all the way to Elon. The Buncher Rail Car Co., a railroad car maintenance business, currently occupies the property at Reusens.

PEDLAR LAKE AND DAM

In "*The Saga Of A City,* Lynchburg, Virginia" published by The Lynchburg Sesqui-Centennial Association, Inc., a section entitled "Water Systems" states that some of the earlier water supplies were springs on Lynch property, Blackwater Creek, and the James River.

"For approximately seventy-five years Lynchburg relied upon James River for its water supply. Shortly before the end of the Nineteenth Century, pollution of that stream became a major problem, for manufactories were springing up above the City's intake, and disposing of their waste in the James and its tributaries. The citizens were alarmed by the possibility of contracting disease from the water and objected to discoloration and the taste."

"John Victor championed a proposal to pipe water to the city from the Blue Ridge Mountains, assuring a better and more palatable supply. It was found that Pedlar River, in Amherst County, was an excellent source and that the supply was sufficient to meet the needs of Lynchburg for many years. A dam site was selected and surveyors discovered the elevation was high enough to assure delivery to the City by gravity."

After some time, approval was obtained from the electorate for the issuance of bonds.

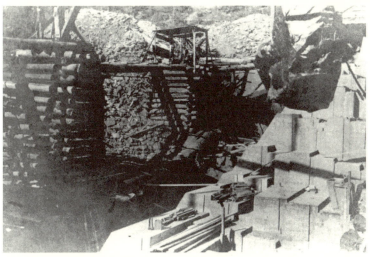

Close up view of construction of dam – *From collection of Bill Dawson*

"The new work was begun in 1904 and three years later a composite wood, steel and cast iron pipe line, thirty inches in diameter, twenty-one miles long, was completed, together with the construction of a concrete dam ninety feet high and four hundred and fifteen feet long.

The sparkling water, direct from the mountains was delivered to

Construction of dam from distance – *From collection of Bill Dawson*

Pedlar Dam in 1941 – *Courtesy Doris Foster*

Lynchburg in September 1907."

By the early 1920s some of the wooden sections of pipe, which were leaking, had been replaced by cast iron pipe.

Some years after originally being built, the dam was enlarged.

According to Daisy (Smith) Oblinger, the redwood pipeline was replaced by cast iron pipe during 1933 and 1934. The work was done by some local laborers and some Civilian Conservation Corps (CCC) workers. The 36 inch cast iron pipe would arrive in Lynchburg on N & W railroad cars and then be loaded onto a truck, using a crane.

Some of the local people who owned trucks that hauled the pipe were: Carey Lamb of Pleasant View, Bennett Harris of Allwood, and Bernard Camden and Bruce

Old California redwood pipeline – *Daisy Oblinger*

Pipe being lifted from railroad car – *Daisy Oblinger*

Pipe being loaded from railroad car onto truck – *Daisy Oblinger*

Stockpile of pipe – *Daisy Oblinger*

"Horse" Johnson, one of the drivers with pipe and cable – *Daisy Oblinger*

Younger of Elon. Addie Brown was one of the drivers for Camden and Younger.

The pipe would then be brought to an area on Route 130, below Elon, near the entrance to the River Road where it would be stockpiled until the weather was suitable to deliver it to the pipe replacement area. There was a bank where the pipe could be unloaded from and then loaded back on to the trucks. The pipe was so large and heavy that they used a cable to unload the pipe and then load it again to take to the work site.

Often the trucks loaded with pipe would stop in Elon at Camden and Younger Store where Daisy Smith helped prepare sandwiches, etc. for the drivers. They would buy gas in Elon also.

Daisy Smith who later married David Oblinger, worked for Camden and Younger in the store. She took the pictures connected with the delivery and laying of the cast iron pipe. She even rode out into the field with one of the truck drivers one day and took pictures. That is why we have such a wonderful pictorial history. Apparently, only two sections of this large pipe could be hauled on a truck at one time.

They completed replacing the pipe in 1934.

In 1963, the dam was raised to its present height of 74 feet.

There are stand pipes atop a hill near Potato Hill Mountain which allow excess water from the line to Lynchburg from Pedlar Lake to overflow into a nearby creek. There are vent pipes on the Jennings property on Lewis Keith Road. Also, there is a pressure valve, in a field belonging to Mrs. Lewis Keith, which releases air pressure in the pipeline to avoid "blowing the line."

Camden and Younger International truck loaded with pipe are: l.-r. Chapman Keith, Bruce Younger, Addie Brown, Bernard Camden, ?, ?, ?; Behind truck: Bob Harris, Willie Burford; ? standing on pipe on truck – *Daisy Oblinger*

Daisy Smith sitting in pipe; standing l.-r.: Beth Younger, Ann Younger, Mildred Camden – *Daisy Oblinger*

In front of Camden and Younger Store with l-r.: Bernard Camden and Bruce Younger beside International truck owned by them loaded with pipe – *Daisy Oblinger*

PEDLAR LAKE AND DAM

Bernard Camden at site where pipe was delivered – *Daisy Oblinger*

Showing the terrain with the long line of pipe – *Daisy Oblinger*

Bulldozer and truck used in laying pipe with l.-r. ?, ?, Bernard Camden, Carey Lamb, ? – *Daisy Oblinger*

Bulldozer and truck showing rough terrain in foreground – *Daisy Oblinger*

Mr. William "Bill" Burford was the caretaker at Pedlar Dam from 1937 to 1963. He took care of the lake and dam. Mrs. Burford would serve delicious meals, usually with two meats, with six or eight vegetables, as well as home-churned butter with hot rolls. Sometimes they would have overnight guests.

Upon their retirement, the Burfords built a home about four miles from Elon.

Bennett Harris' truck fording one of the streams they had to cross – *Ruth Foster collection*

House at Pedlar Dam – *Courtesy of Hannan Marshall "H. M." and Beth Younger Burford*

PEDLAR MILLS

Excerpts from "Memoirs of Life in and Around Pedlar Mills by George T. Pleasants" written by him in the 1960s for the Pedlar Mills Home Demonstration Club Scrap Book.

"My memories of Pedlar Mills as a boy are these:

The first merchant mill at Pedlar Mills was at the mouth of Minors Branch. Eighty years ago, some of the old timber could be seen in the banks of Pedlar River. The second mill was located where Carrington Gillispie's home is known as the 'Mill Site' (data handed down by my grand-mother). The third mill was built during or just after the War Between the States by Mr. Hazel Williams. This mill was located on the west side of Pedlar River, some 200 yards above the mouth of Horsley's Creek. This was a very imposing building for this date. It was some five stories high and built of the very best material to be had at the time. The mill passed from the Williams' family to Silas Ogden; the next owner was Ben Davidson; he sold it to Ott Bailey. It was next owned by John Mitchell who sold it to B. C. Franklin. When the river was low, they used a gasoline engine to replace the water power in the 'Big Mill.' Somehow a spark caused an explosion

Mitchell's Mill "Big Mill"

and it burned in 1939. [After the Big Mill burned, Mr. Ashby Woods ran a small mill, which was run by a gasoline engine, to grind corn.]

Some years after the Big Mill was built [often referred to as Mitchell's Mill] a great quantity of wheat was raised in the Pedlar Valley, more than the Big Mill could grind, so Messrs' Sam and Pomp Turner built a mill almost as large as the Big Mill, about 100 yards above the site of the second mill, 'Mill Site,' on Horsley's Creek. In the 1920s, lightning struck and burned this mill to the ground.

Pedlar Mills used to be a busy place. My first recollection of it was, it consisted of five stores owned and operated by M. D. Ray, Captain Bibb, Albert Padgett, Armstead Feagans, and Bill Carper. Three out of the five stores sold whiskey along with general merchandise.

In addition to the stores, there were two blacksmith shops, one saddle and harness and tannery operated by Bill Tucker, and one distillery, run by Armstead Feagans. They would make brandy from your apples—one gallon of brandy for every eleven bushels of apples.

Turner's Mill – *Ginnie Keith*

Later the building was used as a cannery by Ellis and Woods.

The post office, at this date was in Albert Padgett's store. He could tell you what every postal card was about. Once, Miss Nannie Tapscott stopped by to get her mail on her way home. He told her that the mail had already been sent to her home, and she got a post card, but he had been too busy to read it so he could not tell her what it was about.

No mail carrier in the United States was allowed to ford high water. When the river was high at Pedlar Mills, the carrier would tie his horse on the side of the river and walk across the footbridge bridge to the post office.

The mail would not go to Pleasant View, Allwood, or Forks of Buffalo until the stream ran down. The mail came from Salt Creek to Pedlar Mills about 9 A.M., from there it went to Pleasant View, Allwood, and Forks of Buffalo. The carrier would feed his horse, eat his lunch at Forks of Buffalo, then he would bring the mail over the same route to Salt Creek. By this schedule, the merchants on the route could reply to their mail the day received.

In those days around 600 people lived in the immediate vicinity of Pedlar Mills. The majority of these people gathered there on Saturday evenings for a friendly get together to discuss current affairs, to watch the drunks fuss and fight, and to spend the few pennies which they had accumulated during the week.

Hitching posts were along each side of the road, because this was horse and buggy days.

A long shed was along the road from M. D. Ray's store to the ford across Pedlar, to accommodate the wagoner's horses hauling tobacco out of the mountains to Lynchburg.

The little Episcopal Church, St. Luke's, served the people of this vicinity. Dr. McBryde was the rector at this time and Bishop Whittle had charge of the state of Virginia. In those days, the bishop would come to Amherst Court House and confirm a class there, hire a horse, ride across the mountain and confirm a class at St. Luke's. On one occasion, his

Swinging footbridge over Pedlar River with Big Mill in background – *Courtesy Bill Woods*

horse lost a shoe coming across the mountain, and was lame when he got to Pedlar Mills. George Ray, the blacksmith, and several others were sitting on the long shed when Bishop Whittle rode up. George had several 'nips' and was feeling pretty high. Bishop Whittle stopped and asked him 'Young man, is there a blacksmith in this town?' George replied 'Yes sir, the damned best in the county, but I wouldn't even shoe a horse for Bishop Whittle today.' Bishop Whittle answered, 'Young man, I am Bishop Whittle and I want this horse shod.' George hurried down from the shed, caught the horse by the bridle and said, 'Yes sir, Bishop, you walk across the bridge to the church and your horse will be shod and waiting for you tied at the church.'

The first rectory was a log house on the site of the Community Club House today. In the flood of 1884, Pedlar River rose three feet in the rectory's first floor. It ruined everything on that floor. J. P. Lawrence occupied the rectory at that time.

Walter Lawrence, son of the rector, conducted a private school across the branch from the first rectory. When we went to school the next morning they were busy cleaning up the damage so we had a holiday.

The first foot bridge across Pedlar River was a heavy wooden bridge built on trestles. This, too, was washed away in the flood of 1884 and replaced by a swinging bridge. Now that has been replaced by a concrete bridge.

Mr. John P. Eubank, who was liked by all that knew him, was a great character in this community. He had a pair of oxen and an old mule with which he did custom hauling. One day he had on a load of wheat and drove the mule and oxen into the ford below the footbridge. The water was deep. The oxen couldn't pull without putting their head down, so the mule couldn't pull the entire load. Mr. Eubank was raising 'sand' trying to get the

George T. "Bud" Pleasants in front of St. Luke's Church with Community Club House on the right – 1956 – *Lynchburg News & Daily Advance*

team out of the river. At that time, Miss Nannie Tapscott was crossing the footbridge. She yelled down at him, 'Hey Mr. Eubank, you seem to be having trouble.'

He yelled back, 'Go on Nannie. Go on and shut-up. Many a yoke of oxen and mule have been drowned by a woman's damned long tongue.'

The muster ground for the soldiers of this community was a bottom owned by the Tompkins, now owned by Mrs. Marshall Foster. Col. J. D. Davis drilled the men twice a week, and if anyone failed to be present without cause, he was fined.

PEDLAR MILLS

The ground was also used as a circus ground. John Robinson Circus traveled on foot and they had certain places they stopped and gave performances. This bottom was used for 'Pedlar Valley Circus.'

The amusements consisted of community dances, tournaments, quilting parties, picnics, dinners, and box suppers.

When the overhead bridge 1½ miles below Pedlar Mills, across Pedlar River, was first built, it was a toll bridge, which was kept by a Mrs. Champ Carter. The toll house was on the south side of Pedlar River at the end of the present bridge on Route 130 across Pedlar River.

Long ago, dotted over the broad acres around here, were large plantations. Each plantation was a community within itself. Each plantation had its own loom, its own smith shop, its own smoke house, and each house had its office.

Today this community has changed hands and changed in every way. It now consists of large plantations, mechanized with very few people living on them. As an example, our place. When I was a boy, there were three sets of tenants, four cabins occupied by negroes, and between 30 and 40 people lived on the plantation. Today the sole occupants are my wife and myself.

This story, I feel is not without value as a contribution to the history of the times of which I speak. I have placed facts and incidents which would otherwise be lost, as a record of daily life of the people at the time."

George T. "Bud" Pleasants and his wife, Mary, lived at the Haywood Plantation Home.

HAYWOOD PLANTATION HOME

This house was located in the vicinity of Pedlar Mills, and Agricola. After the bridge was built on Route 130/Elon Road over the Pedlar River, it was a little closer to Agricola.

Haywood owned by Mr. and Mr. G. T. "Bud" Pleasants

According to articles in the *Daily Advance* and *The New Era-Progress*, the original Davis home was called Society Ridge and it stood on a tract of 2000 acres, part of a land grant by Queen Anne in 1710. This home was destroyed by fire.

The construction of Haywood was started in 1850 by Mr. Pleasants' maternal grandfather, Col. John Dudley Davis. By then it was a 450-acre plantation. The two-story house was built of brick and covered with weatherboard.

On February 15, 1963, there was a fire which apparently started from an open fireplace. Mr. and Mrs. Pleasants, who were retired and had taught school at Naola, lost their lives. They were buried in the family cemetery on the property, which is now owned by Lt. Gen. and Mrs. John Albert.

CHURCHES, SCHOOLS, AND OTHER BUILDINGS AT PEDLAR MILLS

ST. LUKE'S EPISCOPAL CHURCH

St. Luke's was organized around 1799 and it was described as a small frame building. In the 1830s the wooden chapel was replaced by a brick church. The church was largely supported by John and Richard Ellis, brothers and merchants at Pedlar Mills who were instrumental in the building of the old brick church. After the Civil War, around 1871 or 1872, the old church was torn down and rebuilt with the same brick.

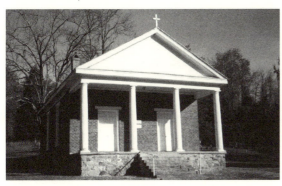

St. Luke's Episcopal Church – *H. R. Nixon*

During the ministry of Rev. Josiah Richard Ellis, the portico with its tall white columns was added to the church building. Rev. Ellis was the grandson and great-nephew of the John and Richard Ellis who had built the old church.

PEDLAR MILLS SCHOOL

Pedlar Mills School was built in 1910 by Mr. Guy Lewis. According to Carlton "Buddy" Gillispie, his family lived at or near Pedlar Mills, and then moved to Elon to the Lawson Younger house. They lived there for a while and then moved back to Pedlar Mills, and lived up near the Warner Rucker place. He and his brothers used to ride the horses to school. Marshall Foster's store was across the road from the school. He said there was a barn to the right of the store building which had several stalls, and

Pedlar Mills School – *Dorothy Harris*

they would put their horses in there. They would bring a bag with corn in it, and at lunch time they would go over and feed the horses some corn. When it was time to plant the crops, they had to walk to school because the horses were needed for farming.

MARSHALL FOSTER HOUSE

This large white house, thought to have been built in the early 1900s, was owned by my Uncle Marshall Foster. It had porches on both floors on the front, and a wide entry hall with rooms on both floors. The wing extending back from the front hall had screened porches on both sides with a bathroom built at the end of one of the porches.

Marshall Foster House – *H. R. Nixon*

A hallway from the kitchen had a concrete spring box. The spring was up the hill above the house and water was piped into the house. Fed by gravity, the water constantly flowed through the "spring" box, keeping the milk, butter, and other items cool.

Facing the store (where gas was also sold), there was a blacksmith shop to the left of the driveway, then the driveway to the house, the store, and then the barn. I don't ever remember seeing the barn, but the school and store were washed away by Camille in 1969.

THE MERIWETHER/WILLIAM "BILL" CROSS HOUSE

The old Meriwether house was built by Dr. George Douglas Meriwether. According to *The News,* (Lynchburg, Va., Sunday Aug. 10, 1958), he began his first practice in Pedlar Mills after graduating from medical school in 1870. He stayed for a few years, and then went to Buena Vista, where he built a house and practiced for many years.

Mr. Cross purchased the house which was on a sharp curve just as you were leaving Pedlar Mills. He stored a cute little wagon under his porch. I remember seeing it when I went to see my grandparents who lived near Pleasant View. The house was torn down when road improvements were made and the big curve was taken out. Mr. Scott Vail bought the brick and used it in a new home he built in the town of Amherst.

Meriwether/Cross house – *Pedlar Mills Home Demonstration Club Scrapbook*

WOODLAWN

This was the Thomas Dabney Woods home. It was later owned by his son Ashby Woods who served on the Amherst County School Board. I was told by his son Bill Woods that after the big mill burned in 1939, Ashby Woods built a small gasoline powered grist mill for grinding corn. It was located in the field not far from the house.

Wood's house – *Pedlar Mills Home Demonstration Club Scrapbook*

THE TAVERN

The date "1813" is inscribed on a brick in the east chimney. It was one of the stagecoach stops on the Lynchburg and Buffalo Springs Turnpike.

There have been several additions and, it has been modernized over the years. In earlier years, in addition to a tavern, it has been used for a private school, and, at different times, Dr. Keith and Dr. Berry practiced medicine there. I remember when the only way to get across Horsley's Creek to the house was by a swinging footbridge. For years it has been a private home. Some years ago, the owners placed pipes with concrete poured around them in the creek, so they could drive a vehicle to the house.

Tavern building – *Pedlar Mills Home Demonstration Club Scrapbook*

BRICK STORE BUILDING

Some publications state that this old store building was originally owned by the Ellis family, and others state that it was owned by the Woods family. Apparently it was built in the 1830s. I don't ever remember seeing it open as a store. In later years it has been owned by the Woods family. It is one of the few building still standing in what was at one time one of the largest villages in the county. It has deteriorated more over the years, and even the front porch roof is falling down.

Old brick store building – *H. R. Nixon*

Mr. Bud Pleasants walking on swinging footbridge beside Jones' Store, heading over Horsley's Creek to Tavern building with old brick store building showing in background – *Lynchburg News & Advance*

BERRY HILL

This was the home of Samuel Turner and his family. The house was located on the right as you turn into Bill Wood's driveway. Mr. Turner was the owner of Turner's Mill which burned in the 1920s. Not only did he lose his mill, but Mrs. Turner, his wife, got very excited about the fire and died the same night. The house was destroyed by fire in the late 1920s.

Picture of Berry Hill taken in 1915 – *Ginnie Keith*

Samuel Turner and son, Sam Turner – *Ginnie Keith*

CHURCHES, SCHOOLS, AND OTHER BUILDINGS AT PEDLAR MILLS

OLD METHODIST PARSONAGE/GILLLISPIE HOUSE

Methodist parsonage/Gillispie house taken in 1992 – *H. R. Nixon*

This house located at the intersection of Buffalo Springs Turnpike and Wagon Trail Road was the Methodist parsonage many years ago. In recent years it has been owned by the Carrington Gillispie family. The property was sold a few years ago, but Eleanor Gillispie who lived there for many years is in her 90s and still living.

TRUSS BRIDGE

One-lane truss bridge over Horsley's Creek – *H. R. Nixon*

There are only a few truss bridges remaining in Amherst County. One is a one-lane bridge on Wagon Trail Road over Horsley's Creek at Pedlar Mills, just beyond the Gillispie house. A plaque on the rail of bridge states "VIRGINIA STATE HIGHWAY COMMISSION CAPACITY 12 TONS BUILT BY CHAMPION BRIDGE CO. WILMINGTON OHIO 1923.

RED HILL FARM

Red Hill

This farm is located on what is now Minor's Branch Road, near Pedlar Mills.

According to Isabel Wallace C. Hundley, the farm originated from a land grant of 1,000 acres to Captain Charles Ellis, and he brought his family to the property in 1754.

The large brick colonial house was built on a high hill, facing Tobacco Row Mountain. The bricks were made on the property, and the plantation was self-sufficient.

Reportedly, Edgar Allan Poe visited at "Red Hill" while attending the University of Virginia. His father was associated in the practice of law with Charles Ellis in Richmond.

The property remained in the Ellis family until 1905. It changed hands several times and was badly neglected. In 1931 the farm was purchased by Col. John W. Hyatt, who restored the property and installed plumbing and electricity. Col. Hyatt fought in WWI and retired from the Army in 1939. Upon his retirement, he moved permanently to Red Hill. He stocked the farm with cows, horses, sheep, and other farm animals.

Upon his death in 1953, his daughter, Kate and her husband, Thomas Cushing Wallace III, inherited the property. Their children, Eleanor, Tom IV, Kate, and Isabel grew up on the farm.

In 1966 the Wallace family sold the farm to Edward Lewis, and shortly thereafter Red Hill was added to the Virginia Landmarks Register. Sometime later renovations were started on the house but were not completed. Upon Mr. Lewis' death, the property was inherited by his son.

MINOR/DODD HOUSE

This home, located up Minor's Branch Road, was built by the Minors. They were the ones who had the Minor's Mill mentioned by Mr. Bud Pleasants.

In later years some of the property and this house were owned by the Dodd family.

Mr. Arthur Dodd owned a fleet of buses. His buses carried students to Pedlar Mills Elementary and Pleasant View Elementary schools, and older students to Madison Heights High School. Some of the drivers besides himself were: Baylor Dodd, Dewey Massey, Stuart Phillips, Earl Meadow, Richard Coleman, and David Jennings.

Minor/Dodd house

CHURCHES, SCHOOLS, AND OTHER BUILDINGS AT PEDLAR MILLS

Arthur Dodd with part of his bus fleet – *Winnie Dodd collection*

EARLY WAYS OF TRAVEL

One of the first automobiles in Pedlar Mills was owned by W. R. "Dick" Ray, who was a merchant. Dick Ray's father, Martin Ray, had a store which closed. Later Dick Ray had a store in a building next to the one that had been run by his father.

Man with no beard in back seat is Dick Ray – *Pedlar Mills Home Demonstration Club Scrapbook*

Men in buggy with horse – *Pedlar Mills Home Demonstration Club Scrapbook*

People in wagon pulled by horses – *Pedlar Mills Home Demonstration Club Scrapbook*

PERA

Old Pera school

The two-room school at Pera was called Edgewood on what is Route 610/Pera Road. There is little remaining in what was the main community except the dilapidated school and old spring house. According to Irene (Foster) Shepherd, in earlier years, as well as these two buildings, there were several houses, a store, post office, blacksmith shop, corn mill, saw mill, and undertaker's shop. Ed Foster owned the store for a while. The store was last owned by Charlie Ware. Tom Powell ran the saw mill and was an undertaker.

After the school closed the building was named Thornton's Chapel and services were held there each Sunday afternoon for a while.

THE THORNTON FAMILY HOME

The Thornton family home is located down a long driveway off Pera Road. Some of the Thorntons were living in Amherst County in the early 1700s and acquired a considerable amount of property in the Dancing Creek area. According to family lore, an earlier home, built of brick, was in the Oak Grove Church area, and that house was destroyed by fire.

The current house is a classic 19th-century farmhouse with large high ceilinged rooms. The date 1856 is inscribed on an old rock chimney. It has served the Thornton family for several generations.

Thornton family home – *Courtesy Becky Pryor*

The Thornton Family cemetery is located on Pera Road, some distance beyond the driveway to the house.

LITTLE OTTIE CLINE POWELL

This marker is located on the left side of Pera Road, heading west, near where he lived.

A story entitled "Little Boy Lost in Mountains of Virginia" was written by J. B. Huffman. This story was related to me by my father many times when I was growing up. A condensed version of this book is written below.

On November 9, 1891, Rev. and Mrs. E. M. Powell, living on the eastern slope of the Blue Ridge Mountains, sent Ottie Cline Powell, almost five years old, to Tower Hill School with his older brothers and sisters.

At afternoon recess, the teacher requested that they bring back some dry wood for the morning's fire. There was a path into the dense forest. Ottie secured some

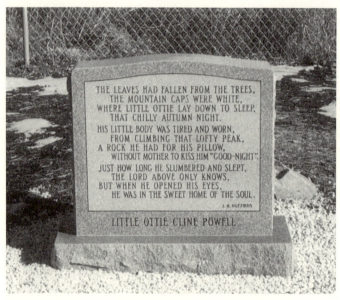

Memorial marker for Ottie Cline Powell – *H. R. Nixon*

wood, but the others were out of sight when he got to the path, and he went in the wrong direction.

About twenty minutes later, the teacher missed Ottie. He wasn't outside playing, and some of the boys went to see if he was where they had gotten wood. Some children went to see if he had gone home.

Soon Rev. Powell, neighbors, men, women and children were searching and continued until about ten p.m. Each day, they went farther and higher on the mountain ridges.

The great search was given up by all except Ottie's father.

On Sunday, April 5, 1892, four young men crossed the Blue Ridge and their dog started barking at something on top of the high peak. They found Ottie's body lying between a rock and an oak tree at the Amherst/Rockbridge County line, seven miles from the school.

According to a physician, Ottie had died within a few hours after leaving the school. Apparently he ran until he fell down, and being fatigued, went to sleep and froze to death before the next morning.

On Monday, April 6, 1892, his funeral was preached, and he was buried in the Tower Hill graveyard.

Henry White house, built around 1850 by the White family – H. R. Nixon

THE HENRY WHITE HOUSE

Henry White moved to Amherst County from Bedford County and built a log house in 1850.

In the attic you can see the very thick and hand-hewn timbers. Another feature is the stone chimneys. Later the house was added on to and clapboarding was put on the outside. In recent years the present owner has taken the clapboarding off and exposed the original logs. There is a large White cemetery on the opposite side of the road, back towards Pera.

White house with logs exposed – *H. R. Nixon*

CIVILIAN CONSERVATION CORPS

CCC Camp No. 10 was located on what is now Pera Road. It was located on property that was later owned by Robert "Bob" and Audrey Ware. There was a rock chimney at the edge of the yard which was left from one of the CCC Camp buildings. Also there are some concrete pads across the road, back near the woods. After the death of the Wares, the house was sold. Unfortunately, within the last year or two, the chimney has been torn down by the new owners. (There were several CCC Camps in different areas of the county.)

Chimney remains from CCC camp – *H. R. Nixon*

l.–r. Robert "Bob" Ware and Roy Ware in driver's seat

PLEASANT VIEW/ NEW PROSPECT

The Gilmer map which was drawn during the Civil War shows New Prospect as the name of the village we now know as Pleasant View. When a post office was established, it became Pleasant View.

NEW PROSPECT BAPTIST CHURCH

In "A History of the Churches in the Piedmont Baptist Association of Virginia" the information shows that New Prospect Church was formed in 1828, and met in a log build-

New Prospect Baptist Church Circa. 1898 – Notice hitching posts in front l.–r. front row: Mr. Tom Davis, Amos Tinsley, Lena Davis; 2nd row: Mrs. Nannie Davis, Mary King, Victoria Bibb, Marshall P. Gatewood, Mrs. Marshall P. Gatewood holding ? Gatewood, Norma Andrews, Ruby Gatewood, Jack Tinsley, Joe Tinsley, Mrs. Joe Davis, Mrs. Joe Tinsley, Lucy Hill; 3rd row: Bernard Tinsley; 4th row: Leticia (Smith) Bibb, Dellia (Bibb) Dodd, Emma Hill, Bessie Watts, Glen Phillips, Willie Anne (Bibb) Hawkins, Carrie Phillips, ?, Alonza Bibb, Robert Harlow, Sammy Carter; 5th row: Joseph Radford Bibb, Miss Blanche Morris, Mrs. Kate Smith, Ollie Tinsley, Annie Carter, Joshua Bibb, Eva Sales, Mrs. Charlie Phillips, Mr. Wilshire, John Lewis Sales, George Bibb; back row: John Andrews, Cephus Bibb, Mrs. R. O. Root, Mr. R. O. Root, Tom Carter, Will Cross – *Lois Foster*

New Prospect Baptist Church – *H. R. Nixon*

Old Pleasant View Elementary and High School taken around 1913

ing on the property. They built a church on the present site in 1847. Some records show that the present church was built in 1871. Over the years, some additions have been made. A field of churches including Midway, New Prospect, Cornerstone, and Elon was formed in 1896. (See more details about the field of churches in the Elon Baptist Church history).

PLEASANT VIEW SCHOOLS

According to Sally Eubank, the Pleasant View High School was built around 1910–1912. There were six rooms: three for grades one through seven and three for high school students.

Sally Eubank also stated that after the High School was built, a three-room school, which was located a few yards away, was converted into an auditorium. My brother, James Foster, attended Pleasant View School and graduated in 1941. Helen (Coffey) Keith, and Ruth (Harris) Foster, along with a number of others graduated with him.

The new Pleasant View Elementary School was built and first occupied in January 1953.

Picture: Taken behind Pleasant View School auditorium in 1930s l.–r.: Back Row: ? Sales, Hesper Franklin, Naomi Harris (with arrow), Irene Hudson, ?, Marie Burks, Owen Foster, Cabell Burks, ?, Billy Jennings, ?, Charles Grant, Essie Grant. Center of picture: Nannie Mae Hudson, ?, ? . Back Row Cont'd.: ? Johnson, ?, William Massie, Everett Dodd, Warren Franklin, Ashby Woods Jr., Robert Franklin, Anne Tyler, Ruth Harris, Margaret Clark, Cecil Burks. Front Row on steps: ?, Edward Franklin, Gladys Maddox, Dolly Jennings, ?, Shirley Eubank, Dot Myers, Nancy Woods, Rachael Franklin, Elizabeth Davis, Nancy Caufield (with arrow), Frances McDaniel, Claudine Johnson, Pauline Davis, Earle Brown, Hal Myers Jr., ? Campbell, John Dudley Davis, Betty Jean Owen, Irene Campbell, Evelyn Hamilton. Front of steps: Odell Johnson, James Foster, Edward "Big Boy" Burch, Dude "Eddie Tom" Anderson, Ralph Anderson Jr., Frank Burks Jr., T. J. Tomlin, Dolly Tomlin – *Ruth Foster collection*

Seniors of Pleasant View High School in 1932: l.–r. Frances Johnson, Martha Watts, "Dimple" Sandidge, ?, ?, ?, Dorothy Crist – *Ruth Tiller collection*

Pleasant View High School with additions, and separate auditorium building

GATEWOOD HOUSE

The house, known as the Gatewood house, was built in the 1850s and was owned by the Harlows. Mr. Harlow and his young son drowned in the James River, down at Pearch. The child fell into the water in the winter. Mr. Harlow jumped into the water to try to save him, but his overcoat weighted him down.

Old Marshall Gatewood house – *H. R. Nixon*

Some years later his widow married Marshall P. Gatewood. Mr. Gatewood served as a delegate to the General Assembly for eight years. His daughter, Mary Gatewood, married Bernard H. Camden of Elon. They had dated for at least 40 years before they got married.

The Jimmy Eubank family purchased the property years ago and have made renovations.

DR. E. M. SANDIDGE

Dr. E. M. Sandidge lived in Pleasant View and traveled many miles taking care of all the people in the area. I am sure he delivered many babies in his day. His home is no longer standing. Dr. Sandidge served on the Amherst County Board of Supervisors.

Dr. E. M. Sandidge's house

Dr. E. M. Sandidge

THE BAPTIST PARSONAGE

The parsonage, built in 1897, was located between the Camden house and Dr. Sandidge's house. At the time it was built, there was a field of churches: Cornerstone, Elon, Midway, and New Prospect. The preacher lived there and preached one Sunday morning and one Sunday night at each church every month. For a while the Home Mission Board helped support the preacher financially. The custom was for a church family to invite the preacher and his family home for Sunday dinner.

Baptist Parsonage – H. R. Nixon

A practice of the Baptists in the field of churches was to hold a "pounding" once in a while for the preacher. It got its name because people would take food items to the parsonage to help supply food since the preacher didn't receive a very high salary. People would take pounds of sugar, flour, potatoes, apples, various canned goods, baked goods (usually including a pound cake), and other items, since people in the country had these things that they could share.

In 1949, Elon Baptist Church felt that we could make it financially on our own, and decided to withdraw from the field of churches in order to have more services at our church. We gave our part of ownership of the parsonage at Pleasant View to the remaining churches.

SOME BUSINESSES

There were several stores: Claude Watts' store, Mose Trevey's store, and Marshall Gatewood's store. Some years ago, Glen Campbell sold his business at Elon and moved to Pleasant View and purchased what had been Watts' Store.

Glen sold the store some years ago, after making additions and changes to the building.

Watts' store – H. R. Nixon

Campbell's store – H. R. Nixon

Emmett Smith's House– *H. R. Nixon*

Bernard Johnson with jitney bus beside Carroll Hotel in Lynchburg – *Ruth Foster*

Mr. Emmett Smith was an undertaker and he built wooden caskets. There used to be an old abandoned hearse sitting beside the road when we would go to visit my grandparents, Bob and Jennie Turner. The property is now owned by Wathena Watts and her family.

According to Edward Paxton "Pack" Sandidge, a Mr. Tinsley had run a blacksmith's shop which was located between the Baptist parsonage and the Camden's house, but the building is no longer standing.

Mr. Bernard Johnson, who lived at Pleasant View, drove a jitney bus into Lynchburg. He would park the bus near the Carroll Hotel which was located at the corner of Eighth and Main streets, and wait for his passengers for the return trip. Sometimes, a black man, John Miller, would drive his truck to haul large items for the passengers. He would follow the jitney bus with the cargo. In later years two buses would run from Lynchburg to Pleasant View on Saturday morning, and then return in the afternoon. They would pick up passengers along the way.

LAMB'S MILL

After the Big Mill at Pedlar Mills burned, Rev. E. E. Lamb had a gasoline powered mill on his property. Some of the millstones are located in front of the old Lamb house. In a conversation with my brother, Gordon W. Foster, in 1982, he told about going to the mill at Pleasant View with other family members. On occasion, when he was about seven years old, he would be sent with corn to be ground. Only one-half of a bag would be sent, and this would be divided with equal portions put on each side of the saddle. He was not big enough to get up and down from the horse, so someone at the mill would take him down out of the saddle and then place him back into it when the meal was ready for him to take home. Of course, he was helped down from the horse when he got back home.

TIMOTHY BAPTIST CHURCH

Timothy Baptist Church is a black church which was built in 1870 and is located on Buffalo Springs Turnpike at Pleasant View. It was a white frame building, and according to the cornerstone, it was bricked in the 1960s.

TIMOTHY SCHOOL

This was a two-room school located on the right side of Timothy Baptist Church which, in the earlier years, had classes through the ninth grade. Mr. Selvy Burton had two buses and he transported the children to school. The school closed in the 1960s and the church used the building as a social hall. Sometime later, road construction was started in the area and the building was torn down.

Timothy Baptist Church – H. R. Nixon

Timothy School – *Tyler Fulcher's Booklet*

EUBANKS' MILL

This mill was located on Dancing Creek Road, on Dancing Creek, approximately 2.4 miles from Pleasant View. The mill was last run by Bob Eubanks. Before him, the mill was run by his father, John Nick Eubanks. My uncle, Earl Foster, told me that it was so dry in 1881, that they cut a channel from Little Dancing Creek and ran that water into Dancing Creek to have enough water to keep the mill going. The mill shut down in about 1915.

TURNER'S STORE

The main house was located back off the road at Knoll, a little ways beyond Pleasant View School, not far from the site of Eubanks' Mill. My grandparents raised their five children there. A great-aunt, Hattie Turner lived with them also.

After the George Foster store, which was located through the cut (the road had literally been cut through the hill) was closed, Grandpa Turner built his store. There was a bedroom over the store with a ladder to get to it. He and Granny would go down and spend the night to ward off burglars.

You had to use a special finger combination to open the cash drawer.

He had beans and sugar in bins which he would weigh in bags and then tie the top of

Turner's Store after it had been sold for a residence
–H. R. Nixon

Bob and Jennie Turner at their
50th anniversary – *Jimmie Ray*

the bag with string from a string holder that was mounted on the ceiling. He sold canned goods, as well as drinks and candy. As did most country storekeepers, he would barter for eggs, etc. He also sold gas. Before they had electricity, he had a gas pump that fed by gravity. As children, we liked to pump the gas up into the top and then watch it flow back down. They had electricity and telephones on the main road leading to Pleasant View, but people living off the main road didn't get electricity until in the mid-1950s. In later years, after he had electricity, he replaced that pump.

In the summer of the late 1940s and early 1950s I would usually go up to the Pedlar Mills and Pleasant View areas and spend two weeks with some relatives, including my grandparents, and Aunt Hattie. As I stated, Granny and Grandpa would spend the night over the store. I would sleep at the big house with Aunt Hattie in a bed that had a straw tick/mattress. (In the winter they would use a feather tick on the bed. The cover would be stuffed with feathers instead of straw). Also, in preparing for bed, the big bolster would be removed and pillows put in its place. After dark, our light came from oil lamps, and/or lanterns. There was a path to the outdoor toilet for the day time, but at night a slop jar was placed beside the bed.

It was a novelty to me to go to the spring for water, and to place items in the spring box to stay cool, since soon after we moved to Elon in 1941, we had electricity, a well with running water in the house and a bathroom. We also had a telephone with eight parties on the line.

FRANKLIN'S STORE

This log building is located on Buffalo Springs Turnpike, a little east of Pleasant View. It was close to the road and run by Nellie Franklin and some of her family. They sold gas and other items. It has not operated as a business for many years. Buddy Watts and his wife now own the property.

Store run by Nellie Franklin and family – *H. R. Nixon*

PEDLAR FARM

According to a newpaper article, Pedlar Farm of over 1,000 acres was a direct grant from the King of England to a Mr. Crist, an Englishman, before the Revolutionary War. Mr. Crist, being loyal to the king was dispossessed after the Revolution.

It was then owned by Charles and Josiah Ellis until purchased in 1809 by George T. Pleasants. He deeded it to his two daughters, Jane C. and husband Ambrose R. Woodroof (they were to take the lower half) and Margaret N. and Alfred M. Woodroof (who were to take the upper half). This deed was written August 15, 1859.

Lower Pedlar Farm – *Courtesy Pedlar Mills Home Demonstration Club Scrap Book*

The Pleasants family owned a large plantation on what is now Wagon Trail Road. The property is shown on the Gilmer Civil War Map.

Ambrose R. Woodroof built the mansion house on lower Pedlar Farm in 1859, the same year they were given the property. The date can be seen on the gable end of the house. The brick were made on the farm from native clay. This structure consists of six rooms with solid brick walls, 18 inches thick. There was a brick kitchen (with servants' quarters) separate from the house.

In later years, Mrs. Ella Dillard owned the lower Pedlar Farm for some time. After her, it was owned by the Malige family for many years. They remodeled the house and furnished it with Parisian furniture. Some years ago, the property was sold by the Malige family.

Alfred M. Woodroof built a large frame house on upper Pedlar Farm sometime after the Civil War. This house has thirteen rooms, with two sets of stairs. There is a front porch, and a porch on the back of the house as well. It is said that Mrs. Woodroof wanted to build on the top of the hill where they would have a good view, but they would not have had water. They built down lower where there was a spring.

The property stayed in the Woodroof family until it was sold to the Lloyd family, in recent years. I understand the house has been beautifully renovated by the Lloyds.

House at Upper Pedlar Farm – *H. R. Nixon*

RIVER ROAD AREA

TWIN OAKS/FLINT HILL

Twin Oaks house circa 1903, with young Victor Wood in foreground

Twin Oaks was built circa 1763. This assumption is based on the way the house is constructed. It was built from hand-hewn timbers and put together with wooden pegs. Of particular interest is the large rock fireplace in the basement with a food warmer built into the side. Evidence of clay pipes running from the spring to the house have been found.

The house was at one time occupied by a family named Stillwell, and during their oc-

Tobacco growing with house in background – *Photo by Victor Wood/Courtesy of Nancy Marion*

Man with cut tobacco – *Photo by Victor Wood/Courtesy of Nancy Marion*

Corn shocks, big pile of shucks, pile of ears of corn, in right foreground – *Photo by Victor Wood/Courtesy of Nancy Marion*

cupancy a private school was conducted in the Stillwell house. Miss Nettie Forbes was the first teacher.

Mrs. Stillwell's mother was Mrs. Ada Old. Mrs. Old was related to the Pettyjohns who lived about two miles beyond there, near the banks of the James River. Mrs. Old was buried in the Pettyjohn Cemetery.

The Wood family owned the farm at the turn of the century. Then son, Victor Wood, took many photos of the area for several decades.

Mr. Wood took pictures around 1905 of tobacco growing near the house and then after it had been cut.

By the time Wade and Martha Camden bought the property in 1972, there was only one oak tree, and the name had been changed to Flint Hill. They have made additions and changes to the house.

PETTYJOHN SCHOOL

This one-room school was built in the late 1800s on a portion of the Pettyjohn plantation. The building has had several additions, and is located across the road from the entrance to Union Christian Church. Some of the teachers over the years were: Alice (Gottshall) Webster, Elsie (Loving) Ware, Odell (Hudson) Candler, and Carrie Belle (Bowles) Watts.

Pettyjohn School –taken in 1932) l.–r. Back Row: Helen Garrett, Elizabeth Tolley, ?, ?, ?, ?, Dorothy Campbell; Front: ?, ?, ?, Lucille Garrett, ?, ? – *Courtesy Helen Ranson*

UNION CHRISTIAN CHURCH

Early Union Christian Church – *Courtesy Helen Ranson*

Union Chapel was organized in 1901. The congregation met in the one-room school house for a while. In 1904, T. L. Wills donated land, and a church building was erected. The name was changed from Union Chapel to Wills Chapel. Some years later the name was changed from Wills Chapel to Union Christian Chapel.

Additional land was donated by the Reuben S. Garrett family, and a new church was erected in 1961.

In the 1970s a parsonage was built, the social hall was enlarged, Sunday school rooms were added, and other improvements were made.

The name of the church is now Union Christian Church.

Present Union Christian Church – *H. R. Nixon*

PETTYJOHN HOUSE

Pettyjohn house – *Elon Home Demonstration Club Scrap Book*

The old Pettyjohn house was built in the 1700s on land near James River that was a grant to James Pettyjohn. The bricks used in the construction were made on the place. The outside walls are 14 inches thick and the inside partitions are also brick. The floors are made of yellow pine and in some areas wooden pegs were used. There were an ice house, many other buildings, and slave quarters, but only the house remains. It has been remodeled and has some additions. It is owned by the Merritt family. The Pettyjohn cemetery and an old slave cemetery covering approximately two acres are located across the road from the end of the house.

RAILROAD TRESTLE

Railroad trestle

Old railroad bridge circa 1903

Southern locomotive is crossing 1,860 foot long trestle over James River. This trestle replaced the railroad bridge where abutments can be seen across from "Old 97 Road." When the leaves are off the trees, you can see retaining wall for old track across from the bridge over Harris Creek.

FLOYD'S STORE

Frank L. and Ruth Floyd ran a store which was located near the abutments for the old railroad trestle. It was just across the road from what is now called "Old '97 Road."

According to Mrs. Floyd, they operated the store from 1951 until the flood of 1985. The store was cleaned up and ready for business when someone torched it. After it was burned, they decided not to rebuild.

Floyd's Store on River Road – *Courtesy Ruth Floyd*

LOVINGSTON BAPTIST CHURCH

Lovingston Baptist Church – *H. R. Nixon*

Lovingston Baptist Church is located on Kings Road just at the top of the hill from River Road. In 1877 a church was established down on the river, and in 1880 Mr. Garland Booker gave the land where the church is presently located. The church took its name from the owner of the property down on the river, Mr. Love.

The new church was built during the administration of Rev. C. J. Davenport who served from 1966–1982. They were without a pastor from 1982–1984 but they continued worshiping and praying. In 1984, Rev. Edward E. Austin became their pastor.

LOVINGSTON ELEMENTARY SCHOOL

This was a two-room black school which was located on Kings Road, just around from Lovingston Baptist Church. Each room had a cloak room. Grades 1-4 were taught in one room, and 5–7 were taught in the other room. There was a cafeteria in the center, between the two rooms. There were two pot-bellied stoves which burned wood and coal.

The children drew water from the Lewis' well and took it back to the school where it was stored in wooden barrels. The teachers were: Rev. E. D. Irvin and Mitchell. This school closed in the 1960s.

Lovingston Elementary School – *Tyler Fulcher's Booklet*

RED AND DOT'S

This store is a located above the Scott's Mill Dam. It has been operated for many years by the Proffitt family. They sell groceries and many other items, as well as fish bait.

They have a boat ramp which can be used for a small fee.

Scott's Mill – *Collection of Jimmie Ray*

SCOTT'S MILL

In 1883, John J. Scott Jr., formed an agreement with the Richmond and Alleghany Railroad Co. and leased land on the Amherst County side of the James River with the right to construct a mill on the end of the stone dam that was extended across to the other side of the river in that year. The familiar landmark, Scott's Mill Dam, is where the mill was operated under the control of R. C. Scott and Co. of Lynchburg.

The mill was destroyed by fire on May 27, 1944. The foundation can still be seen as you pass the north end of the dam on the River Road.

Williams Viaduct, Scott's Dam and Mill, and railroad bridge in the far back – *Courtesy of Nancy Marion*

Lover's Leap on bluff side, near dam

WILLIAMS VIADUCT AND JOHN LYNCH MEMORIAL BRIDGE

The building of Williams Viaduct was begun in 1916 and completed in 1918. Williams Viaduct was replaced by John Lynch Memorial Bridge which was dedicated on April 18, 1988. The new bridge was opened for the first traffic on April 19, 1988. The demolition of Williams Viaduct was started shortly after that date.

New John Lynch Bridge and Williams Viaduct taken day of dedication – *Courtesy of The News & Advance*

SNOWDEN AND AREA

According to Mrs. Moses Kyle (Margaret) Williams, Rope Ferry became Snowden after the Williams brothers moved there from New York. They were first generation Welsh from slate mining country in Wales.

Over the years, a number of quarries were operated in the area. The Williams brothers operated a slate quarry from the 1880s into the 1900s, and supplied slate for the roofs of many of the local houses as well as Amherst County Court house, per information supplied by Doug MacLeod.

There was a C & O Railway station with a post office located in the station building. Mr. Williams operated the telegraph.

Between 1929 and 1936, most of the building was torn down leaving only a waiting room which was torn down some time later. Tickets then had to be purchased at the Williams' Store.

Horses and wagon, probably hauling slate, with James River in lower left background – *Louise Tyler Williams collection*

Snowden Railroad Station – *Courtesy Wanda Gilbert*

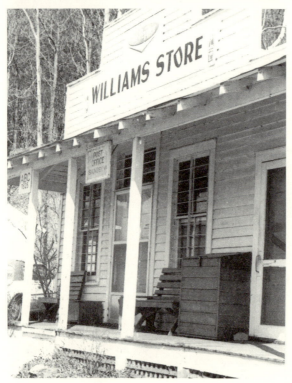

Williams Store – *Amherst Co. Museum and Historical Society collection*

Hikers on the Appalachian Trail would stop at the store to replenish supplies and catch up on the news.

In August, 1979, the Snowden post office, which by then was located in Williams' Store, was closed. Mrs. Williams as "officer-in-charge" was given a choice of two local post offices: Big Island, six miles away, and Monroe, twenty miles distant. Not unnaturally, she opted for the nearer one but this gave rise to several unforeseen problems for the reason that Big Island is in Bedford County whereas Snowden is in a remote section of Amherst County. According to Mrs. Williams, this caused a number of problems.

Snowden voters were ordered to have their names removed from the county records or to appear at Amherst Court House to explain the situation. In January, when the purging of records came to the attention of the Snowden citizens, it was inconvenient to drive 33 miles to the county seat, but finally it was established by telephone and correspondence that they lived just where they had been for the last 45 years. The only change was in the mailing address; all of them paid hundreds of dollars in taxes to Amherst, etc., and their names were restored to the voters list.

The same difficulty was encountered with insurance. The company based in Lexington wanted the exact location of the property concerned and maintained that higher rates prevailed in Bedford Co., etc. Mrs. Williams explained that they were still in exactly the same place they had been all these years, in Amherst County. The insurance representative said "AMHERST," I thought you were in "ROCKBRIDGE"! Anyway they had to pay the higher rate since they were in a different county from the carrier.

Tombstone of James McClarty, native of Scotland – *H. R. Nixon*

Taken in 1938: Moses Bennett Kyle and son, Winfield Nelms Kyle, with river in background before bottom was flooded – *Louise Tyler Williams collection*

Another problem was that the automobile registration had to state the location where the car was garaged, among other data. Well, it certainly wasn't garaged in Big Island, six miles down the road. They had to drop "Snowden" and show their route and box number and Big Island as their address. The curious coincidence was that she still got junk mail and begging letters with nothing but her name and "Snowden, Va." without even the zip code in the latter days.

There is a small cemetery in the rock quarry area where some Scot-Irish workers are buried. They were helping build the Kanawha Canal and died due to the smallpox epidemic.

There were private dwellings, a building which served as church and school, a boarding house and commissary located near the mine. There was a tavern which was used as a dwelling in later years.

The James River was dammed in about 1929 or 1930 and this flooded the bottom land of the Williams family.

After having been contacted by Mrs. Williams, the Hercules Corporation leased and reopened the quarry in 1969. They produced an inflated rock product marketed as "Snowden Lightweight Aggregate" and used a tipple and conveyor over Route 130 to load railroad cars. It ceased operation in the early 1990s. .

The store has been closed for some years now, and a few of the houses are still occupied.

There was a Civilian Conservation Corps camp at the present location of the wayside which is on the left side of Route 130/Elon Road just as you start up Snowden Mountain. It is about 1.8 miles west of the intersection of Route 130 and Route 501. At the back side of the park you can see where there was a canal lock for the Kanawha Canal.

Conveyor over Route 130 with tipple and railroad cars – *H. R. Nixon*

Canal to Power Plant below Snowden per Bill Dawson – *Bill Dawson collection*

FRANK PADGET STORY

January 21, 2004, marked the 150th anniversary of the death of Frank Padget. A four foot high granite obelisk once overlooked an abandoned canal lock beside the CSX railroad tracks, about halfway through the James River water gap between Snowden and Glasgow, near the Amherst-Rockbridge Co. line. The inscription read:

> IN THE MEMORY OF FRANK PADGET
> A COLOURED SLAVE, WHO DURING
> A FRESHET IN JAMES RIVER IN
> JANUARY 1854 VENTURED AND
> LOST HIS LIFE BY DROWNING IN
> THE NOBLE EFFORT TO SAVE SOME
> OF HIS FELLOW CREATURES WHO
> WERE IN THE MIDST OF THE
> FLOOD FROM DEATH.

In 1854, there had been rain for several days. An especially heavy rain raised the North (now Maury) River several feet higher than it had been the day before.

Approximately 50 people were on board the canal boat *Clinton*. Just after passing the North River Bridge, the towline broke and the boat drifted down James River towards the Mountain Dam. The water was too deep to touch bottom with poles. About 100 yards before reaching the dam at the cement kilns, seven people jumped off and attempted to swim to shore; four reached the shore safely and three went over the dam and perished.

The captain of the boat was advised to straighten up his boat and prevent her from going broadside. The awful crisis came, to run through the White Rock, the Little Balcony, the Great Balcony Falls, and the Tobacco Hills.

The boat passed within a foot of the White Rock. The captain and four or five other persons jumped onto the rock, and were in the middle of the James River. The boat reached the head of the Tobacco Hills where she hung lightly on a rock in the middle of the river.

Some people on the shore obtained a boat, dragged it over the towpath and launched it in James River below the cement kilns, to try to save the people.

Among those volunteering was an old Negro boatman, a headman named Frank Padget. Frank was requested to take the head of the boat. He selected two assistants, Sam and Bob. William Matthews and Mr. McCollogan, employees of the James River and Kanawha Company volunteered to assist.

They were driven back to the shore by the rough river. They then went towards the White Rock and threw a towline. Frank skillfully shot the head of his boat into the eddy under the rock, saved these men and got them to shore.

The canal boat continued down the river, heading through the Tobacco Hills. One man jumped off unto a rock, before it hung in the small timber of a small island. They reached the canal boat and all hands were taken off and safely brought to shore.

They went back to rescue the man on the rock and when the man jumped, the craft collided with the boulder and broke into two large parts.

Three of the six men scrambled to safety on the rock. The slave Bob clung to the drifting stem oar and made his way safely to shore, down river. Frank Padget and the man he came to rescue were thrown into the river and drowned.

The next morning, an old ferryman, Sam Evans, went out with six volunteers and rescued the half-frozen men from the rock.

A marker was erected at canal lock 16 by Capt. Edward Echols, a prominent Glasgow resident who assisted in the rescue attempts, and was a witness to all that took place. In 1975 another marker was placed beside the original marker since the engraving was so hard to read. This was sponsored by Rockbridge Historical Society using the John C. Echols Memorial Fund.

In 1997, the original marker was moved to Glasgow and is located just outside Glasgow Town Hall.

In 2007, a highway marker was placed beside the highway on Route 501 at the Amherst-Rockbridge County line and dedicated by the Virginia Department of Historic Resources.

– H. R. Nixon

Original marker, now in Glasgow's Centennial Park – *H. R. Nixon*

New marker placed in 1975, beside original marker (mile post 173 on the CSX Railroad) on right – *H. R. Nixon*

TOBACCO IN AMHERST COUNTY

Some of my ancestors moved to Amherst County from Buckingham County and Bedford County in 1840s and 1850s. They bought property in the canebrakes which was in the vicinity of Pedlar Mills, Knoll, and Pera to raise dark tobacco.

At one time Amherst County was known for raising dark tobacco, as well as having a lot of fruit orchards.

My father didn't raise any tobacco after we moved to Elon, so I just have to go by what others tell me about the hard work. Marshall Mays in the *Amherst County Heritage Book* Vol. II gave a good account about raising tobacco and the work involved.

Over the years fewer and fewer farmers in Amherst County kept allotments to raise tobacco. By 1994, there were only about four local tobacco growers.

My husband, Holcomb, and I took pictures of tobacco being grown and ready to go to market that year. We went to Jack Davis' place in Pleasant View.

By this time there were no tobacco warehouses and markets in Lynchburg. The closest market for selling tobacco was in Danville, Virginia.

Tobacco field in fall about a week before tobacco was cut – *H. R. Nixon*

Plant bed in spring with plowed field in background – *H. R. Nixon*

Tobacco being cut and laid in field to be put on tobacco sticks – *H. R. Nixon*

Tobacco barn at Pleasant View – *H. R. Nixon*

Tobacco on tobacco sticks laying on trailer with stack of wood for firing the tobacco – *H. R. Nixon*

Tobacco on sticks being hung at different levels – *H. R. Nixon*

This shows where fires were burned to fire the tobacco – *H. R. Nixon*

TOBACCO IN AMHERST COUNTY

Cured tobacco hanging in tobacco barn – *H. R. Nixon*

Percy Davis, who was ninety years old, stripping tobacco, getting it ready for market – *Florence Foster Nixon*

Jack Davis putting stripped tobacco into bundles – *Florence Foster Nixon*

Planters Tobacco Warehouse – *Wayland Rice collection*

In early 1900s teams of horses were lined up after leaving their wagon loads of tobacco at Planters' Tobacco Warehouse. The warehouse was located in Lynchburg on Main Street below 13th Street. It has been torn down and there is a parking lot where it was located.

There are still tobacco farmers in Campbell and Pittsylvania Counties, but they raise mostly bright tobacco and burley tobacco. Most of that is harvested by the leaf as it ripens (not the whole stalk like dark tobacco).

My mother told me that in the early 1900s her father took his tobacco to the tobacco market in Lynchburg and sold it. This was their main source of income. He would purchase food items for the coming year. He usually bought: 5 pounds of coffee (he and Granny drank only one cup of coffee each a day), 100 pounds sugar, 100 pounds pinto beans, 100 pounds great northern beans, and a keg of salt fish. This was for family use, many years before he owned a store.

Of course, they had their home-canned fruit and vegetables, as well as potatoes to supplement their diet. They had pork from the hogs they raised each year. They always kept cows, so they had milk and butter.

At that time they would have grown wheat and corn to take to the mill to be ground into flour and cornmeal.

WAUGH'S FERRY AND AREA

According to article in *Amherst County Heritage Book* –1761–1999, a petition was made in May 1763 to establish Waugh's Ferry. The ferry was to go from Thomas Waugh's farm on the Amherst side of James River to a landing near the mouth of Cabin Creek in Bedford County. James Waugh, son of Thomas Waugh, had the first commercially registered ferry at Waugh. Some of the operators, besides James Waugh, over the years, were: Walter Leslie Bailey, James Andrew Bailey, and Mallie Dameron Burford. The last person to operate the ferry was Jack Burford.

BURFORD'S WAUGH'S FERRY FARM

According to Aileen Burford Young, Burford's Waugh's Ferry farm has been in the Burford family for over 250 years. Dameron Burford built the Waugh's Ferry homestead in 1918 after the original house burned. In addition to the ferry on this property, there were some water powered mills. This is still a working farm. Eddie and Shelby Burford are the current owners.

Burford's Waugh's Ferry Farm house – *Courtesy Burford Family*

Waugh's Ferry (Operated from approx. 1783 to 1937) Walter Leslie Bailey's casket being ferried across the James river. Picture taken December 1937 –Courtesy Josephine Bailey Woods

BAILEY'S FARM HOME

The house was built in 1911 by Walter Leslie Bailey and his wife, Delia (Hill) Bailey, on their farm near Waugh's Ferry. They lived there with their four children: Edwin, Walter, Hill, and Eleanor. The teachers for the Bailey School boarded there and walked several miles each day through the woods to the school with the Bailey children.

Bailey's Home – *Pedlar Mills Home Demonstration Club Scrap Book*

The house has four rooms up and four rooms down. There is a front staircase, and a staircase leading up from the kitchen to the bedroom where the cook lived. There are two separate basements, a lattice cellar, and a rock cellar used for food storage. There is a screened porch on the back where the family ate in the summer. There are two porches on the front. The upper one was a sleeping porch used in the hot summer. The lower porch was used for rocking, and admiring the view of the James River, where you could see the railroad tracks and highway 501.

Walter L. Bailey Jr. bought the home place from his brother Hill and he and his wife, Beulah (Thornton) Bailey, raised two children, Josephine and Walter III.

By the time Josephine was school age, there was no longer a school at Naola, and the roads were not good from the farm. She went to live with her grandmother and aunt and attended school in Lynchburg. She only went home for the holidays and the summer for three years. When her brother, W. L., became school age, her parents rented an apartment in Lynchburg, and the family stayed together. Her father had to go back to the farm every day to take care of the stock. He would travel Rt. 501, and then cross the river by boat to get to the farm. Once there was a bad snow with the roads really bad. He tried to ride the bus and then the train, and finally got across from the farm, but could not cross the river. He had to call a neighbor to feed his stock. He watched the neighbor, from across the river, as he went on his tractor to feed the stock.

When Josephine was older, she would row the boat across the river and pick their mail up since they had a Big Island mailing address. In later years, after improvements to the roads, they had rural delivery from Naola.

VERDANT VALE

According to Mrs. C. H. Prather, sister of Jas. Pembroke Woods, Verdant Vale was owned by their great-grandmother, Isabella McCulloch Waugh and her husband, Edward Waugh.

Verdant Vale – *Pedlar Mills Home Demonstration Club Scrap Book*

Drawing of Verdant Vale by Nancy McDearmon – *Courtesy of Leah Settle Gibbs*

The estate was bought from Cornelius Thomas, and from her brother, Roderick McCulloch.

The old house was built in 1795. The bricks were made on the place. It was four stories with wainscoting in the large hall and rooms. There were two chimneys on each end, and very high and beautiful mantels. It was considered a fine mansion in that day. A cemetery nearby contains graves of Waugh and allied families.

In later years, the property was owned by Jas. Pembroke Woods. It is now owned by Leah Settle Gibbs.

BUSINESSES IN AREA IN 1880S

The Lynchburg City Directory for 1883-'84 listed businesses using their mailing addresses, as follows:

ALLWOOD: M. L. Berry, physician; James Cashwell, shoemaker; Arthur Coleman, constable; Geo. E. Cunningham, flour and grist mill; James Miller & Son, genl. mdse.

HARRIS CREEK: (this would have been in the area of Burford), a station on the Virginia Midland Railway, nine miles south of Amherst Court House, and five north of Lynchburg. Listed are: W. A. Ballowe, trial justice; G. A. Baldock, miller; S. N. Burford, undertaker; D. Carson, shoemaker; G. T. Clark, constable; A. Christian, lawyer; Kunz & Ewers, genl. mdse.; Wm. B. Roberts, physician. Farmers: E. A. Phillips, M. H. Garland, V. H. Rucker, E. F. Hudson, G. B. Mason, F. N. Farrar, J. J. Ewers, B. H. Ewers, B. M. DeWitt, R. Fairfax, E. M. Tinsley, J. C. Long, R. M. Burford, Geo. Haley, Chas. Ramsey, Jas. Roberts, Richard Roberts, W. H. White, Geo. W. White, J. S. White, T. W. White, E. McIvor, S. C. Williams, Jas. T. Williams, Geo. K. Kunz, Jas. Ware, Fred Johnson, John G. Perry, L. D. Stillwell, Joseph Watts, R. Watts, R. I. Kidd, S. L. Blanks, W. A. Grubb, A. C. Rucker, W. I. Rucker, P. C. Farrar, J. J. Ewers, Zach Mason, J. A. Hunt, J. T. Ammonett, Benj. Ammonett, W. F. Ammonett.

PEDLAR MILLS: M. L. Berry, physician; A. N. Feagans, saloon; T. J. Frazier, shoemaker; S. Ogden, flour and grist mill; A. J. Padgett, genl. mdse. and hotel; M. D. Ray & Son, genl. mdse.; D. H. Rucker, trial justice; S. F. Turner & Bro., flour and grist mill.
Farmers: W. L. Brown, W. P. Brown, W. C. Bibb, Ro. H. Brown, S. C. Caldwell, B. R. Caldwell, Jno. Dud Davis, M. Dameron, Z. Dameron, Whiting Davis, R. N. Ellis, Jno. E. Ellis, R. Newman Ellis, R. H. Eubank, John N. Eubank, W. H. Feagans, J. T. Feagans, M. E. Feagans, A. N. Feagans, F. M. Godsey, Ro. J. Hill, O. P. Jones, J. H. Jones, P. C. Jones, M. W. Jennings, Jno. A. Jennings, J. E. Jennings, C. L. Jones, N. C. Keith, R. D. Landrum, L. Minor, W. P. Newcomb, R. C. Newcomb, C. E. Nicholas, Silas Ogden, S. F. Turner, John W. Pleasants, T. B. Pleasants, Mrs. J. C. Pleasants, Jas. Powell, A. J. Richeson, D. H. Rucker, N. D. Rucker, D. T. Swisher, Hugh Snead, Arthur Snead, P. C. Taylor, Sam'l. Taylor, Wm. Taylor, Jas. Williams Sr., Jas. Williams Jr., Marshall Williams, Chas. D. Williams, C. B. Woodroof, Jno. H. Woods, J. T. Woods, L. C. Ware, H. C. Phillips, A. J. Bailey.

PLEASANT VIEW: M. C. Harlow, genl. mdse.
Farmers: L. P. Pleasants, George T. Pleasants, James W. Phillips.

SALT CREEK; A station on the Richmond & Alleghany R. R. Listed are: Chas. H. Buchanan; Post Master; Chas. H. Buchanan, genl. mdse.; W. E. Powell, genl. mdse.
Farmers: Edward Fletcher, Henry Johnson, Henry Gray, R. G. Scott.

The Elon Post Office had been established by 1885 because it shows in the Lynchburg City Directory for 1885-'86, as well as in Chataigne's Lynchburg City Directory for 1887-'88.

The Lynchburg City Directory for 1885-'86 listed Post Offices including the following: Allwood, Elon, Harris Creek, Pedlar Mills, Pleasant View, Salt Creek and Snowden.

ALLWOOD: Coach and Wagon Builder, L. M. Rogers; General Merchant, John H. Parr; Mills – Corn and Flour, Cunningham's; Millwright, H. J. Wright; Physician, Henry L. Berry; Physician, Hazel Williams Jr.; Tanner, J. J. Wright; Undertaker, L. M. Rogers.
Principal Farmers: A. F. Burks, Wm. H. Barnes, R. N. Carter, James N. Pryor, Jas. S. Richeson, Jno. R. Cunningham, Jas. M. Millner, George W. Dodd, James N. Eubank, W. L. Millner, Bluford Morris, Thomas Shepherd, L. P. Hawkins, P. M. Rucker, J. W. Rucker, G. T. Rucker, L. F. Parr.

ELON: Attorney-at-Law, Dudley A. Alexander; Coach and Wagon Builders, L. F. Wood, M. Wright; General Merchants: Charles Robinson, Gustavus Rose; Mills – Corn and Flour, William Brooks; Saddler and Harness Maker, Wm. Dornin; Tanner, Thornton Rodes.
Principal Farmers: Thornton Ricketts, M. Mays, Walter Brooks, Patrick Wood, Patrick Edwards, Samuel Coleman.

HARRIS CREEK: Civil Engineer, M. H. Garland; Coach and Wagon Builder, B. S. Pendleton; General Merchant, Wm. H. Morton; Mills – Corn and Flour: G. A. Baldock, A. L. Burford, J. C. Long; Mills – Saw, G. A. Baldock, J. C. Long; Undertaker, S. M. Burford & Co.
Principal Farmers: John W. Ammonett, E. McIvor, R. M. Burford, S. M. Burford, M. H. Garland, V. H. Rucker, G. B. Mason, L. D. Stillwell, R. Fairfax, J. E. Ewers, B. H. Ewers, E. Kunz.

PEDLAR MILLS: Dentist, J. F. Fristoe; Distiller, A. N. Feagans; General Merchants: Ogden & Feagans, A. J. Padgett, M. D. Ray & Son, J. T. Woods; Hotel: A. J. Padgett; Mills – Corn and Flour: Ogden and Feagans, W. N. Seay, Snow Flake, S. F. Turner & Bro.; Mills – Saw: Lewis Burford & Co., John N. Eubank, W. N. Seay; Millwright, W. N. Seay; Physicians: M. L. Berry, G. D. Meriweather; Saddler and Harness Maker, W. H. Tucker; Schools and Academies, J. P. Lawrence; Tanner, W. H. Tucker; Undertaker, W. N. Seay.
Principal Farmers: R. H. Brown, W. L. Brown, W. C. Bibb, I. R. Bibb, G. J. Burford, S. C. Caldwell, B. R. Caldwell, W. F. Carter, Ro. Caufield, John Dud Davis, John Dan Davis, M. Dameron, Z. Dameron, R. N. Ellis, John E. Ellis, R. H. Eubank, John N. Eubank, W. H. Feagans, J. T. Feagans, H. Fourqurean, W. W. Foster, G. W. Foster, Jo Hamner, Julius Hamner, O. P. Jones, John H. Jones, P. C. Jones, J. E. Jennings, Jno. A. Jennings, M. W. Jennings, L. Minor, A. J. Richeson, L. Phillips, Silas Ogden, S. B. Dabney, Jas. Williams, John W. Pleasants, Thomas Caldwell, James T. Woods, James Martin Jr., James A. Bailey, James H. Woods, Dr. Robert Dabney, David B. Cheatwood, William Barrett, Seth Perrow.

PLEASANT VIEW: General Merchant: M. C. Harlow.
Principal Farmers: Robert C. Wilcher, M. C. Harlow, Robert Hudson, Parks Rucker.

SALT CREEK: Attorney-at-Law, Daniel Rothel; Dentist, E. W. Scott; Druggists, Charles Buchanan, Robert Thompson; Foundry and Machine Shop: George Wright; General Merchant: Thos. E. Williams; Hotel, D. H. Hawks; Land Agent, R. G. Scott; Mill – Corn and Flour, J. J. Scott; Mill – Saw: R. G. Scott; Millwright, D. W. Wash; Physicians, W. B. Roberts, E. W. Scott.
Principal Farmers: Edw. Fletcher, R. G. Scott, Ambrose C. Rucker, George H. Dameron, W. Tinsley, John J. Old, J. T. Plunket, M. Wright, Clarence Deering {Dearing}, Jane Deering {Dearing}, Mattie Blanchard, David Teese, John Moorman, William R. Terry, John Dameron.

SNOWDEN: Mills – Corn and Flour, W. H. Jordan.
Principal Farmers: C. H. Wood, G. W. Noell, John R. Burks.

DO YOU REMEMBER?

Rural milk delivery?

Dry cleaner and laundry pick up and delivery?

Frozen food lockers? In the 1950s there was just enough space in a refrigerator freezer for a few trays of ice. A business, Blue Ridge Frozen Locker, opened on Kemper Street in Lynchburg. It was located at the site of what is now Lynchburg Transit Company. You could rent different sized locker boxes. They would give you access to a big main freezer room, and then you used your key to get in your individual freezer box. People would freeze sausage and tenderloin instead of canning it. This gave you fresh-tasting meat all the time. They would freeze bacon, but it did not have the flavor of side meat which had been salted down and smoked. After so many people had home freezers, the business closed.

Ice cream packed in dry ice?

Mr. Hubbard's fruit stand and him plugging watermelons to see if they were ripe? He also sold blocks of ice.

Church ice cream socials?

Church watermelon feasts?

Church picnics at Miller Park, Bedford Lake, and Eagle Eyrie?

Making holes in wash tubs with ice picks when chipping pieces off a block of ice to make homemade ice cream?

Turning the crank by hand on the ice cream freezer?

Helping your mother churn butter using a churn with a hand crank?

Hog killing when the weather was cold enough to chill the meat at night?

Seeing the meat salted down to preserve it?

Seeing the meat smoked with hickory wood in the smoke house and leaving the hams and shoulders hanging from the rafters so rats and mice couldn't get to them?

Gathering eggs from nests in the hen house?

Feeding the chickens and encouraging them to go up the roost pole into the hen house at night?

Picking huckleberries (now called blueberries) from the side of the country roads?

Picking blackberries and dewberries from pastures and other places? (Dewberry vines did not have as many thorns, and the berries were not as seedy as blackberries).

Picking wild strawberries? (They were smaller than cultivated strawberries, but much sweeter).

When you were on an eight-party line and heard rings for four parties?

Picking the telephone receiver up to see if the line was busy?

When there were no dials on the telephone so when you picked the telephone up, if the line wasn't busy, the operator would say, "Number please," and then she would connect you to your number if it wasn't busy?

When families had only one vehicle to drive?

When there were no shopping centers?

Shopping in Lynchburg on Main Street, since that was where all the stores were located?

Riding the elevator in stores on Main Street to get from one floor to the other with the operator asking which floor you wanted?

Little conveyors for handling money in department stores?

When sweaters, gloves, blouses, slips and stockings, were kept in boxes and store clerks took items out separately for you to make a selection?

When people looked for matching feed bags to be able to have enough material to sew aprons, dresses, or other items?

Your mother having to fill the electric washing machine with water and after the clothes had washed, running them through the wringer into a big tub of water behind the machine to rinse the clothes. After the clothes had soaked a little while in the rinse water, they were run back through the wringer to get as much water out as possible, and then they were taken outside and hung on a clothes line to dry. If the line was very long, forked limbs were placed to keep the line from sagging and the clothes dragging the ground?

Rural churches baptizing in the river because they didn't have baptistries?

Gas pumps were hand-cranked back to zero?

Gas was $0.30 a gallon?

Automobile inspections were every six months?

Commuter buses between Lynchburg and Amherst via Monroe and Sweet Briar?

No shopping on Sunday?

No fishing or hunting on Sunday?

High School picnics at Bedford Lake and Holliday Lake?

SOME SOURCES OF INFORMATION:

Amherst County Virginia Heritage, Vol. I & II
History of Monroe, Virginia, prepared by the Monroe Home Demonstration Club
Histories of different churches
History of Elon Civic Betterment League
History of Elon Home Demonstration Club
The News & Advance, Lynchburg, Va
Amherst New-Era Progress Bicentennial Edition and other issues
The Southern Railway Road of the Innovators by Burke Davis
The Amherst County Story by Alfred Percy
Passages: A History of Amherst County by Sherrie S. McLeRoy and William R. McLeRoy
More Passages: A New History of Amherst County, Virginia by Sherrie S. McLeRoy and William R. McLeRoy
Monroe United Methodist Church 2003 – Cookbook
Personal interviews with people in communities from 1982 to present
Amherst County Circuit Court Clerk's Office
Campbell County Circuit Court Clerk's Office
Elon Home Demonstration Scrap Book prepared in 1960s
Pedlar Mills Home Demonstration Scrap Book prepared in 1960s
Personal knowledge
Richmond Times-Dispatch
Southern Railroad *Ties* magazine
Jones Memorial Library
The Saga of a City, Lynchburg, Virginia 1786–1936
Lynchburg City Directory – 1883-'84 – Commercial Directory of Lynchburg and Directory of Each Post Office in Amherst, Appomattox, Bedford and Campbell Counties
Lynchburg City Directory – 1885-'86 – Commercial Directory of Lynchburg and a Directory of Each Post Office in Amherst, Appomattox, Bedford and Campbell Counties
CHATAIGNE' S Lynchburg City Directory – 1887-'88 – Contains a General and Business Directory Of the Citizens of Lynchburg also a Complete Business Directory of the Counties of Amherst, Appomattox, Bedford and Campbell also a List of Post Offices of the State of Virginia

INDEX

A

Abbey Aldrich Rockefeller Folk Art Center 130
Abert 147
Abert Ferry 146, 150
Academy 7, 13
Academy Theatre 105
Adams, Erma 189
Adams, Jessie 172
Adams, Mrs. Bill 189
Adcock, George "Buck" 168, 169
Agricola 77, 78, 133, 137, 138, 223
Albemarle Association 15
Albert, Lt. Gen. and Mrs. John 38, 224
Allcock, Gay 98
Allen, Gene 168, 169
Allen, Virginia 97
Allwood 141, 142, 144, 209, 214, 267, 268
Ambler's Mill 162
Amelon 184
American Legion 19, 52, 53, 95
Amherst County Fair 108
Amherst County High School 32
Amherst County Service Authority 76
Amherst drive-in theatre 105
Amherst Elementary 32, 184
Amherst High School 184
Amherst Junior High School 32
Amherst, Lord Jeffery 3
Amherst Presbyterian Church 87
Amiss, Betty Jo 168, 169
Ammonette, Ben 132
Anderson, Betty 190
Anderson, Dude "Eddie Tom" 239
Anderson Jr., Ralph 239
Anderson, Kimberly 32
Anderson, Mrs. Horace 94
Anderson, Nancy 189, 190
Anderson, Pansye Franklin 137
Andes, Jane 32
Andrews, John 237
Andrews, Norma 237
Anthony Rucker 150
Appalachian Power Company 149
Arnold, Jay 96
Arnold, Mr. 7
Aronovitch, Mr. 201
Arthur, Dorothy (Johnson) 211
Austin, Rev. Edward E. 251
Ayers, Douglas 31
Ayers, Julia 122
Ayers, Tommy 30

B

Baber, Jane 122
Bailess, Billy 97, 117, 118
Bailess, Hugh 31
Bailess, Linda 15, 117
Bailess, Melvin 38, 97, 114, 118
Bailess, Mrs. Melvin 118
Bailess, Sharon 15
Bailess, Shelby 15
Bailey, Beulah (Thornton) 265
Bailey, Daniel E. and Judith L. 193
Bailey, Delia (Hill) 264
Bailey, James Andrew 263
Bailey Jr., W. L. 83, 265
Bailey, Kendall 77
Bailey, Ott 219
Bailey School 264
Bailey, Susan 122
Bailey, W. L. 263, 264
Baldree, Robert 168, 169
Ballard, Jean Ogden 98
Ballowe, Frances 39
Ballowe, James 49, 55, 99
Ballowe, Miss Virginia 49
Ballowe, Mrs. Fannie (Shelton) 48
Ballowe, Mrs. Jim 49
Ballowe, Mrs. John 52
Ballowe, Mrs. Willard 49, 50, 52
Ballowe, Ragland 39
Ballowe, Virgie 39
Bank of Monroe 186
Banton, Bonnie 168, 169
Banton, J. T. 168
Barnes, Scott and Judy 204
Barnes, Trooper J. H. 90
Barnes, Will 204
baseball 99
basketball 103
Beard, Charlie 96
Bear Mountain 191
Beasley, Mrs. 188
Belk, Frances 18, 19, 68, 107, 115
Belk, Fritz 19, 43, 53, 85, 86, 87, 92, 114, 115
Belk, Mattie Belle 40, 43, 53, 116
Belk, Sam 34, 35, 43, 60, 62, 74, 114, 115
Bell, Mrs. 186
Bernard, Kevin 30
Berry, Dr. 227
Berry Hill 228
Berry, Mr. 146
Berry, Mr. and Mrs. John 49
Best, Frances 189
Best, Sally 189
Bethany United Methodist Church 155, 161, 162
Bethel 13, 145, 147, 153
Bethell Lock 146
Bethel/Salt Creek 150
Bibb, Alonza 237
Bibb, Buddy 190
Bibb, Captain 220
Bibb, Cephus 237
Bibb, George 237
Bibb, Herman "Bucky" 185
Bibb, Jeffery 202
Bibb, Joseph Radford 237
Bibb, Joshua 237
Bibb, June (Rucker) 27, 88, 94, 96, 116, 167
Bibb, Leticia (Smith) 237
Bibb, Monyeene 88
Bibb's Esso Station 133
Bibb, Victoria 237
Bibb, Wallace 68, 88, 97, 202
Big Island 254, 255
Big Mill 219, 220, 221, 242
Bill's Barn 106
blacksmith shops 220
Blanchard, Mattie 146
Blanks, Dorothy 118
Blount, Richard 168
Blue Ridge Parkway 108
Blunke, Marie 168, 169
Bolton, Hugh 29, 31, 57
Booker, Garland 251
Boonsboro High School 212
Boydoh, Melody 117
Boy Scout troop 39
Bradshaw, Mr. 49
Branch, Garland 163
Branch, Jeanette 117
Brandt, Etta 24, 27
Branham, Carolyn 30
Branham, Darlene 29

Branham, Delia 29
Branham, Dennis 29
Branham, Dwain 28
Branham, Edith 29
Branham, Gail 30
Branham, Herman 29
Branham, Larry 31
Branham, Linda 30
Branham, Marilyn 31
Branham, Marshall 28
Branham, Ray 30
Branham, Ricky 28
Bratton, Mrs. 39
Brightwell's Mill 63
Brizendine, Martha 168
Brizendine, Mrs. 188
Brooks, Becky 98
Brown, Addie 45, 61, 74, 97, 114, 115, 166, 215, 216
Brown, Alma 115
Brown, Ashby 114
Brown, Dot 25, 116
Brown, Earle 239
Brown, Ella 97
Brown, Garne 112
Brown, Helen 115
Brown, Henry 88, 114
Brown, Ila 45, 74
Brown, James M. 19, 21, 25, 94, 95, 96, 97, 102, 107, 108, 166
Brown, Janice 25, 167
Brown, Joyce 25, 167
Brown, Keene C. 138
Brown, Lois 18
Brown, Maggie 40
Brown, Pearl 40, 45, 51, 53, 62, 95, 115
Brown, Shirley 97
Bruner, Mrs. 188
Bryant, Joyce 168
Bryant, Patsy 168, 169
Bryant, Preston 168, 169
Bryant's boarding house 185
Bryant, Winfred 169
Bryant, Winnie 189
Buchanan, Charles 146
Buck's Place 104
Buffalo Springs 140
Buffalo Springs Hotel 139, 140
Buffalo Springs Turnpike 139, 140, 209, 229, 243, 244
Bumgarner, Ardie 32
Buncher Rail Car Co. 212
Bunts, Annie Laurie 130
Burch, Bill 88

Burch, Deborah 29
Burch, Ed 88, 94
Burch, Edward "Big Boy" 239
Burch, Ernest 88
Burch, Eva 40, 95
Burch, Helen 88
Burch, Jimmy 31
Burch, Lena 19, 115
Burch, Lois 21, 115
Burch, Marilyn 21, 115
Burch, Tom 19, 62, 115
Burch, William (Bill) 87
Burch, W. W. and Bessie V. 154
Burford 151, 152, 173
Burford, A. L. 152
Burford, Aubrey 70
Burford, Billy 19
Burford, Bob 97
Burford, Calvin 19, 21, 25, 67
Burford, Carrie 21, 22, 45
Burford, Charlotte 115
Burford, Dameron 263
Burford, Eddie and Shelby 263
Burford, Edith 95
Burford, Emma Grey Jennings 83, 198
Burford, Frank 87, 88, 205
Burford, George 19, 87, 88
Burford, H. M. 85, 87
Burford, Hon. W. D. 84
Burford house 44
Burford, Jack 263
Burford, Mallie Dameron 263
Burford, Marshall 19
Burford, Rosalie 168
Burford, Ross 49, 70
Burford, Russell 154
Burford, Sam 53, 97
Burford, S. L. 152
Burford, Sylvester M. 151
Burford, Tommy vi, 110, 154, 155
Burford, William "Bill" 218
Burford, Willie 45, 74, 115, 216
Burford's Chapel 151, 182, 184
Burford's Mill 151
Burford's Station 151, 199
Burks, Cabell 239
Burks, Cecil 239
Burks Jr., Frank 239
Burks, Marie 239
Burks, Mrs. 188
Burton, Mary Katherine 122
Burton, Mr. Selvy 243
Butcher, Rev. R. G. 182
Byrd, Senator Harry 204

C

Cabellsville 3
Cabin on Triple Oaks Farm 131
Caldwell, Basil "Babe" 85
Caldwell, Buck 168
Caldwell, Sherman 54, 85, 97, 110, 112
Caldwell, Sherwood 169
Camden, A. J. 83
Camden and Younger 41, 68, 74, 111, 165, 166, 215
Camden, Bernard H. 6, 7, 26, 43, 44, 45, 59, 60, 61, 62, 63, 68, 74, 76, 83, 84, 90, 91, 95, 112, 114, 115, 116, 199, 214, 216, 217, 240
Camden, Bob 62
Camden, Buddy 88, 97
Camden, Charles Waidwich 53
Camden, Charlie 61, 71, 88, 97
Camden, Charlie and Margaret 104
Camden, Dewey 44
Camden, Hon. B. Frank 84
Camden, Hon. Jordan 84
Camden house 43
Camden, H. P. 44, 55, 56, 59, 60, 99, 112
Camden, John 44
Camden, Lois 52
Camden, Margaret 88, 97
Camden, Mary 59, 68, 95
Camden, Mildred 114, 216
Camden, "Miss Cutie" 88, 115
Camden, Mrs. Bernard 116
Camden, Robert 44
Camden, Sam 125
Camden Store 59
Camden, Todd 144
Camden, Virginia (Rhodes) 43, 44
Camden, Wade and Martha 248
Camille 226
Camm, John Jr. 47
Camm, Rev. John 47
Campbell, A. N. (Abe) 153, 154
Campbell, Angela 28
Campbell, B. Clark 84
Campbell, Dorothy 249
Campbell, Eleanor v
Campbell, Faye 30, 31
Campbell, Flora 25
Campbell, Glen 68, 241
Campbell, Glenda 28
Campbell, Gwen 31, 53, 118
Campbell, Hazel and O. D. 90

Campbell, Irene 239
Campbell, Margaret 26
Campbell, Maynard 132
Campbell, Mrs. R. T. 29
Campbell, Myrtle 168, 169
Campbell, Paul 190
Campbell, Rev. Eugene C. 16, 17, 118
Campbell, Vicky 29, 117
Candler, Odell (Hudson) 249
Carper, Bill 220
Carrington III, Richard A. 155
Carrington, Roy 132
Carroll, Helen Jean 97
Carson, Debbie 29
Carson, Dorothy 168, 169
Carson, Earl 101
Carson, Teresa 28
Carter, Annie 237
Carter, Mrs. Champ 223
Carter, Sammy 237
Carter, Tom 237
Carter, Walter 90
Carter, W. H. 84
Carver, Ervin 114
Cash, Ernest 185
Cash, Janie 189
Cash, Jimmie 83
Cash, Lloyd 168, 169
Cash, Pam 30, 31
Cash, Richard 168
Cash's Mill 162
Cash Sr., Marvin S. 162
Cash, T. W. 84
Cash, William 162
Cassidy, Betty 44
Catlette, Nat 132
Caufield, Nancy 239
Cedar Gate Farm 153, 154
cement kilns 257
Centenary Methodist 161
Chaplin, Dwayne 57
Cheatwood Farm 137
Chesapeake & Ohio Railroad 207
Chestnut Grove Baptist Church 157, 158
Chestnut Grove School 158
Christian, Elizabeth 122
Circle View Farm 138
Civilian Conservation Corps 214, 236, 255
Civil War 119, 173
Clark, David 30
Clark, Margaret 239
Clarkson, Barbara 97

Clarkson, Barry 29, 57
Clements, Clyde 166
Cloudcroft 138
Cloverdale 47
Cobb, Kate 128
Cocke, Thomas 145
Coffey, Betty Jean 19, 21, 25, 115
Coffey, Carolena (Mays) 71
Coffey, Demarest 85
Coffey, Early 114, 135
Coffey, Frank 84
Coffey, Freddie 168
Coffey, Glen 19, 85, 87, 114, 115
Coffey, Helen 11
Coffey, Hiter 84
Coffey, Joyce 168, 169
Coffey, Marshall 88
Coffey, Mrs. Early 115
Coffey, Mrs. Marshall 88
Coffey, Ray 97
Coffey, Robert 71
Coffey, Rufus 19, 115
Coffey, Sandra 97
Coffey, Talmadge 53, 71
Coleman, Alfred and Rebecca 45
Coleman, Aubrey and Lilly Taylor 197
Coleman, Leah 30, 31
Coleman, Mrs. V. A. 29
Coleman, Regina 117
Coleman, René 16
Coleman, Richard 230
Coleman, Virgil 28, 96
Coles, Betty 29
Coles, David 31
community spring 22
Connelly, Audrey 190
Connelly, Beth 16
Connelly, Cheryl 29, 117
Connelly, Danny 31
Connelly, Greg 30, 57
Connelly, Helen v
Connelly, Shirley 190
Conner, E. R. 173
Coolwell 173
Cooper, Jerome 168, 169
Cooper, Lawrence 168
C & O Railway 253, 258
Cornerstone 15, 238, 241
Correll, Aileen 116
Correll, Ann and Spence v, 76
Correll, Ann (Younger) 206
Correll, Spence 97, 114
Country Corner Market 67
courthouse 4

Cowherd, Rev. K. 7, 17
Cox, Miss Lucille 84
Cox, Mrs. 49
Craddock, John 132
Craven, Donnie 96
Craven, Janet 168, 169
Crawford, Dr. Lucy 84
Crawford, John 84
Crawford, Mr. 49
Creasey, George 169
Creasy, Miss Atala 49
Crews, David 29
Crews, Yevonne 31
Crist, Dorothy 239
Crist, Lena Belle 39, 42
Crist, Mayo 97
Crist, Mr. 245
Crist, Mr. Tallifero 49
Crist/Thomas house 42
Cronin, Edna Jackson 183
croquet 103
Cross, Will 237
CSX railroad 257
Curd, Dewey 190
Curd, Shirley 169, 190
C & Y Service Station 63, 64, 107, 111

D

Dameron, Alpha 19, 39
Dameron, Charles 51
Dameron, C. W. 49
Dameron, George H. 146
Dameron, John 146
Dameron, Miss Alpha 21, 22
Dameron, Mr. 6, 50
Dameron, Mrs. Charles 49, 52
Dameron, Mrs. George H. 119
Dameron, Will 119
Danville Prisoner of War Branch 89
Daura Gallery 130
Davenport, Rev. C. J. 251
Dave, Ronald 98
Davidson, Ben 219
Davies family 146
Davies, Henry Landon 145
Davies' Lower Ferry 145
Davies, Nicholas 145
Davis, Ashby 84
Davis, Carl Ray 15, 117
Davis, Charlie 85
Davis, Col. J. D. 222, 224
Davis, Corinne B. 138
Davis, Donald 50
Davis, Dottie 117

Davis, Ed 84
Davis, Elizabeth 239
Davis, Evelyn 168
Davis family 138
Davis, Freda 15, 117
Davis home 224
Davis, Isham 197
Davis, Jack 259, 261
Davis, James 168
Davis, James W. 83
Davis, James Wood 138
Davis, Jane 16
Davis, Jimmy 28
Davis, John Dudley 239
Davis, Kim 28, 117
Davis, Laura 16
Davis, Lena 237
Davis, Miss 8, 50
Davis, Mr. 9
Davis, Mrs. Joe 237
Davis, Mrs. Ruth (Woods) 196
Davis, Nannie 237
Davis, Nathaniel 197, 198
Davis, Pauline 239
Davis, Pembroke 94
Davis, Percy 261
Davis, Ray 117
Davis, Rev. Bailey F. 1
Davis, Rhonda 15, 97, 170
Davis, Robert 198
Davis, Ronnie 30
Davis, Ruth Wood 138
Davis, Sam 16
Davis, Tom 237
Davis, Warren and Eleanor 141
Dawson, Ethel 21, 115
Dawson, Mrs. Walter 116
Dawson, Rebecca 97
Dawson, Walter 62, 202
Day, Hunter 49
Day, Rev. S. S. 87
Dean, Shirley 168
Dearing, Alfred 153
Dearing, Clarence 146
Dearing, Jane 146
Dearing, William 34
Deekens, Dr. Arthur 47
Deekens, Mrs. A. H. 49
deer hunting 102
Delancey, David 15
DeLancey, Rebecca 15
Dews, Mack 168
Dillard, David Hugh 35, 36, 43, 45, 46, 83, 101, 110, 121, 130, 134, 199

Dillard, Elizabeth 88
Dillard, Ella 36, 37, 122, 123, 158, 246
Dillard Fine Arts Center 130
Dillard, James Spotswood 129
Dillard, Jean 114
Dillard, John v, 36, 37
Dillard, Leonora Rosa van Gelder 35, 121, 130
Dillard, Margaret 18, 212
Dillard, Mrs. D. D. 30
Dillard, Mrs. James 49
Dillard, Mrs. John 39, 49, 52, 88
Dillard Paper Co. 121
distillery 220
Dobyns, Bruce and Rosa 45
Dodd, A. B. and Winnie 42
Dodd, Arthur 230, 231
Dodd, Baylor 230
Dodd, Dellia (Bibb) 237
Dodd, Everett 239
Dodd, Gladys 62, 63, 64, 85, 115
Dodd's Service Station 64
Dodd, Will 62, 64, 114
Dodd, Winnie 115
Donigan, Edward 29
Donigan, Evelyn 30
Donigan, Everett 29
Douglas, Betty 32
Doug MacLeod 253
drag hunts 101
Drake, Charlie 203
Drumheller, Jimmy 176
Drumheller, L. F. 84
Drummond, Camm 84
Duff, Burgess 54
Duff, Eleanor 114
Duff, Glenn 29
Duff, Harry 50
Duff, Lois Jean 30
Duff, Mrs. 95
Duffield, Suzanne 98
Dunne, Rosemary 4

E

East, Mrs. 168
Echlebaum, Bobby 122
Echols, Capt. Edward 258
Echols, John C. 258
Edgewood 233
Edmunds, Billy Wilson 132
Edmunds, Easley 130
Edwards, Rev. Jonathan 20
Eggleston, Darlene 31
Eggleston, Joan 25

El Bethel Church 143, 144
El Bethel Community Association 143
Elder, Frances 9
Eley, Addie 28
Ellington, Rev. R. P. 17
Elliott, Dossie 16, 118
Elliott, Pete 118
Elliott, Rev. S. W. 17
Ellis, Captain Charles 229
Ellis, Charles and Josiah 245
Ellis, Charles I. 197
Ellis, Col. Charles 34
Ellis family 228
Ellis, Jane 34
Ellis, John and Richard 225
Ellis Sr., Josiah 197
Elon 5, 6, 7, 8, 9, 10, 11, 13, 35, 37, 40, 41, 43, 44, 45, 68, 69, 73, 76, 77, 95, 109, 121, 130, 133, 140, 154, 163, 184, 212, 215, 225, 238, 241, 244, 268
Elon Baptist Church 7, 15, 17, 22, 34, 52, 75, 241
Elon branch Monelison Fire Department 54
Elon Civic Betterment League 49, 50, 51, 58, 93
Elon Community Pool 53, 103
Elon Elementary 165
Elon Elementary and High School 24
Elon Elementary School 19, 23, 27, 32, 110, 212
Elon High School 9
Elon Home Demonstration Club 52, 206
Elon Home Demonstration Scrap Book 59
Elon Library 50, 52
Elon Militia 84, 86, 92
Elon Post Office 7, 45, 62, 67, 77, 154
Elon Presbyterian Church 13, 16, 17, 18, 20, 21, 23, 39, 42, 52, 77, 87, 191
Elon Ruritan Club 52, 54
Elon School 32, 74, 87, 103, 133, 167
Elon Self Service Market 66
Elon Village Library 51, 104
Elon Water Works 75
Emerson, Henry 27
Emurian, Rev. E. K. 87, 88
Ernest, Marion 83
Eubank, Claude Melvin 53

Eubank, Dorothy 211
Eubank, Jimmy 240
Eubank, John P. 222
Eubank, Kelly 16
Eubank, Lisa 16
Eubank, Opal 16, 118
Eubank, Roy 84
Eubank, Sally 238
Eubanks, Bob 243
Eubank, Shirley 239
Eubanks, John Nick 243
Eubanks' Mill 243
Eubanks, Sallie 189
Eubanks, T. 189
Eubank, W. T. "Tucker" 89, 100
Evans, Sam 258
Ewers, Arnold 168
Ewers, B. H. 153
Ewers, George 62
Ewers, Harry 50
Ewers, Mrs. George 39, 49, 52
Ewers, Ned 49, 54
Ewers, Robey 115, 118
Ewers, Stephen 110

F

Fairfax, Judith S. 45
Fairfax, R. Cary 45
Falwell, Calvin 109
Falwell, Jerry 154
Fauber Funeral Home 68
Fauber Jr., J. Everette 35
Faulconerville 76
Faust, Tommy 57
Feagans, Armstead 220
Fenimore House Museum 130
Ferguson, Jeff 28
Ferguson, Tracy 29
Ferry boat 208
Fifer, David 30
First Baptist Church of Monroe 181
fishing 103
Fletcher, Edward 13, 146
Fletcher, Frank 37
Fletcher, Mr. and Mrs. Frank 36
Fletcher, Ned 6, 37, 158
Flippin family 155
Flowers, Bobby 32
Floyd, Barbara 189, 190
Floyd, Frank C. 194
Floyd, Frank L. and Ruth 251
Floyd Jr., R. D. 188
Floyd, Maggie (Brown) 206
Floyd, Preston 188
Floyd, R. Don 187, 188

Floyd, Robert v, 109, 155
Floyd, Shelby v, 168, 189
Floyd, Shirley 168, 169
Floyd's Store 194, 251
Folkers, Carolyn 138
Forbes, Miss Nettie 248
Ford, J. C. 184
Forks of Buffalo 139, 221
Fort Early Theatre 105
Foster, Addie 40, 115
Foster, Bill 100
Foster, Bonnie 31
Foster, Broadus 53, 85, 86, 87, 88,
    92, 97, 114, 116, 118
Foster, Carolyn 16
Foster, Cecil 15, 16, 52, 118
Foster, Connie 16, 57, 117, 118
Foster, Debbie 16
Foster, Debrell 31
Foster, Doris v, 16, 65, 117, 118
Foster, Earl 243
Foster, Ed 233
Foster, Eddie 30, 31
Foster, Edith 15, 16, 115
Foster, Eleanor 11, 18, 166
Foster, Elmer 85, 88, 96, 109
Foster family 12
Foster, Florence 11, 15, 21, 25, 27,
    81, 97, 108, 118, 169
Foster, George 243
Foster, Gordon 11, 25, 108, 116,
    166, 242
Foster, Helen 15, 27, 108
Foster, James 11, 53, 79, 88, 118,
    238, 239
Foster, Jimmy 63, 65, 66
Foster, Joe and Lois 70
Foster, Joshua Lyle 53
Foster Jr., Talmadge 15, 108, 117,
    133
Foster, Judy 16
Foster, Leigh 72
Foster, Linda 15, 98, 117, 134
Foster, Lois v, 71, 117, 118
Foster, Lyle 11, 96, 100, 101, 102,
    111, 154
Foster, Lyle and Massie 11, 12
Foster, Marshall 83, 225, 226
Foster, Mary 15, 16, 53, 88, 94,
    95, 114, 117
Foster, Mary and Broadus 113, 134
Foster, Mr. and Mrs. Ed 45
Foster, Mrs. Addie 53, 88
Foster, Mrs. Lyle 11, 22, 79, 117
Foster, Mrs. Marshall 222

Foster, Nancy 29, 117
Foster, Owen 239
Foster, Ralph 65, 66, 97
Foster, Ray 30, 57
Foster, Ronnie 15, 117
Foster, Russell 114
Foster, Ruth v, 116, 238
Foster, Sallie Walthall 197
Foster, Sue 30
Foster, Talmadge and Florence
    (Horton) 110
Foster, Tom 46, 205
Foster, Tommy Joe 15, 117
Foster, Will 70, 197
Foster, William Leigh 72
Foster, William Massie 53
fox hunting 100
Franklin, Annie Mae 189
Franklin, B. C. 219
Franklin, Burks and Grace 138
Franklin, Edward 239
Franklin, Hesper 239
Franklin, Margaret 168
Franklin, Nellie 244, 245
Franklin, Rachael 239
Franklin, Robert 239
Franklin, Russell 97, 170
Franklin's Store 138, 244
Franklin, Warren 239
Freeman, David 29
Freeman family 34
Freeman, Rose 28
French, Dan E. 76
Fulcher, Tyler 17, 24, 27, 89, 167,
    212

G

Gaines, Mrs. Tom 189
Gallagher, Joe 168, 169
Gallo, Betty 169
Galts Mill 162
games 107
Garland, M. H. 13
Garrett, Betty 25, 26, 27, 168, 169
Garrett, Helen 249
Garrett, John 31
Garrett, Lisa 28
Garrett, Lucille 249
Garrett, Marie 25
Garrett, Reuben 87
Garrett, Reuben S. 249
Garrett, Stanley 30
G. A.'s 16
Gatewood house 240

Gatewood, Marshall P. 237, 240, 241
Gatewood, Mrs. Marshall P. 237, 240
Gatewood, Ruby 237
General Electric 128
Gerhardt, Anne 122
German Prisoners 89
Gibbs, Leah Settle 266
Gilbert, Wanda 254
Gillispie, Carlton "Buddy" 225
Gillispie, Carrington 219, 229
Gillispie, Charles "Buck" 168, 169
Gillispie, Eleanor 229
Gilmer, Rev. Graham 114
Girling, Lorriane Shiels 34, 201
Girling, Mary "Mae" 201
Girling, Philip 201, 203
Girling, Phillip and Mary (Mae) 34
Girling, Rowland Lea 34, 201
G. J. Thomas & Sons 67
Glasgow 257, 258
Glass, Carter 154
Goad, Rev. T. E. 17
Goff, Gene 168, 169
Goff, Paul 168, 169
Gold, Dr. Marvin C. 17
Gorrell, Donald 188
Gowen, Bernard 15
Gowen, Betty 97
Gowen, Edith 118
Gowen, Ellen 16, 118
Gowen, Nancy 97
Gowen, Sanford 87
Graham Creek Reservoir 76
Grant, Charles 239
Grant, Essie 239
Grant, Mrs. Abner 49
Graybeal, Ida Gwynn 190
Great Oaks Estate 45
Green, Delores 15
Green, Nancy 117
Grekos, Paul 84
Grubbs, Mr. 6
Grubbs, Mrs. 45
Guggenheimer Jr., Max 64
Guggenheimer, Max 44, 60, 62, 63, 74, 77, 111
Guthrie, Fred 132

H

Hall, Cheryl 29
Hall, Rebecca 31
Halsey, Liza 171
Hamilton, Donna 28
Hamilton, Evelyn 239
Hamilton, Norma Jean 29
Hannon, Dr. John 161
Hans Hill 130
Harding, Mr. 6
Harding, W. O. 17
Harlow, Mr. 240
Harlow, Robert 237
Harper, Joan 168, 169
Harper, Mr. and Mrs. W. W. 171
Harper, Owen 122
Harper, Richard 172
Harper, Teddy 122
Harris, Bennett 141, 214, 218
Harris, Betty 18, 166, 167
Harris, Bob 216
Harris, Eva 40, 115
Harris, Fred 96
Harris, Kathy 30
Harris, Marie 115
Harris, Marilyn Burch vi
Harris, Melanie 31
Harris, Naomi 239
Harris, Ned 18
Harris, Nina 25
Harrison, Miss Caroline 49
Harrison, Randolph 132
Harrison, The 105
Harris, Ruth 11, 115, 239
Harris, Sadie 40, 43, 44, 51, 141
Harris, Sara 117
Harris, Susan 28
Harris, Wayne 29, 57
Harvey, Dorothy (Kent) 161
Harvey's Drive-In 105
Haskins, Dunbar 122
Haskins, Lloyd 122
Hatcher, Mrs. T. T. 84
Hawkins, Miss 8
Hawkins, Willie Anne (Bibb) 237
Hawks, D. H. 146
Haywood Plantation Home 223, 224
Henderson, Mr. 144
Henry L. Lanum Jr. Water Filtration Plant 75
Hercules Corporation 255
Hicks, Annie Mae 169
Hicks, Benny 190
Hicks, Glen 84
Hicks, Hazel 39
Hicks Jr., Ted W. 114
Hicks, Lillian 21, 22, 40, 65, 116
Hicks, Littleberry 189, 190
Hicks, Miss Virgie 52
Hicks, Mrs. T. W. (Edna Ballowe) 48, 49, 50, 52, 88, 89, 115
Hicks, Mr. W. M. "Will" 46, 64, 65, 68, 74, 114
Hicks, Nelson 84
Hicks, Seth 83, 186
Hick's Store 64
Hicks, T. W. 48, 50, 62, 88, 89, 97, 98, 114, 115
Hicks, Wallace 88
Higginbotham 167
Higginbotham, Carl 26
Higginbotham, Cecil 25
Higginbotham, J. H. 84
Higginbotham, Lewis 114
High Peak Road 159, 160, 161, 162
Hill, Alicia 28
Hill, Danny 29
Hill, Emma 237
Hill, Lucy 237
Hill, Munsey 83
Hill, Tommy 29
Hite, Thornton 84
Hobbs, Joe 150
Hodges, Mrs. James A. 94
Hodges, Robert 96
Hodnett, Debbie 30, 31
Hodnett, Rhonda 31
Holcomb Rock 212
Hollins Mill 152
Hollins Mill Drive-In 106
Homewood Farms 13, 35, 36, 38, 54, 77, 121, 122, 123, 134, 158, 199
Horsley, Carolyn 21, 25, 70, 97, 116, 168
Horsley Jr., Abbitt v, 85
Horsley, Ruth 107
Horsley Sr., Abbitt 118
Horton 212
Horton, Arlene 19
Horton, Billy 85, 86
Horton, Cathlene 19, 115, 166
Horton, Frank 88
Horton, Harry and Mary 62
Horton, Harry Wayne 18, 53, 86, 94, 96
Horton, Henry 114
Horton, Jim 112
Horton, Madeline 19
Horton, Mrs. 88
Hot Springs 139
Howard, June v
Howell, Mrs. J. V. 84
Hudson, Ed 6, 186

Hudson, Edith 166
Hudson, E. F. 146
Hudson, Frances 19
Hudson, Frank 59
Hudson, Hope 84
Hudson, Howard and Rosemary 67, 130
Hudson, Irene 239
Hudson, Lena 115
Hudson, Luke 30
Hudson, Lydia 168
Hudson, Mr. 7
Hudson, Mrs. Martha 83
Hudson, Nannie Mae 239
Hudson, Val 198
Hudson, Walker 84
Hudson, W. E. 59
Huffman, Garland v, 96
Huffman, Jackie 28, 117
Huffman, J. B. 234
Hume, Edward 57
Hume, Mrs. 188
Humphreys, Gail 28
Humphries, Archie and Vernell 155
Humphries, Chancer 29
Humphries, Cynthia 16
Humphries, Darlene 30
Humphries, Landon 85
Humphries, Leroy and Brenda 154
Hundley, Isabel Wallace C. 229
Hunt Club 45, 74, 102
Hunt Club Subdivision 43, 45, 46
Hyatt, Col. John W. 22, 230

I

Indian Mission 191, 192
Inge, Doug 117
Inge, Douglas 15
Inge, Frank 179
Inge, O. B. 189
Inge, "Sissy" 15, 117
Irvin, Rev. E. D. 251
Isis 105
Ivey, Ed 132
Ivy Hill Baptist Church 195
Ivy Hill School 196

J

Jackson, Mrs. George 39
James River and Kanawha Canal 146, 255, 258
James River Post Office 7
James River Steel Manufacturing and Mining Company 212

Jennings, Arlene (Brown) 206
Jennings, Billy 239
Jennings, David 230
Jennings, Dolly 239
Jennings, Doris 168, 169
Jennings, Harold 96, 114
Jennings, John W. 198
Jennings, Lloyd and Vickie 134
Jennings, Wilma 97
jitney bus 242
John Lynch Memorial Bridge 252
Johns, Danny 30
Johns, David 28
Johns, Jerry 31
Johnson, Bernard 242
Johnson, Billy 118
Johnson, Claudine 239
Johnson, Frances 239
Johnson, "Horse" 215
Johnson Jr., Billy 16
Johnson, Nancy 25, 168, 190
Johnson, Odell 239
Johns, Rillie 31
Johns, Roy 28
Jolley, Rev. Charles 17
Jones, Fay 30
Jones, Mrs. 34
Jones, Sharon 29
Jones, Will 83
jousting tournament 100

K

Kaiden, Mr. 134
Keaton, Mr. 6
Keefer, Barbara 122
Keefer, Verne 122
Keith, Chapman 216
Keith, Dr. 227
Keith family 137
Keith, Harry 44
Keith, Helen (Coffey) 238
Keith, Lewis 44, 94
Keith, Mrs. Lewis 215
Keith, Mrs. Tilden 49
Keith, Tilden 62
Kelley, J. J. 175
Kennedy, Rev. J. Renwick 20
Kessler, Judy 122
Kessler, Mr. 201
Kidd, Mary Lou 168
Killey Kranky Farm 36, 37, 158
King, Donald 28
King, Douglas 28
King, Mary 237
King, Mike 30

King, Mr. 30
King, Naomi 115
King, Richard 31
Kinner, Freeland 132
Kirkwood, Rev. 17
Knight, Mayo 30, 31, 57
Knight, Tucker 122
Knoll 78, 243
Knowles, Rev. Joe 17
Kuhn, Rev. Harold V. 20
Kyle, Moses Bennett 255
Kyle, Winfield Nelms 255

L

Ladd, Mrs. 86, 99
Ladies Aid Society 18
Lamb, Carey 214, 217
Lamb, Rev. E. E. 17, 242
Langhorne, D. A. 132
Langley, Buddy 116
Langley, Carol 15, 117
Langley, Glenna 116
Langley, Ruth 116
Laughon, Rev. T. G. 84
Laurel Cliff 153, 154, 155
Lavino, E. J. 212
Lawrence, J. P. 222
Lawrence Trucking Company 105
Lawrence, Walter 222
Layne, Billy 88, 115
Layne, Johnny 21, 25, 26
Layne, Kenneth "Bibbie" 168, 169
Layne, Lois 21, 25
Layne, Mrs. Nannie 15
Layne, Randall P. 16, 17, 116
Layne, Warren 87
Lea, Phyllis 51, 52, 102, 116
Lea, Rowland 34, 49, 50, 83, 94, 201
Lea, Theadora 34, 49, 50, 52, 94
Leggett, Billy 122
Lendy's Big Boy drive-in 106
Lewis, Edward 230
Lewis, Florence 25
Lewis, Mrs. Guy 22, 40, 115, 116
Liberty University 154
Litchford, Jack 18, 53, 85, 87, 97, 166
Litchford, Margie 18, 95, 115
Little Elmo's Place 105
Livesay, Mrs. Lillian 84
Lloyd family 246
Long, Armistead 132
Long, John C. 163
Long, Miss Fannie 130

Long, Miss Sallie 49
Long, Mrs. John 49, 132
Long's Mill 163, 164
Loop, Mrs. 27
Love, Mr. 251
Loving, Ann 116
Loving, Celia 168, 169, 189
Loving, Daniel 53, 88, 97
Loving, Daryl 31
Loving, Dorothy 19, 88, 115
Loving, Elmer 96
Loving, Elmer and Ann 71
Loving, Greg 30
Loving, Helen Jean 19, 21, 25, 115
Loving Jr., Elmer 53, 85, 86, 87, 88, 92, 94, 114, 205
Loving Jr., Mrs. Elmer 94, 205
Loving, Lewis 71, 85
Loving, Marita 115
Loving, Percy 92, 114, 115, 205
Loving, Robley 19, 21, 25, 96
Loving, Shirley 19, 115
Loving Sr., Elmer 85, 92, 114, 115
Loving Sr., Mrs. Elmer (Helen) 205
Lovingston Baptist Church 251
Loving, Sylvia 21, 97, 115
Loving, Vera 21, 97, 115
Loving, Vicky 29
Loyd, Frank Stone 154, 155
Lynchburg 101, 155, 163, 173
Lynchburg and Buffalo Springs Turnpike 227
Lynchburg Baptist Association 15
Lynchburg–Buffalo Springs Turnpike Company 140
Lynchburg College 121

M

MacLeod, Douglas 212
Maddox, Gladys 239
Maddox, Hazel 169
Maddox, Hilton 168, 189
Madison 145
Madison Heights 7, 67, 77, 78, 184
Madison Heights Baptist Church 117
Madison Heights Elementary 165
Madison Heights High School 24, 165, 167, 169, 184
Madison Heights Methodist Church 87
Madison Heights Negro School 158
Madison Heights Sanitary District Utilities 76
Magann, Rev. Talmadge 17
Malige family 246

Manley, Thomas 168, 169
Mann, Jackie v
Manse 204
Marion, Nancy v, vi
Marks, Mary 117
Martin, Ann 122
Martin, Catherine 116
Martin, Claude 40
Martin, Jack 99
Martin Jr., Walter P. 53
Martin, Margaret 97
Martin's Store 105
Martin, Valarie 16
Martin, W. P. 166
Mason, Billy 30
Mason, Calvin v
Mason, Dot 98, 117
Mason, Earl 87, 114
Mason, Joe 87, 115
Mason, Joyce (Coffey) 71
Mason, Mr. and Mrs. Joe 46
Mason, Mrs. 52
Mason, Mrs. Evelyn 115
Mason, Tommy 28
Massey, Dewey 230
Massie, Ann 98
Massie, Barbara 16, 57
Massie, David 31
Massie, Debbie 117
Massie, Emma 110
Massie, Homer 168
Massie, Ira, I. D. and Homer 205
Massie, Maggie 117
Massie, Mr. 13
Massie, Randy 57
Massie, Tommy 117
Massie, William 239
Matthews, William 258
Mayes, Rev. Walter 17
Mayo, R. C. 179
Mays, David 29
Mays, Don 31
Mays, Dr. M. D. 196
Mays, Earnest 25
Mays, E. H. 83
Mays, H. P. 84
Mays, Jimmy 30
Mays, John H. 83
Mays, Johnny 28
Mays, Kathy 29
Mays, Linda 28
Mays, Marshall 259
Mays, Rev. M. D. 195
Mays, Sharon 31
Mays, Shirley 27

Mays, Theodore 25
Maze, Delores 168, 169
McBryde, Dr. 221
McClarty, James 255
McCollogan, Mr. 258
McConnell, Lynn 29
McConnell, Sonny 87
McCraw, Donald 169
McCraw, Gerry 168, 169
McCraw, W. D. "Bill" 202
McCulloch, Roderick 266
McDaniel, Frances 239
McDonald, Jo Anne 189
McFadden, Beverly 30, 31, 57
McFarland, Mrs. A. W. 49
McGlothlin, Barbara 118
McGlothlin, Gilbert 24, 88, 94
McGuire, Harry 179
McIvor, Carolyn 168, 169, 189
McIvor, C. E. 185, 186
McIvor, Christine 83, 161, 175, 184
McIvor, Christopher 171
McIvor, Gene 179
McIvor, Judson 183, 186
McIvor, Kit 173
McIvor, Mrs. 188
McIvor, Nancy 111, 189, 190
McIvor Station 153, 171, 173
McLeRoy, Sherrie and William 145
McPherson, Virginia 169, 170
Meadow, Earl 230
Meeks, Judge Edward 84
Meeks, Miss Dabney 84
Meredith, Rev. Wayne 20
Meriwether, Dr. George Douglas 226
Meriwether, J. A. 194
Merritt family 250
Metzl, Glen 68
Metzl, Margarete 68
Metzl, Mrs. Rudolf 94
Metzl, Robert "Bobby" 68
Metzl, Rudolf 68
Metzl's Barber Shop 68
Midway 15, 238, 241
Miller, Aileen 48, 88, 95, 104, 115
Miller, Jackie 26
Miller, John 242
Miller, Lloyd 53, 88, 114, 115
Miller, Mary Ellen 104
Miller, Mrs. Lloyd 89
Miller, Susan 31
Miller, Susanne 104
Miller, Ted 29
Mills, Bea 188
Mitchell 212, 251

Mitchell, Calvin 84
Mitchell, John 219
Mitchell, Mr. 211
Mitchell's Mill 219
Monacan Indians 150, 192, 199
Monacan Park 34, 146, 149, 150, 153
Monelison Middle School 32
Monroe 76, 78, 109, 155, 172, 173, 174, 176, 184, 254
Monroe Baptist Church 181, 182
Monroe Education Center 184
Monroe Elementary 165, 184
Monroe Home 89
Monroe Presbyterian Church 182
Monroe United Methodist Church 161, 183, 186
Montague-Betts 128
Montrose Fruit Farm 8, 201
Montrose Orchard 201
Montview 154, 155
Moore, Catherine v
Moore, Dorothy 5, 10, 24, 39, 59
Moore, Mrs. James 49
Moore, Ola 39, 52
Moore, Zelma 39
Moorman, John 146
Morris, Alex 36, 115, 205
Morris and Camden 6
Morris, Annie 40, 41, 115
Morris, Blanche 237
Morris, Bob vi, 19, 85, 86, 97, 115, 135, 166, 204
Morris, Bobby and Eleanor 62
Morris, Charles Houston 53
Morris, Clara 40
Morris, Doris 18, 19, 42, 88, 167
Morris, Earl 41, 69, 74, 85, 86, 133, 205
Morris, Ethel 189
Morris Filling Station 69
Morris, Frances 18, 19, 22, 42, 65, 112, 166
Morris, Harry 84
Morris, Herbert Thomas 87
Morris, Houston 85, 88, 92, 94, 96, 102, 114, 115
Morris, Jenny 115
Morris Jr., Earl G. 41, 53, 60, 62, 87, 88, 94, 97, 114
Morris, Lena 204
Morris, Margaret 5, 24, 39
Morris, Mrs. Alex 116
Morris, Mrs. O. P. 49, 52

Morris, Nancy 19, 21, 65, 108, 112, 115, 133
Morris, O. P. 6, 13, 39, 44, 60, 62, 64, 65, 73, 74
Morris, Randolph 54
Morris, Robert P. 41, 114
Morris Sr., Earl 53, 84, 92, 97, 114, 115
Morris, Sue 64
Morris, Vernell 19, 115
Morris, Virginia 19, 21
Morris, William 65, 74, 204, 205
Mosby, Alex 132
Moseley, Althea S. 122
Moser, Chris 57
Moser, Gil 31
Moser, Mark 29
Moss, Bessie 15, 16, 70, 107
Moss, Betty 16
Moss, Charles 87
Moss, Clayton 53, 70, 87, 96
Moss, Daniel 87
Moss, Gerald 87
Moss, Joe 71
Moss, John 87
Moss, Judy 168
Moss, Martha 16, 118
Moss, Mary 16, 118
Moss, Preston 87, 94
Moss, Robert 15, 117
Moss, Wanda 168
Moss, William 53, 87
Mt. Carmel Presbyterian Church 87
Mt. Sinai Baptist Church 136
Mt. Tabor 137, 138, 161
Mt. Tabor United Methodist Church 137
Murphy, Nancy 111
Musselman, Mr. 7, 37, 59
muster ground 222
Myers, Dot 239
Myers, Eddie 139
Myers, Henry S. 198
Myers Jr., Hal 239
Myers, Margaret G. 197, 198
Myers, Mary L. 139

N

Nance, Kathy 32
Naola 78, 194, 195, 197, 212
Nash, Mrs. John 84
Neblett, Jean (Dillard) 33, 36
Neblett, Nancy 168, 169
Nelson, Louis and Helen Loving 138
Newcomb, Pete 168

New Hope Church 182
New Prospect 15, 237, 238, 241
Nichols, Richard "Dick" 168
Nixon, Amy Rodgers 40
Nixon, Dakota 32, 200
Nixon, Drake 32, 200
Nixon, Dylan 32, 200
Nixon family 12
Nixon, Florence 57, 117
Nixon, Holcomb vii, 11, 118, 168, 169, 189
Nixon, Jacqueline 200
Nixon, Jennifer 32, 40
Nixon, Kelly 32, 40
Nixon, Maurice Alan 29, 31, 40, 57, 111, 188
Nixon, Maurice William 40
Nixon, Scott 16, 66, 188, 200
Norberg, Phyllis 168, 169
Norman, Everett 190
Norvell, Owen 109
Nowlin, Helen 22
Nuckles, Jimmy 30
Nuckols, Franklin 190
Nuckols, Marie 168, 169

O

Oakes, Doris 115
Oakes, Esther 88, 115
Oak Grove Church 209, 234
Oak Park Farm 121, 124, 125
Oaks, Five 4
Oaks, The 4
Oblinger, Daisy v, 52, 54, 88, 115, 214
Oblinger, David 88, 215
Odgen, John 97
Ogden, Barbara 26, 27, 118
Ogden, Billy 25, 26, 169
Ogden, Buddy 87
Ogden, Diane 31
Ogden, Dorothy 25
Ogden, Elizabeth v
Ogden, Haywood 88
Ogden, John 87
Ogden, Lori 28
Ogden, Mark 28
Ogden, Mike 30, 57
Ogden, Raymond 87, 97
Ogden, Silas 219
Old, Ada 248
Old, John J. 146
Oliver, Rev. R. A. 17, 87, 88
Orange and Alexandria Railroad 173
Oriskany 212

Overstreet, Ann 190
Owen, Betty Jean 239
Owens, Bob 189
Owens, Helen 189
Owens, Jean 189
Owens, Mrs. 188

P

Padget, Frank 257, 258
Padgett, Albert 220
Page, Ambrose 49, 59, 99, 112
Page, Elmo 5, 24
Page, Mary Lou 5, 24
Panzario, Mrs. Wlliam 94
Paramount 105
Parent Teachers Organization (PTO) 58
Paris, Benny 97
Paris, Frances 118
Paris, John 88
Paris, Mary Due 88
Parkway Restaurant 104
Parr, Mrs. L. V. 84
Pasco 6
Patterson, C. G. 102
Patterson, Hazel 168, 169
Patterson, Mr. 9
Patteson, Marie 84
Pearch 197, 207, 208, 209, 211, 212, 240
Pedlar Dam 213, 214, 218
Pedlar Farm 38, 123, 245, 246
Pedlar Ford Church 17
Pedlar Lake 213, 215
Pedlar Mills 22, 78, 123, 140, 209, 210, 219, 220, 221, 223, 225, 226, 229, 230, 231, 242, 244, 267, 268
Pedlar Valley Circus 223
Pekar, Mrs. 32
Pera 233, 235
Percy, Alfred 53, 84, 85, 89, 132
Percy, Mrs. Alfred 86
Perry, E. V. 45
Peters, Gene 25
Peters, June 26, 27
Peters, Neil 21
Peters, Pete 168, 169
Peters, Ryland 16
Pettyjohn Cemetery 248
Pettyjohn, Jack 168, 169, 189, 190
Pettyjohn, James 250
Pettyjohn, Mary 169
Pettyjohn, Samuel 188
Pettyjohn School 249

Peyton, Mrs. O. I. 175
Peyton's Mill 152
Phelps, Calvin 169
Phillips, Carrie 237
Phillips, Essie 40
Phillips, Glen 237
Phillips, Mrs. Charlie 237
Phillips, Stuart 230
Pick, Brian 28, 57
Pick, Ethel v, 15, 16, 19, 53, 57, 94, 115, 118
Pick, Gary 29, 57
Pick, Walter 15, 117
picnic 107
Piedmont Baptist Association 15, 237
Piney Hill Baptist Church 142
Pixley, Kathryn Spencer v, vi
Planters Tobacco Warehouse 262
Pleasants, Bud 230
Pleasants Chapel 161
Pleasants family 246
Pleasants, George T. 219, 222, 223
Pleasants, Mary 223
Pleasants, Mr. and Mrs. 224
Pleasant View 15, 16, 68, 78, 140, 147, 194, 209, 214, 221, 226, 237, 240, 241, 242, 243, 244, 267, 268
Pleasant View Elementary 165, 238
Pleasant View High School 194, 238, 239
Pleasant View School 144, 230, 243
Plunkett, J. T. 146
Poe, Edgar Allan 230
Poindexter, G. 173
Pollard, Mary Spence 122
Poston, Trueheart 35
Potts 173
Potts, Betsy 122
Potts, Nancy 122
Powell, Elizabeth 47
Powell, Ottie Cline 234
Powell, Rev. and Mrs. E. M. 234
Powell, Tom 233
Prather, Mrs. C. H. 265
Presbyterian Manse 18, 69, 74
Proffitt, Red and Dot 251
PTA 52
Pugh, Bobby 170
Pugh, Harold 168
Purvis, Bob 190
Purvis, Bruce 176
Purvis, Frank 179
Purvis, Mildred v

Purvis, Soule 168, 169

Q

Quality Dairy 125

R

race track 134
Ragland, Shirley 168
Ramey, "Pinky" 98
Ramsey, Carl 99
Ramsey, Charlie 188
Ramsey, Chip 99
Ramsey, Elmer 9
Ramsey, Eunice 189
Ramsey, J. E. 7
Ramsey, Mrs. 188
Ramsey, Perry 188
Ramsey, Rev. R. R. 20
Ranson, Emery 96
Ranson, Tommy 30
Ray, George 221
Ray, Martin 231
Ray, M. D. 220, 221
Ray, Rev. George H. 18, 20
Ray, W. R. "Dick" 231
R. C. Scott and Co. 252
Red Brick Church 13, 15, 17, 19
Red Hill 22, 229, 230
Red Level 48
Reusens 212
Rhodes, Margaret "Maggie" 44
Richerson, W. H. 84
Richeson, Celia v
Ricketts, Bobby 85
Ricketts, Joanne 94, 116
Ricketts, Joanne and Dick 98
Rigsby, Johnny 98
Riley, Audrey 25
Riley, Russell 78
Riley, Shirley 168, 169
Riner, Robert 169
Rivermont Presbyterian Church 21
Riverview 149, 153
Roberts, Lori 28
Robertson, H. Clay 83, 186
Roberts, Sonny 66
Roberts, Virginia 115
Roberts, W. B. 146
Robinson, Goode 122
Roosevelt, Franklin D. 176
Root, Mrs. R. O. 237
Root, Rev. E. R. 17
Root, R. O. 237
Rose, Bernard 202

Rose, William 202
Rose, Yosie 110
Ross, Lisa 117
Ross, O. B. 84, 203
Rous and Hicks Country Store 70
Rowbotham, Agnes (Brown) 211
Rucker 45
Rucker, A. C. 146
Rucker, Ambrose C. 146
Rucker, Anne 30, 31
Rucker, Anthony 150
Rucker, Benjamin 150
Rucker Brothers' Orchard 203
Rucker, Hannon 25, 26, 51, 85, 203, 204
Rucker, Harry 50, 203
Rucker, Harry Clark 30, 31
Rucker, Helen 28, 116
Rucker, June 19, 21, 68, 166
Rucker, Nay 27
Rucker, Parks McDaniel 137
Ruckers' Fruit Farm 153
Rucker, Warner 225
Rucker, Warren 21
Rutledge, Oscar 62
Rutledge, Rebecca (Keith) 62

S

Sale, Mr. and Mrs. Emmett 140
Sales, Charles 30
Sales, Debbie 30
Sales, Eva 237
Sales, Harriette 189, 190
Sales, John Lewis 237
Sales, Robert L. 179
Salmon, Austin 99
Salmon, Bill 99
Salt Creek 6, 145, 146, 147, 148, 157, 221, 267, 268
Sam 258
Sanders, Loretta 168, 169
Sanders, Roger 168
Sandidge, "Dimple" 239
Sandidge, Dr. E. M. 84, 240
Sandidge, Edward Paxton "Pack" 242
Sandidge, F. B. 84
Sandidge, Mrs. Harriet 84
Sandidge, Oneal 31
Sandidge, William E. 53, 84
Sands & Company 174, 176, 185
Sardis 161
Saunders, Gordon 87
Schermaker, Buddy 88
Scott, Angie Woodruff 157

Scott, David P. 153, 154
Scott, Dr. H. Don 153
Scott, Dr. William 197
Scott, Eva Davies 153
Scott, E. W. 146
Scott, Florence 34, 153
Scott Jr., John J. 252
Scott, Mr. 33, 34, 200
Scott, R. C. 252
Scott, R. G. 146
Scott, Rice 54
Scott, Robert "Bob" 149
Scott, Samuel B. 153
Scott, Stuart D. 153
Seeds, Emily Gay 189, 190
Seeds, Jerry 189
Sellick, Jimmy 30
Sellick, Kaye 30, 31
Selvage, Donald 84
Sexton, Freddie 29
Sexton, Gary 31
Sexton, Gerald 29
Sexton, Kathy 31
Sexton, Rita 28
Sexton, Shirley 30
Shaner, Jean 168
Shaner, Stewart 190
Shelter, The 33, 35, 36, 43
Shelton 6
Shelton brothers 34
Shelton, Captain E. L. 48
Shelton, David B. 57
Shelton, Howard 115
Shelton, Major Jack 48
Shelton, Russell 88, 114, 115
Shelton, Sally Bell 48
Shepherd, Ambrose 51, 84, 85, 86, 92, 114, 115, 202, 203
Shepherd, Bea 114
Shepherd, Ed 115
Shepherd, Edwin M. 114
Shepherd, Irene 114, 115, 233
Shepherd, Mrs. Ed 115
Shrader, Hubert 97
Shrader, John T. 84
Shrader, Mr. L. H. 84
Shrader, Thelma 19
Shrader, W. E. 84
Shumaker, Mrs. 15
Sigmon, Annie 40, 200
Sigmon, Becky 16
Sigmon, Catherine 200
Sigmon, Cathy 29
Sigmon, Gene 25
Sigmon, Mr. John 112

Sigmon/Plunk Camden house 74
Sigmon, Robert 25
Sigmon, Ruth 31
Sigmon, Timmy 117
Sigmon, Toppie 23
Simmons, Carl Dewey 114
Simmons, Donnie 169
Simmons, June 168
Singleton, Charles vi, 85
Singleton, Charles William 53
Singleton, Harold 1
Slaughter, Mr. 157
sleigh riding 107
Smiley, Althea 102
Smith, Alvin 107
Smith, Aubrey 54, 115
Smith, Cassie Lee 39
Smith, Cornelia 39
Smith, Daisy 39, 115, 216
Smith, Don 179
Smith, Emmett 242
Smith, Hoge 19, 114
Smith, Jack 54
Smith, Jenny Lind 190
Smith, Judy 29
Smith, Kate 237
Smith, Kenneth 30
Smith, Mac 19
Smith, Margaret 114
Smith, Martha 19
Smith, Mrs. Aubrey 49
Smith, Mrs. Cassie 52
Smith, Ruth 114
Smith, Thelma 107, 163, 164
Smith, Virginia 114
Smoot's grocery store 185
Smyrna 161
Snowden 78, 209, 253, 254, 255, 256, 257, 268
Snyder, Jannetta 96
Southerner Drive-In 106
Southern Railroad 153, 155
Speed-the-Plow 40, 43, 153, 201
Spencer, Alice 189
Spencer, Kathryn 168, 169, 189
Spencer, Mrs. Roy 175, 188
Spring Garden 171, 172
Spring Hill Cemetery 155
Springston, J. E. 83
Stallings, Larry 29
Stallings, Rosa 29
Stanley, L. L. 90
Staples, Shelby 188
Staton, Anne 30
Staton, Randy 29

Staton, Robin 169
Staton, Sharon 28
Staton, Terry 168
Steele, Beulah 211
Steele, Ralph 32
Steuart, Jimmy 168
Steuart, Joyce 168, 169
Stevens, George 34, 35, 43
Stevens, Mr. E. G. 49
Stillwell 247, 248
Stinnett, Edna 30
Stinnett, Frank 188
Stinnett, Mrs. 189
Stinnett, Russell 179
Stinnett, Scott 66
Stinnett, Tony 28, 57
Stinnette, Barbara 15, 16, 116, 117
Stinnette, Connie 21, 25, 115, 168
Stinnette, Dick 85, 87
Stinnette, Fred 19, 21, 25, 75, 108
Stinnette, Harold 25, 118
Stinnette, J. M. 153, 154
Stinnette, Ruby v, 202
Stinnette, Sam 29, 57
Stinnette, Snooks 19, 21, 25, 74, 75, 108, 116
Stinnette, Terrell 84, 86, 92, 114, 115, 202
Stinnette, Tim 31
Stinson, Charles vi
St. Luke's 221, 222, 225
Stonehurst 35
Story, James 168
Story, J. R. 83
Stovall, Bob 29
Stovall family 130
Stovall, Jonathan Breckenridge "Brack" 129
Stovall, Queena 36, 38, 47, 49, 50, 52, 96, 129
Stowe, Bertha 97
Stowe, Caleb 25
Stowe, Mrs. Jerry 94
Stowe, Ollie Mae 25
Stowe, Patsy 118
Stowe, Ronnie 26
St. Paul's Mission 191, 192
Stuart, Coke 68, 149, 150
Stuby, John 45
Sullender Chevrolet 95
Sunside Farm 205
Sutherland, Jean 107
Sutton, Rev. Charles E. 20
Swisher, Daniel 198

T

Tabor, Becky 29
Tabor, Eleanor 45
Tabor, Frank 56, 87
Tabor house 44
Tabor, Jessie 56
Tabor, Lena 47
Tabor, Melissa 29
Tabor, Robert 54
Tabors 45
Tabor, Triggy 54
Tabor, W. T. 47
Tait, Robert 172
Talbot family 18, 41
Talbot, George 21, 41, 115
Talbot, Mrs. George Bird 22, 40, 88
Talbot, Patty Bird 15, 41
Talbot, Rev. George Bird 15, 20, 21, 22, 27, 39, 84, 87, 88, 89, 90, 115
Talbot, Wade 21, 25, 41, 108, 115
Tankersley, Dennis 97, 190
tannery 220
Tappman, Marcia 122
Tappman, Mary 122
Tapscott, Nannie 220, 222
Tavern, The 227
Taylor, C. W. 163
Taylor, Ed 53, 70, 87, 94, 97, 116
Taylor, Elizabeth 96
Taylor, Fleming 107, 163, 164
Taylor, Garland 87, 113, 164
Taylor, John 197
Taylor, Laura Jenkins 197
Taylor, Lillian 107
Taylor, Marita v, 70, 71, 94, 97, 200
Taylor, Matt 164
Taylor, Michael 26
Taylor, Opal 212
Taylor, P. G. 163
Taylor, Robert W. 113, 163
Taylor, Rodney 29, 57
Taylor's Mill 163
Taylor, Willie 77, 78, 85, 86
Teese, David 13, 17, 20, 146
Temple, Rev. Edward O. 17
Tennis 103
Terry, William R. 146
Thacker, Donna 168, 169
Thackston, Charles S. 153
Thomas, Cornelius 266
Thomas, Ellen 188

Thomas, Gerald James 42, 55, 62, 67, 74, 77, 78, 114
Thomas, Gerald "Jerry" 85, 100, 109, 114
Thomas, Grover and Janet 41
Thomas, Jack 116
Thomas Jr., W. T. 83
Thomas, Mildred 22, 67
Thomas, Mitzi 52, 115
Thomas, N. J. 21, 25, 51, 67, 114
Thomas, Peggy and Jerry v
Thomas, Rev. J. A. 8, 20
Thomasson, Mary Harper 96
Thomas, W. T. 186
Thompson, Carolyn 97
Thompson/Dawson home 152
Thompson, Robert 146
Thornton, Becky 170
Thornton, C. D. 83
Thornton family 234
Thornton's Chapel 233
Thornton, T. D. 168, 169, 189
Throneburg, Christy 16
Throneburg, Gloria 15, 16, 117, 118
Throneburg, Harold 24, 71, 114
Throneburg, Norman 108
Throneburg, Roy 205
Throneburg, Scottie 29, 117
Throneburg, Stephanie 16
Tibbs, Virginia 97
Tiller, Clara 16, 117
Tiller, Margaret Jean 16
Timothy School 243
Tinsley, Amos 237
Tinsley, Bernard 237
Tinsley, Ethel 25, 27
Tinsley, Jack 237
Tinsley, Joe 237
Tinsley, Mary L. 153
Tinsley, Mr. 6, 242
Tinsley, Mrs. Joe 237
Tinsley, Ollie 237
Tinsleys 45
Tinsley, W. 146
Tinsley, Zack D. 153, 154
Tobacco Hills 257
Tobacco Row Mountain 5, 95, 191, 199, 230
toll bridge 223
Tolley, Elizabeth 249
toll house 223
Tomlin, Annie 40
Tomlin, Dolly 239
Tomlin, Lois 168, 169
Tomlin, Louis 168, 169

Tomlin, T. J. 239
Tompkins 222
Torode, Mr. 114
Torodes 19
Torrey, Tom 90
Tower Hill graveyard 235
Tower Hill School 234
Townley family 33
Townley Tan Yard 34, 157
Townley, Thomas 157
Townsley's farm 158
Traylor, R. E. 168, 169
Trenton 105
Trevey, Mose 83, 241
Triple Oaks School 47, 51, 129, 130, 131, 132
Tucker, Barry 20, 115
Tucker, Bill 220
Tucker, John 30
Tucker, Nehemiah 102
Turman, Eddie 28
Turman, John 87
Turner, A. L. 84
Turner, Bob and Jennie 242, 244
Turner, Carolyn 28
Turner, Deacon Silas 182
Turner, Dennis 29, 57
Turner, Hattie 243, 244
Turner, Junior 170
Turner, Nellie 168, 169
Turner, Sam and Pomp 220
Turner, Samuel 228
Turner's Mill 228
Turner's Store 243, 244
Turner, Walter 85
Tyler, Anne 239
Tyree, Boyd 118
Tyree, Corrine 168
Tyree, Doris 16, 117, 118
Tyree, Jean 168
Tyree, Joe 188
Tyree, Joyce 168, 169
Tyree, Rev. Steve 17

U

Union Christian Church 249
Union Church 7, 15

V

Vail Jr., Charlie L. 1, 2, 118
Vail, Scott 226
Vaughan, James 188
Vaughan, Lewis 188
Vault Hill 150

Verdant Vale 265
Vest, Mr. 7
Vic-o-Bel Stables 198
Victor, John 213
Virginia Funeral Home 68
Virginia Midland Division 173
Virginia Midland Railroad 173
Virginia Nail and Iron Works 212
Vosburgh, Annmarie 30

W

Wade, Mrs. 188
Waidelich, Mary (Camden) 44
Walker, Bill 19
Wallace, Ashley 32
Wallace girls 22
Wallace III, Thomas Cushing and Kate 230
Wallace, Joe 118
Wallace, Lurleen 118
Walsh, Mrs. Alma 39
Walsh, Rev. and Mrs. 39
Walsh, Rev. Clyde J. 18, 20, 39, 54, 56
Ware, Charlie 83, 233
Ware, Elsie (Loving) 249
Ware, Mabel Mitchell 198
Ware, Mike 30
Ware, Owen 198, 209
Ware, Patty 16
Ware, Phil 30, 57
Ware, Robert "Bob" and Audrey 236
Ware, Roy 236
Ware, Virginia 16
Warm Springs 139
Warner 105
Warner, John 96, 153
Warner, Mary S. 153
Wash, D. W. 146
Watson, Kelly 189
Watts, Albert 184
Watts, Andrew 146, 148
Watts, Bessie 237
Watts, Buddy 244
Watts, Carrie Belle (Bowles) 249
Watts, Cecil 27
Watts, Claude 241
Watts, Donald 54, 205
Watts, Dr. D. L. 84
Watts, Elizabeth 147
Watts, Gary 29
Watts, Howard 99, 188
Watts, James Monroe 173
Watts, Jimmy 122
Watts, Junior 29

Watts, Kenneth 29
Watts, Lela Watts and Rufus 160
Watts, Lenna 147
Watts, Linda 28
Watts, Martha 239
Watts' Mill 161
Watts, Mrs. Claude 83
Watts, Mrs. Dave 49
Watts, Oscar 153, 205
Watts, Ray 25, 118
Watts, Rufus 205
Watts, Ruth 114
Watts, Samuel L. and Nora 161
Watts, Sandra 28
Watts store 160
Watts, Wathena 242
Watts, Wayne 118
Watts, William 26, 27, 118
Waugh, Amy 28
Waugh, Annie 29
Waugh, Edward 265
Waugh, Isabella McCulloch 265
Waugh, James 263
Waugh, Nicholas 193
Waugh's Ferry 263, 264
Waugh's Ferry farm 263
Waugh, Thomas 263
Webb, Mrs. John 49
Webb, William and Lily 45
Webster, Alice (Gottshall) 249
Weeks, Margaret Camden v, 37
Wee Tee Playgrounds 104
Weir, Hon. James 84
Welch, Rev. Carroll B. 17
Wells, Terry Jean 98
Wetmore, Edwin 114
Wheaton, Hon. Don C. 84
White, Catherine 24, 25
White cemetery 235
White, George Henry 89
Whitehead, Floyd 25
Whitehead, Joyce 31
Whitehead, Rosa 16
Whitehead, Withers 25, 168
White, Henry 235
White house 236
White, Marie 169
White, Mildred 11, 25
White, Rose 168
White Sulphur Springs 139
Whitlock, Carl 132
Whitmore, Mr. and Mrs. John 140
Whittle, Bishop 221
Wigwam 38, 46, 47, 129, 134
Wiley 7

Wiley, Barbara 21, 22, 108, 168
Wiley, Bertha (Camden) 59
Wiley, Bob 54
Wiley, Bruce 45
Wiley, Calvin 59
Wiley, Earl 15, 21, 54, 108
Wiley, Earl and Vernie 70
Wiley, Gloria 21
Wiley, Ivan 108
Wiley Jr., Earl 97, 108, 170
Wiley, Sylvia Kaye 15, 108, 117
Wiley, Vernie 40
Wilkerson, Donald 168
Wilkerson, George 168
Williams, Ed 194
Williams, Hazel 219
Williams, James "Jim" 195
Williams, J. D. 83
Williams, John 194
Williams Jr., E. Crawley 146
Williams, Katherine Elizabeth Watts 147
Williams, Moses 83
Williams, Mr. 8, 253
Williams, Mrs. Lelia 195
Williams, Mrs. Moses Kyle (Margaret) 253
Williams, Mrs. W. R. 28
Williamson, Carrie 117
Williamson, Dot 97
Williamson, Frank 97
Williams, Ruby 117
Williams' Store 194, 253, 254
Williams, T. S. 84
Williams, Uncle Harry 113
Williams Viaduct 252
Wills, Ashby 54, 99
Wills, Barbara 21, 115, 118, 128
Wills, Betty 128
Wills, Buck 96, 99
Wills, Buddy 85, 86, 88, 92, 96
Wills, Charles 21, 26, 108, 128
Wills, Charles Raymond 53
Wills, Dick 54, 99, 205
Wills, Edward (Buddy) 88
Wills, Eleanor 27, 108, 128
Wills family 151
Wills, Frank "Dick" 127, 128
Wills Jr., Frank 19, 128
Wills, June 19, 21, 25, 115
Wills, Junior 21
Wills, Lena 95
Wills, Lula 22, 40, 128
Wills, Malcolm vi, 19, 85, 86, 92, 114, 115

Wills, Mike 30, 57
Wills, Nancy 21, 25, 26, 27, 108, 115, 168
Wills, Raymond 18, 85, 86, 87, 92
Wills, R. H. 19, 21, 25
Wills, Rita 57
Wills, Roy 54
Wills, Shelia 29
Wills Sr., Frank 114
Wills, T. L. 249
Wills, Vera 115
Wills, William Edward 53
Wills, W. P. "Buck" 47, 53, 84, 85, 86, 92, 95, 114
Wills, W. P. "Buck" and Lena 70
Wilsher, Eloise 25, 26
Wilsher, Mrs. 188
Wilshire, Mr. 237
Windy Hill Farm 138
Winesap 173
Winesap Station 152, 184, 199
Winfree, Chris 132
Winfree, Robert 132
Winnia, W. W. 96
Winridge Bed and Breakfast 151, 152
Womack, Patsy 30
Wood, Harry 83
Wood, J. E. 84
Wood, J. S. 84
Woodlawn 227
Wood, Lee 28
Wood, Marie 168
Wood, Miss Inez 84
Wood, Monyeene 97
Wood, Mrs. Edgar 49
Wood, Ran 96
Woodroof, Alfred M. 246
Woodroof, Ambrose R. 246
Woodroof, Jane C. and Ambrose R. 245
Woodroof, John 100
Woodroof, Joyce 170
Woodroof, Margaret N. and Alfred M. 245
Woodroof, Rev. Pitt 143
Woodruff, Angela 29
Woodruff, James Earl 157
Woodruff, Mary Fannie 147, 157, 158
Woodruff's Café and Pie Shop 157
Woodruff's Store 157
Woodruff, Walter 157, 158
Woodruff, Wyatt 157
Woods, Ashby 196, 220, 227

Woods, Bill 227
Woods family 228
Woods, Isabella 194
Woods, Jas. Pembroke 265, 266
Woods, Josephine Bailey 193
Woods Jr., Ashby 239
Woods, Mrs. Isabell "Belle" 196
Woods, Nancy 239
Woodson, Gordon 84
Woods, Pembroke 196
Woods, Thomas Dabney 227
Wood, Victor 132, 247, 248
Wooldridge, Mike 28
Wooldridge, Mr. Haywood L. 20
Wooldridge, Walter 29
World War II 87
Worley, N. M. 83
Wortham, Mr. and Mrs. Ned 49
Wright, Aubrey 83
Wright, George 146
Wright, Lynn 168
Wright, M. 146

Y

Y. M. C. A. 174
Young, Aileen Burford 263
Young, Edwin 87
Younger, Ann 19, 21, 43, 107, 216
Younger, Beth 18, 19, 21, 43, 88, 115, 166, 216
Younger, Bruce 40, 44, 51, 59, 60, 61, 62, 63, 74, 83, 88, 96, 99, 102, 114, 115, 133, 214, 216
Younger, Lawson 40, 225
Younger, Lizzie 39, 40, 42, 53, 62, 74, 115, 116
Young, June 168
Young, Robert 114
Young, Robert and Mildred 119

IN THE SHADOW OF TOBACCO ROW MOUNTAIN